CASTLES IN IRELAND

CASTLES IN IRELAND

Feudal Power in a Gaelic World

—·◆·—

Tom McNeill

London and New York

First published 1997
by Routledge
11 New Fetter Lane, London EC4P 4EE

Simultaneously published in the USA and Canada
by Routledge
29 West 35th Street, New York, NY 10001

© 1997 Tom McNeill

Reprinted 1997

Typeset in Garamond by
Florencetype Ltd, Stoodleigh, Devon

Printed and bound in Great Britain by
Redwood Books, Trowbridge, Wiltshire

British Library Cataloguing in Publication Data
A catalogue record for this book is available from the British Library

Library of Congress Cataloguing in Publication Data
McNeill, T. E.
Castles in Ireland: Feudal power in a Gaelic world/Tom McNeill.
p.   cm.
Includes bibliographical references and index.
1. Ireland–History–1172–1603. 2. Power (Social sciences)–
Ireland–History. 3. Social history–Medieval, 500–1500
4. Architecture, Medieval–Ireland. 5. Military history, Medieval.
6. Feudalism–Ireland–History. 7. Castles–Ireland–History.
8. British–Ireland–History. 9. Civilization, Celtic.
I. Title.
DA933.M46   1997
941.503–dc21   96–46689
                                                      CIP
ISBN 0-415-16537-7

In memory of J. C. McNeill, 1902–93

CONTENTS

——— .◆. ———

— *Contents* —

ILLUSTRATIONS

—— •◆• ——

PREFACE

———— .•. ————

This book has had a long period of gestation. During this time, I have had the benefit of many discussions with colleagues, both within Ireland and outside it, and have had to explain the facts and problems to many students. From the first, I have derived much information and many ideas. It is so difficult to disentangle the sources of them in the memories of discussions that I hope they will take it as flattery when they recognise them here, understanding that I have been so convinced by them that I have thought of them as my own. I have been lucky to supervise the work of many students on specific castles; at least with these the written product can be acknowledged. To all of the two overlapping groups, I am very grateful. All the mistakes are my own, however.

I am grateful to a number of sources for specific illustrations. My colleague, Barrie Hartwell took the photographs for figures 33, 44, 49, 103 and 123, and helped me with many others. The Office of Public Works, Ireland supplied nos 22, 43 and 65 and the source for nos 19 and 28; no. 19 is also derived in part from B. Hodkinson. Figure 3 was taken by C. O'Rahilly. Figures 59 and 61 are in part based on original plans supplied by courtesy of Cadw: Welsh Historic Monuments. Figure 26 is based on the plan in Buckley and Sweetman, 1991, fig. 248; figure 53 similarly from the plan in Knight, 1992, fig. 14. My students' dissertations provided the surveys for the plans in figs 46 (G. McCool), 107 (P. Stitt), 109 (G. Nuttall), 114 (E. McFadden), 120 (A. Blacoe), 124 (P. Mitchel), 125 (K. Neill).

The maps were drawn by my colleagues Maura Pringle (figs 1, 37, 99, 124, 125) and Gillian Alexander (figs 4, 5, 38, 41), who also arranged for much of the processing. Although the rest of the drawings were drawn by me, from my field notes, the final arranging of them owed everything to the firm (if not ferocious) guidance and standards of Maura Pringle. To both I owe a great debt.

Finally, to Penny, David, Richard and John who have put up with my absences and my obsession for many years.

INTRODUCTION

———— •◆• ————

Castles remain, with the great cathedrals, the most evocative monuments of the middle ages. They come down to us from a time when the aristocrats of Europe controlled the rest of society through their possession of great landed estates. They built castles to serve them as centres of their lives, the administration of their estates and the means to hold on to them in times of war. For the last 150 years scholars and others have been studying and writing on castles in western Europe. This often started with the more military parts, the castles' defences and sieges, but then moved on to considering their wider, civil aspects. As a result, we think we know the main lines of development of castles and the life they represented. This is no static picture, but one subject to great variation. It changes according to time, as the builders adopted new fashions and developments; according to the resources of the lord who built any castle, and the skill of the workmen whom he employed; and (above all) because of the rooted objection of medieval lords to build a castle exactly like any other existing one. As objects meant to display their lord's power and prestige they had to be impressive, and uniformity denied that. It is in this endless variety, as well as in the humanity of their bombast and in the ingenuity of the individual designs, that the appeal of castles lies.

Ireland is remarkable among the countries of western Europe for its scholarly neglect of its castles after the early years of this century. Then there were at least two major scholars working on the study, Thomas Westropp and Goddard Orpen. The latter was one of the key figures writing in English on the study of castles in the decade before the First World War. His greatness rests on two things. He recognised, as early as the more famous Ella Armitage in England, that earthworks were as much castles as were masonry structures. He also was a great historian, who combined the physical and the documentary evidence when he wrote about an individual castle. To him castles told a story just as much as did royal documents, and on the one hand he used their evidence in his histories, while on the other he never stopped at mere description in his account; the castles were evidence to be interpreted and expounded. Westropp was less concerned with the grand sweep of history. He was a great gatherer of information about individual castles, from documentary sources and particularly from the field evidence; he was also concerned not just with the medieval period but with monuments of all dates, but mainly in his native south-west of Ireland.

After them, in 1941, came H. G. Leask to uphold the standard of castle studies, but he never had the time to produce a study of castles comparable to his three-volume work on the ecclesiastical buildings of medieval Ireland; his book remains a sketch of what it might have been. Leask's publication of churches rather than castles, whatever his individual reason, represents a certain ambivalence in the study of the secular world of the later middle ages in Ireland. As in many of the countries to emerge into independence after 1918, the study of history and archaeology in Ireland was closely affected by the politics of nineteenth- and twentieth-century nationalism. It was difficult to divorce castles from the fact that many of the lords who built them ultimately came from England and owed allegiance to the king of England. Especially as long as the emphasis of castle studies was on their military role, it was inevitable that they should be seen as the symbols, not of national freedom but of the beginning of English domination. As such, they were unwelcome guests at the academic feast, a situation exacerbated by the overt Unionism of Orpen. It must be significant that much of the archaeological study of early Dublin, even after it became a city under the English Crown, is often presented as the study of Viking Dublin; similarly, the medieval lords of Ireland who were not Irish are often called Normans. It avoids reopening futile disputes. The situation also intimidated outsiders; it is curious, and unfortunate, that Ireland was excluded from the publication of the *History of the King's Works* which played such a seminal role in the study of castles in Britain and beyond in the 1960s.

For obvious reasons people in Northern Ireland, reacting to the nationalism of the rest, were less affected by this view of the middle ages. The amateur tradition, with such men as H. C. Lawlor, continued to include the middle ages and castles as part of their antiquarian writings. The first professional archaeologist to work in the North, O. Davies, did the same, which also ran counter to the tendency visible in Britain to cut professional archaeology short at the Romans or Vikings. A new era opened in 1948 with the appointment of an overtly medieval archaeologist, E. M. Jope, to a lectureship (later to a chair) of archaeology in the Queen's University in Belfast. He was followed two years later by D. M. Waterman, appointed to a position in the newly created Archaeological Survey of Northern Ireland. Between them, with A. E. P. Collins, they revolutionised the study of archaeology there, especially in the medieval period and the study of castles. A systematic programme of excavation of the castles of Co. Down was started which saw more such activity in the county during the 1950s than probably any other area of Europe. Waterman produced a whole series of studies of castles, either already in State Care, or else as they came into it, in advance of conservation work. By 1966, with the publication of *An Archaeological Survey of Co. Down* (Jope, 1966), Northern Ireland was one of the leading regions in Europe for the study of castles.

Since then, things have evened out between the two parts of Ireland. Medieval archaeology in general, and the study of castles in particular, has advanced greatly in the South, while there has been an unfortunate relative decline in the North. In both, the activity has mainly been publication of excavations of individual castles;

essential in themselves but not the complete studies of the upstanding fabric and documentation combined into one study which the subject needs to establish its basic evidence. The tradition of Westropp, rather than that of Orpen, perhaps, has been the dominant force, in Ireland as elsewhere. Leask's book of 1941 has continued to be reprinted, with the last edition in 1977, because there has been no attempt to replace it as a source of information about the castles of Ireland in general.

Against this background, there need be no apology for a new book on castles in Ireland as such. It may cast light on what was the period when Ireland became, for better or for worse, intimately tied to the social and economic fabric of western Europe, through the medium of England. How that happened is clearly a significant object for study. The lack of work on the castles still leaves the field open for one of two kinds of books on the subject. The first would be to take Leask's approach, which he used in both his major works, and concentrate on presenting the reader with descriptions of individual castles. The other would be Orpen's, where the aim is to weave the evidence from the castles into a story, to give an explanation of their meaning in history, in the wider sense of that term.

This book aims to be one of the latter kind. Working from a university gives one neither the time nor the resources in the field to undertake the massive programme of recording that the descriptive book would demand. The role of detailed recording is best done from within the state organisations entrusted with the care of the monuments. On the other hand, facing up to sceptical students impresses the habit of explanation on to a lecturer. While obviously I hope that I have made no false statements in this book, I would be shocked if the subject was left to rest here. More work will inevitably give us more information, more evidence of the complexity of the castles and new interpretations of them. Waiting for this, however, and rewriting each remaining bit around the new story, would make the whole process unending, as likely to be completed as giving the final coat of paint to the Forth Bridge. We cannot wait until everything is in place, not least because some of the castles will no longer be so. The pressures on castles are mounting again, often in the guise of well-meaning but over-enthusiastic restoration and interpretation. In these circumstances I am prepared to face the criticism and take the plunge into trying to tell the reader what I think these sites mean.

This aim dictates the structure of the book. It is divided into three parts, corresponding to three periods which present us with different questions to ask about the castles of the time. Within these period divisions, I have tried to let the study of the physical remains of the castles, their archaeology, play the dominant role in the account, rather than the historical documentation. The accounts, and in particular many of the drawings, must be seen in the light of the foregoing remarks. They are often based on a one-person attempt at survey which is aimed at giving an explanation of the remains rather than a total record of them; that is for another operation, just as assembling the complete documentary record of the castles is. In a sense all this adds up to a plea of *caveat lector* but it is not meant as such; rather it is a plea for this book not to be judged for not being what it was never meant to be.

PART I

EARLY CASTLES: TO *c.* 1225

CHAPTER ONE

BEFORE 1166

—— .◆. ——

Society in Ireland during the eleventh and twelfth centuries was in a state of flux. The establishment of a number of coastal towns, initially by Scandinavians, of which the most prominent was Dublin, meant that Irish goods were able to be marketed abroad in much greater quantities and much more regularly than before. Political affairs were marked by the rise to power of a small group of pre-eminent provincial kings, whose military power allowed them to suppress lesser kingdoms within their areas, and to contend for a position of supremacy over their peers, as so-called High Kings of Ireland. Their power was based on controlling armies (a steady increase in the length and ferocity of wars followed) and on their vast herds of cattle, which they used to buy support from other lords. They captured cattle in war and, along with them, slaves; both could be marketed through the Scandinavian towns for silver to be used for display and for buying more support. The twelfth century saw a determined attempt to transform the traditional Irish Church institutions into ones in line with the rest of Europe, most notably in the introduction of new monastic orders and territorial bishoprics, leading eventually to a network of parishes over the country.

The impulse for change seems to have come from the top levels of society, typified by the alliance of reforming churchmen with some of the new, aggressive kings. The resources that we hear of being deployed by the new powers were essentially mobile forms of wealth, particularly cattle, that could be captured in war. In the rest of Europe new forms of lordship were being introduced (lumped together by historians as 'feudalism') which were based on tighter control of smaller estates linked to increased grain production, through machines such as the great plough and the water mill. The changes in Ireland might be similar or they might involve the new kings simply seizing a greater share of existing resources for themselves at the cost of their inferiors. Elsewhere a key element in the changes was the use of private fortifications as the skeleton of control of the fields and estates. In Ireland there are hints of such things in the eleventh and twelfth centuries.

SITES OF THE TENTH CENTURY AND BEFORE

For centuries before structures which we now identify as castles were built, men in Ireland erected enclosures and fortified sites. Some of these were essential components of the early medieval (or 'early Christian') society of Ireland from the fifth or sixth centuries onwards. The commonest of these were the 'normal' raths, or ringforts, scattered in their thousands across the landscape of the island. These are circular enclosures, up to about 60 metres (200 feet) across, although usually only half that size, defined by a single bank of earth inside a ditch (for a discussion of these and other sites, see Mallory and McNeill, 1990, 184–225). In their lack of defensive equipment, notably their often open entrances and the lack of maintenance of their enclosing banks and ditches, and in their social position associated with the free farming class rather than with aristocrats, these 'normal' raths can hardly be considered in the same context as castles.

More complex, because less well understood, are the variety of sites which appear to be more strongly fortified raths. In the sort of buildings found within the enclosure, and the size of the enclosure itself, they resemble raths. Their perimeter, however, is defined not by a bank and ditch, but by elevating the whole area on to a mound. The result gives us sites which appear (without excavation) now to be very similar to the mottes of later castles. Many of these raised raths are marked by ramped entrances which break the perimeter of the raised mound, to provide easier access to the top. Similarly, some sites, such as Gransha, Co. Down (Lynn, 1985), are sited along ridges and the raised appearance is produced only along the greater part of the perimeter: the central part, along the ridge top, is hardly raised at all, and again offers easy access to the 'mound' top. At Ballynarry (Davison, 1962) or Rathmullan (Lynn, 1982), both in Co. Down, the raised mounds were produced in small increases in height over a long period of time. At Rathmullan in particular, this is in contrast with the conversion of the site in around 1200 into a motte, when the pre-existing mound was doubled in height in a single effort.

The sites where the raised effect is either not carried around the whole perimeter, or that perimeter is deliberately breached to provide easier access, would seem to be significantly less effective defensively than we would expect from a castle. With the sites which have been developed into mounds by gradually adding to their height, it is true that the same effect has been found in the Rhineland, and there it is associated with the origins of castle building; the type site for this process is the Husterknupp (Herrenbrodt, 1958). It must be pointed out, however, that the Rhenish sites, and those of the Low Countries where we may see the same phenomenon, are sited in low-lying, waterlogged situations, often in preference to drier sites nearby. One could instance here the site of Leichlingen (Müller-Wille, 1966, no. 52) where it is placed in the valley bottom in preference to a steep bluff only a few hundred metres to the south-east; these sites relied on water for their defences, not on the height of their perimeter, as a true motte did. This is not the case in Ireland, where the gradually mounded sites are set, like the 'normal' raths, well up slope from ground liable to flood, and so give protection. Defence in Ireland comes from height alone, not from water.

The crux of the matter comes with two sites, Big Glebe in Co. Londonderry (Lynn, 1982, 167) and Deer Park Farms in Co. Antrim (Hamlin and Lynn, 1988, 44–7). At Deer Park Farms, at one point during a long occupation involving several small-scale increases in the height of the site, some 1.5 m (5 ft) of gravel and soil was dumped on the site, partly contained by a redundant house. At Big Glebe the whole mound, some 6 m (20 ft) high, was constructed in a single effort, not gradually in several stages over time. At this site at least, we have something which, if excavation had dated it to around 1200 instead of several centuries before that, we would not hesitate to call a motte. Neither Deer Park Farms nor Big Glebe is mentioned in documentary sources, so that we cannot locate either of them directly in the social or political structure of the time. In some cases, notably at Rathmullan, the raised site (however produced) was in occupation in the twelfth century, and overlapped in time with the construction of castles; indeed the Rathmullan mound was doubled in height then to convert it into a true motte castle. Relationships between the traditional sites and castles are possible, but not proven.

The artificial islands constructed in lakes, known as crannogs, were lived in by kings and aristocrats and are clearly defensive in their siting and purpose. As military structures, they were revived at the end of the middle ages, and proved to be effective strongholds during the Tudor wars in Ireland. Unfortunately, there have been few excavations at crannogs, and there is a real dearth of chronological information about their use as opposed to their construction, where dendrochronology has given us dates which place them clearly in the seventh century or before. Whether any individual crannog was continually used thereafter until the late middle ages, or in the same way, is unclear.

If, however, we take the definition of a castle, published in 1977 (Saunders, 1977, 2), as 'a fortified residence which might combine administrative and judicial functions, but in which military considerations were paramount', then crannogs pose a real problem for the students of castles. On the one hand, there can be no doubt that crannogs may meet this definition as well as many castles. On the other, they are not generally accepted as castles, usually, if silently, because of two lines of argument. The first is because of the link which is always at the heart of the question of castle origins and definition: in no way were crannogs linked to the territorial estates and system of lordship called feudalism. The problem is that, while this link can be maintained (if only with difficulty) in France or England, if we move to the Gaelic worlds of medieval Scotland or Wales, there we find structures which can only be called castles, and yet which were built and used by lords whose power was not feudal. We shall see the same in Ireland later: the feudal link is not universal. The second argument against the crannog as castle is even cruder, if more powerful. It is that they are found far earlier than any castle, and they do not look anything like what we think of as a castle; this is, of course, a classic circular argument.

That the arguments are weak does not alter the probability that they are right: crannogs were not castles. The problem is not with the crannogs but with our attempts to produce a simple definition for such a protean thing as the castle. There are two problems here. The first is that the link to feudalism is real but not absolute: it was clearly possible for the structure to be used without the institutions which brought it forth. When castles were used in societies which we consider as non-feudal, we must ask questions as to the nature of the power structure involved, and whether the lord was borrowing more than the physical castle. A Gaelic lord might build a castle to live in, in imitation of feudal lords elsewhere, but the key word is imitation; this would have nothing to do with the origin of castles, or even with their early use, except in the Gaelic world concerned. The second general problem is that of extrapolating from the form of the site to the function, particularly relevant to the raised rath sites. They are too simple to make conclusions about the institutions which accompanied them. Just because a circular, enclosed site develops into a mound over time, this is not sufficiently peculiar to demand that we attribute the development to importing ideas from a world of castles. This can go further, for the builder of a castle might not use it in the way it was intended; castles of the nineteenth century were not built by feudal magnates, but they have the form of those that were.

POSSIBLE CASTLES OF THE ELEVENTH AND TWELFTH CENTURIES

We want to find sites where both documentary and physical evidence exist which can be used to argue that there were other, new and different structures in twelfth-century Ireland which could relate to later castles. The documentary evidence has been assembled by O'Corrain (1974) and consists of brief entries in Annals. Most are from the Annals of Tigernach and relate to sites of the O'Connor kings of Connacht from 1124 onwards. They use a word new to Irish to describe a number of sites as 'caistel', or 'caislen', loan-words from Latin *castellum* or medieval French *chastel*. The same Annals use the word to describe the castles of the English after 1169. Another reference, in the seventeenth-century Annals of the Four Masters for 1166, states that the enemies of Diarmait Mac Murchada burned his stone house at Ferns (fig. 1) and the 'longport' there. It should be noticed, however, that the entry reads as though his house was not actually in the longport or fortress. A fort separated from the residence of the king is not the sort of thing that we are looking for in a castle. With the places named in the Annals, we do not know whether it is right to accept that a new word must mean a new thing. The period was one of dynamic political change which could either have seen new kinds of sites deployed, or it could simply have seen men attracted to new, fashionable or boastful words: English people had eaten pigs before they started to call their meat pork.

There has been an attempt to link these Connacht references to physical evidence of a new type of site, so that we could talk of castles from the century before 1166 (Graham, 1988). Unfortunately, the only one of the list which Graham specifically identifies as a new type physically is Dunmore, which he identifies as a motte, i.e. as an artificial mound of earth (ibid., 115). In fact, the site is one whose present remains are those of a later thirteenth-century masonry castle set on a natural rock outcrop: in no sense can it now be identified as a motte. Other sites which he claims as early castles cannot be distinguished from the traditional corpus of raths or ringforts, and so the connection between the new word and a new type

Figure 1 Map of possible castle sites in Ireland from before 1166

of site is not made, nor does he establish any way of recognising such new sites, other than by references in documents. The argument is not advanced beyond that of O'Corrain.

In fact two sites do exist which combine physical and documentary evidence of being something new. The site of Duneight, Co. Down, should be the starting point for discussion of the physical evidence, for it has both been excavated and identified as a place mentioned twice in the Annals of Ulster (1983, s.a. 1003/4 and 1010/1). On the second occasion, Flaithbertach ua Neill of the Cenel Eoghain is recorded as burning the fort and destroying the township of Duneight, before extracting the submission of the king of Ulaidh. Royal associations may have led to its inclusion in the dower charter of John de Courcy, the first English lord of Ulster and in a sense continuator of Ulaid kingship (Otway-Ruthven, 1949, 78–9:

Dunechti should be identified with Duneight rather than Donaghy, Co. Antrim).

The excavator (Waterman, 1963) considered that the large inner ditch and the reinforced bank which went with it were both of the tenth or eleventh century and rightly stressed their difference from the normal rath enclosure. It is possible, and the excavation was not by any means perfect, that this ditch cut through an earlier, much shallower one, and the strongly military defences might be later than this date, indeed date to the time of de Courcy. It would still leave the fact of the large size of the enclosure, and its associations with both royalty and a township, distinguishing it from traditional raths.

The best physical evidence, although unexcavated, comes from the so-called 'English Mount', a large enclosure set at the edge of the Quoile marshes north-east of the hill on which Downpatrick cathedral is sited (Jope, 1966, 202–3). The enclosure is enclosed by particularly massive defences (a ditch and a bank rising 6 m (20 ft) higher than the interior, and up to 15 m (50 ft) above the ditch fill) on the line of approach from the ridge leading up to the cathedral hill (fig. 2), while the marshes reinforce the defences of the other sides. Inside is a motte which looks unfinished, with a smaller ditch on the north side where the mound perimeter is incomplete. The motte is sited awkwardly against the enclosure bank, and the bank at that point is higher than the motte; it is unlikely that builders of a motte and bailey castle would proceed to build the bailey first and then start in on the motte. The whole makes no sense as a motte and bailey, but it is likely to be an enclosure with an unfinished motte added later.

There is no direct evidence of the date of the enclosure, but it is very tempting to identify it with the royal, secular site of the eleventh and twelfth centuries situated at Downpatrick (Flanagan, 1973). The documentation of Downpatrick in the earlier twelfth century is also interesting for it associates the royal site with the site of a cathedral, the hallmark of the contemporary Church reform. Two centres of the new power were apparently set side by side here, and it is surely significant that this was the site of a town soon after the seizure of the kingdom by de Courcy in 1177. The centralisation of wealth would attract merchants in the classic configuration of eleventh century power.

Recent excavations have added two other sites to the list. Excavations at Limerick castle in 1990 exposed the remains of an enclosure earlier than the extant remains of the stone castle (Wiggins, 1991, 43–4). It was strongly defended by a ditch up to 2.8 m (9 ft) deep and over 11 m (36 ft) wide in front of a bank revetted by a dry-stone wall (fig. 3). The remains look too strong to be a temporary camp occupied before the construction of the castle shortly after 1210 (see chapter 2), but yet with their use of dry-stone revetment do not look like an early English castle, where one would expect timber. It is very tempting to identify it with a twelfth-century Ua Briain fortification within the city.

The later castle of Dunamase dominates the Midland plain of Laois from the hills to its south. Excavations in 1994 and 1995 have greatly extended our knowledge of the site. Along the line of the present main curtain wall, Hodkinson found two earlier periods (Hodkinson, 1995). The first was a dry-stone wall cut into the rising hill-slope: the second was a mortared stone gate house inserted into this dry-stone wall. We cannot be absolutely precise about the dating of either of

Figure 2 'English Mount', Downpatrick: view along the defences on the land side

these, or indeed about that of the main curtain wall and gate house, but it seems likely that the dry-stone walling pre-dates the arrival of English lords in the area, but not by much. Its construction is similar to that of the dry-stone facing of the Limerick ditch, and it is certainly a site of much greater size and strength than any 'normal' Irish fort of the eleventh or twelfth centuries.

The sites named by O'Corrain from the Annals and those identified on the ground as belonging to the earlier twelfth century (fig. 1) share some characteristics. They are mostly associated with the provincial kings, the major players in the politics of the period, not with the lesser kings who were slipping into a merger

Figure 3 Limerick: the defences of the pre-castle enclosure, with the castle gate house in the background

with the aristocracy. A high proportion of them have evidence of being reused as the sites of later castles. Limerick was a royal castle; Dunamase the *caput* of a section of the lordship of Leinster; Duneight retained by John de Courcy and the site of a motte. Downpatrick is not known as having had a castle of the Earl of Ulster (McNeill, 1980, 13) but the unfinished motte may mark an abandoned attempt to build one there, and the town of Downpatrick was certainly a key place in the Earldom. Of the documented sites, Ferns had been an important place since the twelfth century, while of the ten Connacht sites five were the sites of important castles. The new sites clearly were at places which the English of the later twelfth and thirteenth centuries, as well as later generations, were to reuse as important. Those sites which can be identified on the ground are very much more powerful militarily than the traditional enclosures of earlier years, and cover a considerably greater area. Whether we should equate this with a greater military strength of the kings concerned, or see it as proof of the fear of attack, there is no doubt that they show an increase in the resources needed to build them over those of their predecessors.

We must sound two serious notes of caution. There are not many swallows here to make a summer. We cannot point to enough sites to argue that castles were regularly used in Ireland before 1166, or that their use requires us to think that the basis of Irish lordship had changed because of them. The power of kings in the eleventh and twelfth centuries in Ireland rested overtly on naked military power, and these sites seem to reflect this. Nor can we point to a widespread use of the new sites, if such they are; those that we know of are associated with the major kings, not with the wider circles of lesser kings and aristocracy. If these sites mark a new departure for secular society, it is like the contemporary reform of the Church; led from the top and starting with the upper grades first, bishops before parishes. In both cases it is legitimate to question how far the new ideas were accepted beyond the power of the major kings. In this context, we might envisage that the lesser lords were those who continued to occupy the reduced number of traditional sites, emphasising their importance with a new stress on mounds and height, but largely formally rather than with a real appreciation of their military potential. It is clear, however, that Giraldus Cambrensis' sweeping statement that the Irish did not care for castles, but instead relied on the natural refuges of woods and bogs (Dimock, 1867, 182), was wrong; some clearly had fortifications.

In many ways the academic position about castles in Ireland before the English lordships were established is a mirror image of the parallel question of whether there were castles before 1066 in England. There the idea that castles were simply a Norman introduction was challenged in the 1960s. The argument that they existed in England before 1066 rested on two legs: that landed lordship of an essentially 'feudal' nature existed in Anglo-Saxon England, and that the lords had built defensive enclosures around their manor houses, which would be recognised in France, or elsewhere, as castles (Higham and Barker, 1992, ch. 1). Of the two legs, the first has stood the test of discussion better than the second. Studies of the pattern of land holding in the English countryside before 1066 show the existence of tightly organised estates, very similar to the later manors, and unlike the earlier extensive but loosely controlled lordship. On the other hand, the documentary references in pre-1066 chronicles are as ambiguous as those in Irish Annals. The sites which are proposed as castles, such as Goltho (Beresford, 1987) or Sulgrave (Davison, 1977), look, to an Irish eye, no more defensive than a rath, with low banks and shallow ditches, and without evidence of gate structures. In Ireland, by contrast, we have evidence of fortification, linked to royal power, but not of the structure of landed lordship parcelling out the landscape.

Here lies the nub of our view of what happened when Diarmait Mac Murchada invited English lords and troops from south Wales, most notably Richard fitz Gilbert (or Strongbow as he was later known), to Leinster after 1166. His immediate need was military force; he had been expelled from his kingdom by the High King and he wanted it back. But he went further and offered Richard his daughter in marriage and the succession to his kingdom (for a full discussion of these political events, see Flanagan, 1989). This may have been simply an added bait, to attract a man who was socially well above any mere mercenary soldier to be recruited for pay or loot alone, but it may be more. The kings of twelfth-century Ireland were well aware of developments outside Ireland. On the one hand they could see the military effectiveness of the feudal lords in England or Wales, but they had also the example of Scotland. There the kings had been steadily granting land to English lords, so that their kingdom would be transformed. The new feudal lords of Scotland introduced the methods of systematically exploiting estates and land for a greatly increased profit, compared to the traditional means of lordship. They did so in a context of a strict hierarchy of institutions, headed by the king, whose power was thus increased, but, above all, who gained greatly in authority. If such ideas were in Diarmait's mind, we shall never know, and he died in 1171 before he had a chance to make it happen. Ireland lay open to the new lords and their system of organisation of the land.

EARLY CASTLES OF STONE

—— •◆• ——

THE ESTABLISHING OF THE ENGLISH LORDSHIPS

Before we consider the castles of the new, English lordships in Ireland, we must glance at the process of their establishment there. Initially, there were the mercenaries recruited by Diarmait Mac Murchada after he left Ireland in 1166, and returned in the following year. The pace quickened in 1169, and a new element was introduced when Richard fitz Gilbert (Strongbow), later Earl of Strigoil and Pembroke, also came over, and married Diarmait's daughter, in 1170. In 1171 Diarmait died, to be succeeded by Richard, but then Henry II also came to Ireland. The king of England was now overtly involved: Henry brought over other men, and made wider grants outside Leinster. It became posible to think, as Giraldus Cambrensis did, of the occupation of the whole of Ireland by English lords under the English king.

Over the next forty years, much of southern and eastern Ireland was seized by English lords. Henry granted the kingdom of Meath to Hugh de Lacy, who proceeded, especially after 1177, to organise what was something of a power vacuum. Early in 1177 John de Courcy was invited into the kingdom of Ulster, where, after four or five years marked by hard fighting for his small force, he succeeded in becoming accepted as in effect the successor king. In the same year Henry granted the kingdom of Cork to Robert fitz Stephen and Miles de Cogan, who won it with the help of Domnaill Ua Briain, king of Thomond. By 1185, when Henry's youngest son, John, first came to Ireland as its lord, he set about defining the boundary of his own lands in Waterford, set between Cork and south Leinster, and then made grants to the north and west of it, towards the town of Limerick (see fig. 4).

It was not until the death of Domnaill Ua Briain, king of Thomond, in 1194, that these grants were followed up. A number of major lordships in Tipperary, held by Theobald Walter, William de Burgh and Philip de Worcester, resulted. In 1199 John made a further series of grants in Munster, splitting up what is now the county of Limerick among a number of lords. Similarly, to the north, the death of Murchad Ua Cerbaill, king of Argialla, was followed by grants to Bertram de Verdon and Roger or Gilbert Pippard, establishing English 'Oriel' (the anglicisation of Argialla),

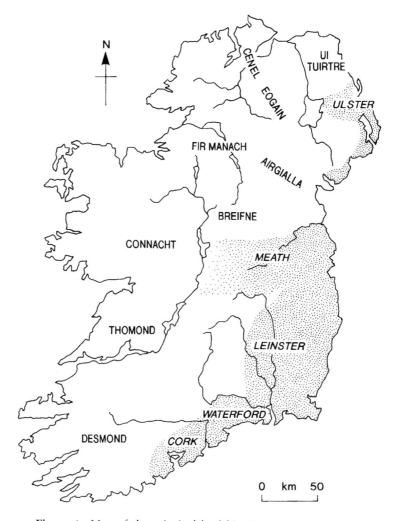

Figure 4 Map of the principal lordships in Ireland, *c.* 1185

now County Louth. In 1185 Domnaill Mac Gillapadraig, the last effective king of Ossory, died. By 1207, when William the Marshal came over to Leinster, which was his by right of marrying Richard fitz Gilbert's daughter and heiress, he was able to make Kilkenny, formerly the centre of Ossory, the chief place of his Earldom of Leinster.

John, king of England since 1199, never forgot Ireland. In 1210 he returned, partly in pursuit of William de Braose, but also to stamp his power on the land. He went a long way to making the royal power effective in Ireland, establishing the basis of its later administration. From the year after his campaign, the Exchequer year 1211–12, survives the only Pipe Roll from Ireland to escape the vicissitudes

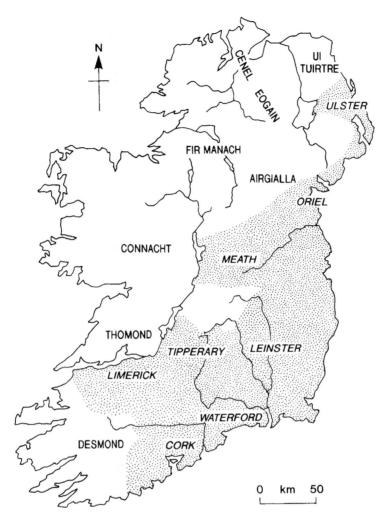

Figure 5 Map of the principal lordships in Ireland, *c.* 1210

of time (Davies and Quinn, 1941). It provides a benchmark of English lordship in Ireland, similar to Domesday in England. By then, the English had seized all the good, corn-growing land of Ireland south and east of a line from Cork to Limerick and Dundalk. North of it there was the English outpost of Ulster, while within it were numbers of areas where the land was still to all intents and purposes Irish (fig. 5).

It is worth emphasising a number of points in this story. First, the progress of the English was remarkably rapid. In forty years they had occupied a much greater area of land than they had conquered in a century of warfare in Wales. Second, this was not an even process, but a staccato one. The occupation or seizure of an

Irish kingdom was usually preceded either by an invitation to intervene (Leinster, Ulster), the death of a strong king and a resultant succession dispute (Munster, Argialla, Ossory) or a straightforward power vacuum, as in Meath. There is no sign either of a planned programme of conquest or indeed of any long-term resistance by the Irish, after the initial battle, or battles, for each kingdom. Third, the beneficiaries of these lordships were not by and large the original soldiers from south Wales, but men who came to Ireland with Henry II and John, men with court connections at the highest level (Phillips, 1984, 97–8). Either they, or their close relatives, were men of wide experience, far beyond that of the Norman lordships of south Wales. These new lords were coming into a land where there was no settled tradition of strong secular centres of power and administration on the lines they knew from England. One of their first needs was to establish these, which would become their baronial *capita*.

CASTLES WITH GREAT TOWERS

From Strongbow's death in 1176 to William Marshal's coming to Ireland after 1200, Leinster was without a resident lord. This left Meath as the greatest Irish lordship, under Hugh de Lacy and his son. In 1174 there was a castle at Trim, attacked and destroyed during Ruadhri Ua Conchabair's raid into Meath. It was rebuilt in stone, as the *caput* of the lordship, and the largest of Irish castles. Its site is undistinguished by nature, set on the south bank of the River Boyne, but its size and grandeur alone mark it out as the *caput* of the lordship of Meath (fig. 6). Ireland's largest castle, its remains consist of the great tower, roughly in the middle of the enclosure; along the river front and towards the town, the curtain has rectangular towers, but towards the south, facing the open country and the approach from Dublin, it has half-round ones (fig. 7). We are not yet in a position to give a detailed description of this castle, because it is the subject of a major campaign of conservation and analysis of the standing fabric, and excavation of the below-ground remains. These studies, when they are complete and published, will greatly amplify our existing knowledge, expressed in the publication of the excavations of 1971–4 (Sweetman, 1978) and an article on the basic outline of the structure and history (McNeill, 1990a).

The great tower still dominates both castle and town by its height and unique design: a central block, to which were attached side towers (fig. 8). It was built in several stages, the first being the central block to first-floor level, but with the walls carried up a floor higher, to support the side towers which rose to that level. This extraordinary structure was roofed, and recent examination of the fabric has shown that it had a wall-walk and parapet on top of the walls of the central block. Later the whole was raised a height of three floors (entry, second and third) in the central block, which also received a north–south dividing wall of stone internally, and four floors (including the ground floor or basement) for the side towers. Its height was then further increased, incorporating the earlier wall-walk into a gallery level above the main third floor (O'Brien, personal communication). Until recently, dating of the great tower at Trim was forced to rely on the traditional mixture of

Figure 6 Trim castle: general view from across the River Boyne

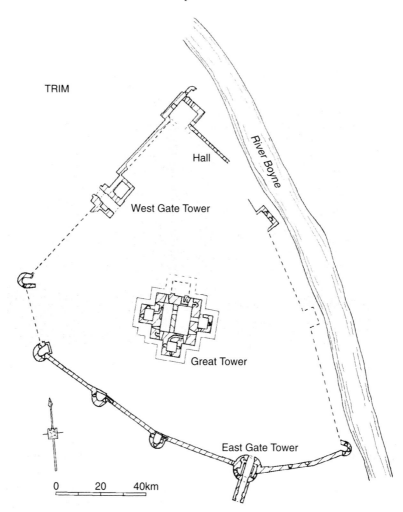

Figure 7 Trim castle: general plan of the castle

scant documentary references, masonry styles or parallels and the general historical context. The position is now greatly clarified by the discovery of oak beams
built into the fabric during construction, which have been dated by dendrochronology. When the detailed sequence of phasing of the tower's construction is
worked out and aligned with these dates, we will know to within a few years the
chronology of its several parts, a remarkable precision for a castle of around 1200,
and a unique insight into the processes and changes of planning which went on.

This great tower was weakly defended. Its entrance was a single door at first-
floor level in the north wall of the east side tower, only partially guarded by a
timber gallery (and that may be later) around the exterior north-east angle of the

Figure 8 Trim castle: view of the great tower from the north (entrance) side

central block. The excavations have shown how this weakness was both recognised in the later thirteenth century and corrected by building a towered screen wall in front of the entrance, to protect it. The loops in the ground floors of the side towers gave no flanking fire, but with their wide embrasures in walls already thin enough, provided obvious points for attack. The side towers were floored with timber (except for the northern one): if an attacker did get in, he would have found access to the rest of the great tower easy.

Display and the provision of rooms were clearly the priority of the design of the completed tower. The varied spaces provided by the plan were used to give a range of different rooms in a number of suites. The entry floor was carefully organised, with a pivotal entry room giving access to the main stair and rooms in the northern and southern side towers. A suite of two rooms occupied the western half, guarding the way from the entry to a stair in the south-west angle of the central block, which led to the second-floor suite and to the great room on the third floor. On the second floor was a suite of rooms, carefully insulated from the main stair in the north-east angle of the main block. The main room was the one which took up the whole of the third floor of the central block, linked to a gallery along what had been the parapet of the first phase. It was clearly the key room, but it is too far from the entrance to be a hall; we should see it as de Lacy's great chamber, not his public hall.

It has always been assumed that the great tower is the earliest stonework surviving at Trim. Its military weakness on the one hand, and the fact that it appears not to provide a great hall among its many rooms on the other, lead us to conclude that the curtain walls, and buildings against them, cannot be much later. In particular, the castle needed a great hall for public life. Its position must be marked by the large windows which can be seen along the Boyne frontage in the northern curtain wall. They have been blocked up later, for they must have been a source of real military weakness along that front. The ground within the courtyard of the castle here is clearly higher than when the castle was in use; a vault below the line of the windows marks the ground level; the great hall was on the first floor.

The curtain walls provide the front and real strength of the castle. Along the lengths of the walls where they are preserved, there are two sets of arrow loops, at courtyard level and along the wall-walk. They are set in good embrasures, and the top ones on the east side have plunging loops of early thirteenth-century type. The walls were studded with towers, mostly destroyed along the Boyne frontage, although now traced through excavation. The north towers are rectangular in plan, but along the south front the towers are semicircular (fig. 9). The walls are dominated by the two gate towers, the west gate to the town, and the south gate to the country and Dublin. Both are single towers with foreworks in front: the stubs of the wing walls of the western tower alone are left, but at the south gate there is a small forward tower linked to the main gate tower by a bridge over the ditch (fig. 10). The towers themselves recall others outside Ireland. The west gate changes from a square to a polygonal plan above the gate passage, like two towers of the de Lacys' home castle of Ludlow (fig. 11). The south gate is more exotic: a circular tower imitating that of Coudray-Salbart in Poitou; it also has deeply plunging arrow slits (fig. 12).

Carrickfergus, the *caput* of John de Courcy in Ulster, provides both a contrast and similarities with Trim: it also has been described in detail in print (McNeill, 1981). The first phase consisted of an oval enclosure at the end of a volcanic dyke projecting into the sea and protecting the harbour of John's new town (fig. 13). For all the fits and starts visible in the masonry, marking individual changes in detail, and annual campaigns, the overall sequence and design of the castle are clear. The early castle, probably started in 1177 or 1178, was an enclosure which was planned from the first to contain a great tower, a hall and at least one other building with good windows. It is worth stressing how small the stone enclosure at Carrickfergus was, less than 45 m long and 25 m wide (145 × 80 ft) internally, while the curtain wall at Trim encloses an area of some 160 by 250 m (500 × 800 ft).

As at Trim, the great tower dominates the whole castle; it faces the line of approach along the rock from the town, and actually occupied nearly a quarter of the area of the enclosure (fig. 14). Unlike Trim, it is a simple rectangle in plan, and was not much subdivided internally; it is likely that the present, sixteenth-century, wall across each floor is the successor of a wooden arcade or wall, necessary if only to provide intermediate support for the floor beams which had to span some 11 m (36 ft). The first floor had a relatively low-status entry room; above it lay a better one and then, at third-floor level, a fine chamber, possibly with a

Figure 9 Trim castle: view along the south front

Figure 10   Trim castle: the main, south gate tower

gallery (described in the published account as a fourth floor). As at Trim, it is difficult to see this room as functioning as a great hall; rather it was John de Courcy's chamber. The great hall was in the courtyard, marked by two windows, with window seats, in the curtain wall east of the keep: it was raised over a low ground floor.

Defensively, the castle is a mirror image of Trim. It relies entirely on the strength of the great tower, commanding the line of approach and providing a genuine strong point. The curtain wall has no projecting towers (the restrictions of the rock might be in part the cause of this) and the gate was a simple arch through the curtain; only after 1215, apparently, was it even equipped with a double arrow loop. The gate is in the east side, which can be approached easily at low tide; once at the gate, the curtain hides an attacker from view from the great tower. In spite of its size and defensive weakness, however, Carrickfergus was a fine castle in other ways. The great tower is not only impressive, but it provided a splendid great chamber for John de Courcy, as well as living space for his household. The surviving remains of the great hall are marked by good windows, and the standard of the ashlar details, cut in fine cream-coloured stone from Cultra across Belfast Lough, is high and they show up well against the dark grey basalt rubble of the bulk of the walls.

The second stone castle associated with John de Courcy's lordship in Ulster is Dundrum, in Co. Down (Jope, 1966, 207–11). It is sited on a rocky hill

Figure 11 Trim castle: the west gate tower, facing towards the town

overlooking Dundrum Bay and the approach to Lecale and southern Ulster along
the coast. Excavation in 1950 (Waterman, 1951) showed that the top of the hill saw
a sequence of four phases of construction: a perimeter bank, the present stone curtain wall, the round great tower, and the inner gate house, in that order. Whether
the bank pre-dated 1177 or not, is unknown: the excavator thought not, but there
was evidence of earlier occupation of the hill top. The curtain wall is quite thin
(around 1.2 m (4 ft)), and polygonal in plan, enclosing an area of some 60 m by 40 m
(200 ft by 130 ft). It had no towers and the entrance was a simple gate with a small
pit in front; it is obvious why it was replaced in the thirteenth century with a proper
gate house (fig. 15). There is a series of holes through the curtain wall at wall-walk
level, usually interpreted as for hoarding. Given how narrow the wall-walk is, however (the parapet is about 65 cm (26 in) wide, leaving a quite inadequate walk of
only 45 cm or 18 in), these were probably designed to widen the fighting platform
inside the curtain, not outside. A double latrine set into the curtain wall at the east
side shows that there were buildings within it of some permanence and pretension,
presumably of timber, for there are no signs of their attachment.

The 1211–12 Pipe Roll records building work at Dundrum (Davies and Quinn,
1941, 59; Quinn, 1943, 36). The entry notes that the work was on the great tower,
the (or a) lesser tower and the hall, as well as a granary and stable: the total sum
expended was only £4–15–2, too small for the buildings to have been totally

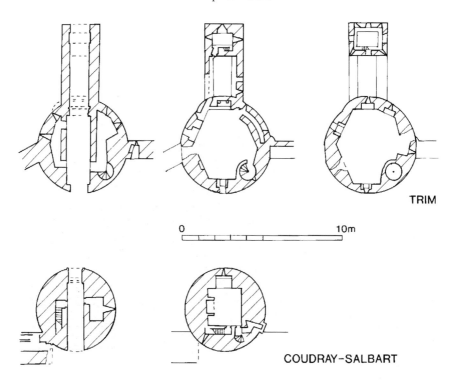

Figure 12 The plan of Trim south gate tower (*l – r* ground, first, second floors) compared with that of Coudray-Salbart (*l – r* ground and first floors)

constructed from nothing in that year. The distinction between the great tower and the hall is confirmed by the design of the present great tower. It is round, with three floors. The ground floor functioned as a basement to the entry floor above; it also gave access to a well. The entry floor is occupied by a fine room, with a fireplace, windows with seats, and access to the wall-walk or a latrine.

One of John's grants in 1185 was to Theobald Walter, of large tracts of what is now north Co. Tipperary (Empey, 1981, 6). Certainly later, and apparently from the beginning, the *caput* was at Nenagh, where the castle is marked by the remains of an enclosure of stone, perhaps 30 m (100 ft) across, with a round great tower and a later gate house (Gleeson and Leask, 1936). The great tower is the finest of the round towers in Irish castles, although it owes the top 7 m (23 ft) of its 30 m (100 ft) height to an addition made in the second half of the nineteenth century, using funds originally collected in America to build a new church (fig. 16). This work restored some of the height lost in the slighting it received in the 1690s, and damage caused in the mid-eighteenth century by an attempt to blow it up.

The ground floor of the tower was originally unlit and reached from the floor above by a ladder. The entry floor has as its only features two deeply plunging arrow loops, and a stair to the second floor. This is a much finer room, some

Figure 13   Carrickfergus castle: general view of the castle from the south-east

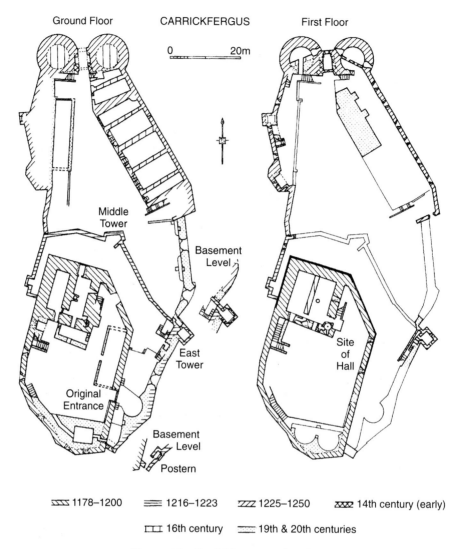

CARRICKFERGUS

Ground Floor   First Floor

0 _____ 20m

Middle
Tower

Basement
Level

East
Tower

Site
of
Hall

Original
Entrance

Basement
Level

Postern

〰〰 1178–1200   ≡ 1216–1223   ⧄ 1225–1250   ⬙ 14th century (early)

⊏⊐ 16th century   ≈ 19th & 20th centuries

Figure 14 Carrickfergus castle: plan

9 m (30 ft) in diameter, with a fireplace, windows with seats, and access to the wall-walk or a latrine. The second floor was the original principal floor: the present third floor is an addition. This is shown by a change in the masonry visible internally a metre below the third-floor offset; by the change in the design of the openings, from round-headed to segmental arches, the insertion of the corbels to carry the third floor; by the change in plan in the stair, from a mural one following the line of the wall, to a circular vice half-way between the floors; and by the mouldings of the two floors. The arch of the embrasure leading to the stair on the second floor has its round arch decorated with a complex chevron, typical of the

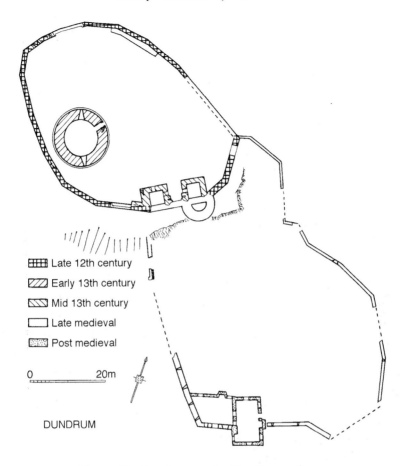

Figure 15 Dundrum castle, Co. Down: plan

Irish Romanesque (fig. 17). The arches and the corbels of the third floor have mouldings and attached shafts of thirteenth-century fashion. The great tower up to the change may be attributed to Theobald Walter before his death in 1206; the third floor (and perhaps the gate house) to his son, Theobald II, who did not take possession of his lands until the end of his long minority in 1221.

Here we may note three other towers in Munster castles: at Kiltinane, Ardfinnan and Inchiquin. Kiltinane and Ardfinnan were both manors granted by John to Philip of Worcester, at the same time as his grant to Theobald Walter, although the massive motte at Knockgraffon probably marks the original *caput* of his lordship (Empey, 1981, 8–10). Both are marked by round towers, with Ardfinnan being the larger, but less well preserved (fig. 18). Both are probably later than the strict limits of this chapter; the only evidence for the date of either is a fine floral chamfer stop on the round-arched door from the first floor to the second or wall-walk at Kiltinane, which may be assigned to the earlier thirteenth century (see fig. 117).

Figure 16 Nenagh castle: general view

Figure 17   Nenagh castle: fireplace and doorway decorated with Romanesque ornament on the second floor of the great tower

Inchiquin was part of the lordship granted in 1177 to Robert fitz Stephen in the kingdom of Cork, and later granted by him to Gerald fitz Maurice (Collins, 1945, 31). The round tower is much ruined now, but the first floor can be seen to have had a fireplace, windows with seats, and a single latrine, in contrast to the poorly equipped ground floor (Hartnett, 1945, 42–5). A last round tower to be noted is the remarkable structure on a small island in Lough Oughter, probably erected by William de Lacy just after 1220 (Orpen, *Normans*, III, 44). It is notable, apart from its situation, for the almost total lack of features that would hint at the use for which it was built; it looks like a plain, purely military outpost.

There was certainly a castle at Dunamase in Co. Laois, at the northern frontier of the English lordship of Leinster, by 1210 (Orpen, *Normans*, II, 218), and it is mentioned in the 1211–2 Pipe Roll (Davies and Quinn, 1941, 17). The castle is superbly situated on a rock with wide views over the lands to the north (fig. 19). The remains of a massively built rectangular block, in part reconstructed in post-medieval times and also badly damaged by explosives, lie at the top of the hill. The current excavations may shed light on the date and the purpose of this

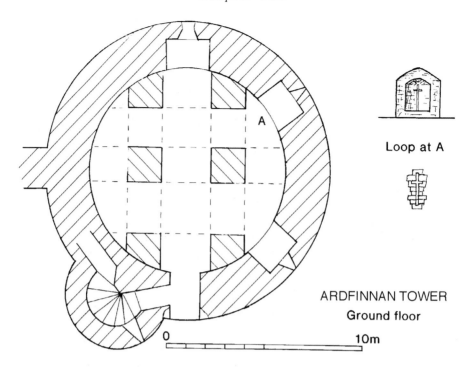

Loop at A

ARDFINNAN TOWER

Ground floor

0   10m

Figure 18 Ardfinnan castle: plan of the round tower

building which is apparently a hall, rather than a chamber tower. The excavations have radically enlarged our knowledge of the sequence of events along the line of the main curtain wall (Hodkinson, 1995). We have already noted the discovery of defences from before 1169. After that comes the insertion of a mortared stone gate house into the earlier wall. This was replaced by a new gate house, square-fronted in plan with a narrow gate passage in the middle. The gate house may be seen as having two narrow towers on either side of the passage, but in fact it is better to think of it as a single, massive tower, pierced by the passage. The gate house was equipped with plunging arrow loops, as was the new curtain wall built on either side of it, where they were placed at precisely regular intervals along it. At least constructionally later is the stone barbican, also equipped with plunging loops, and an earthwork outer barbican (fig. 20).

Hodkinson proposes that the first gate house, reinforcing the earlier dry-stone wall, might be the work of Meiler fitz Henry before 1207, and that the great tower at the top of the hill might be his work too. We may surely identify the second curtain wall and gate house with the work of William Marshal between 1208 and 1215. The date of the stone barbican might be later, perhaps the work of his sons, reinforcing what was by then a gate house of clearly obsolete design.

The castle of Maynooth became the principal place for the barony which emerged later as the core of the Earldom of Kildare. The castle is now hard to interpret,

Figure 19 Dunamase castle: general view from the east

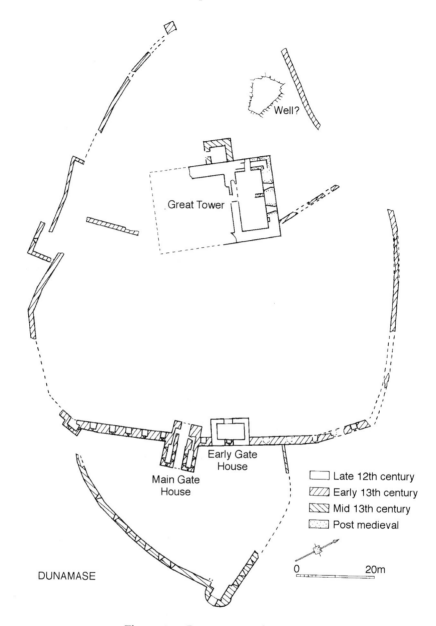

Figure 20 Dunamase castle: plan

with much of the stonework lacking features, and it has been the subject of heavy restoration (fig. 21). Much is later, but there is a large rectangular structure at the western side of the present enclosure, which is usually known as the keep, and ascribed to around 1200 (Leask, 1977, 36). On the east side are the toothings for

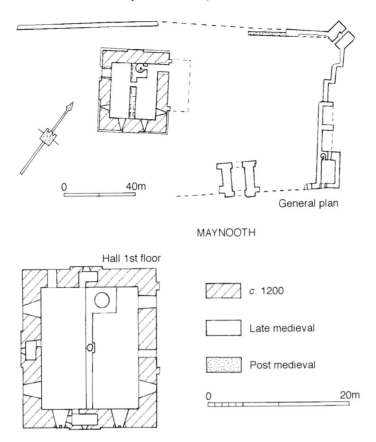

MAYNOOTH

Hall 1st floor

▨	*c.* 1200
☐	Late medieval
▦	Post medieval

0   20m

General plan

0   40m

Figure 21 Maynooth castle: general plan and plan of the first floor of the great tower

the forework for a stair to the first-floor entry, at the north end of the wall. The ground floor has a number of loops of uncertain age, and an inserted spine wall, or arcade, running north–south up the middle. This wall carries the base of a pier in the centre of the floor, which presumably supported an arcade dividing the floor space into two; as with Carrickfergus, it is likely that this later stone arcade effectively replaced an original timber one.

The building shows signs of three periods of stonework. The external quoins change from granite to tufa at the level of the first floor. How significant this is in terms of an absolute chronology is unclear, but the top two or three metres of the building are clearly an addition; the shallow projections on three walls are abruptly terminated, and the walling (not just the quoins) changes nature. This heightening of the building included a mural gallery or elaborate wall-walk. The only windows are the large, but much restored, ones at first-floor level. At this level, too, are three small chambers contrived partly in the thickness of the south, west and north walls and partly in shallow exterior projections from the walls. A door midway along the east wall presumably led to a room over the stair in the forework. There are now the traces of three sets of floors below the level of the later addition: corbels, joist holes and an offset. Not only can none of these be co-existent, but it is very difficult to understand how a floor carried on the first two could have functioned, for there are no signs of windows to go with it. As it stands, the tower at Maynooth appears to have been purely a large, first-floor hall, quite possibly open to the roof until floors were inserted, with very little else originally provided in it, and as such may be compared to the structure at the top of Dunamase hill.

CASTLES APPARENTLY WITHOUT GREAT TOWERS

The most substantial survivor of the early castles of Limerick is that of Adare, *caput* of Geoffrey de Marisco's lordship granted in 1199 (fig. 22). It is now very overgrown but was the subject of a detailed nineteenth-century survey (Dunraven, 1865). Its site, beside the River Maigue, has no natural defensive qualities apart from the riverside. In plan it is now divided into an inner and outer ward, but when this dates to is quite unclear (fig. 23). It is always assumed that the inner is the earlier, but the walling at the junction shows no sign of change on the exterior, while on the inside the inner ward wall can be seen to be butted against the outer curtain, and the gate into the inner ward is undoubtedly late. Three elements concern us here: the hall and gate in the outer ward and the tower in the inner. The gate is a simple, round opening, only later strengthened with a small tower, containing a portcullis, added behind.

At the south-west corner of the outer courtyard, just within the gate, stands the early first-floor hall. There are two double windows east of the door in the long, northern wall, and one in the east, gable wall; the south wall, overlooking the river, is less well preserved, but there are the remains of two more double windows and, at the west end, a door to a latrine tower built over the river. The windows are of fine quality, with two lights set in the one opening, with heavy continuous roll mouldings of the Western Transitional style, and comparable to the west window of the nearby Cistercian monastery of Monasternenagh (Leask, 1977, 35). As such, they are datable to the years immediately after 1200.

The tower has lost its southern half above ground-floor level, but the south wall survives to its battlements. In plan it is rectangular (fig. 24): each corner has a projection to east and west which Leask described as buttresses but, with their shallow projection in only one direction, their function as such may be doubted. The tower shows the gable in the north wall of the original roof over the first floor. At some later date, a second and third floor were added, and a vault was inserted over the ground floor. This work may be dated to the late medieval period (fourteenth to sixteenth centuries) by the punched dressing on the limestone jambs of doors in the west wall of the ground floor and north wall of the first floor, which were also apparently inserted then. As originally built, a two-storey building, possibly with an attic, this is an unconvincing great tower. If it were the great tower of the castle, its relationship with the undoubted hall would be interesting.

Figure 22 Adare castle: aerial view of the castle from the north

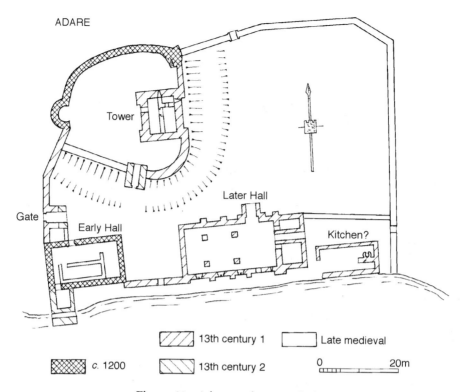

ADARE

Figure 23 Adare castle: general plan

The hall is sited against the outer curtain, next to the gate. Its windows, like those of Trim and Carrickfergus, breached the curtain, although they were given some protection by the river. Not only was it a source of military weakness to the whole castle, but its siting made it very vulnerable if the castle were to be attacked. This is especially true if the division into inner and outer wards is original, for the valuable hall would then have been left in the outer one, close to the weakly defended outer gate.

Carlingford castle was built on a rock promontory overlooking the harbour and town of Carlingford (fig. 25), which was the *caput* of the lordship, in north-eastern Oriel, granted to Hugh de Lacy, younger son of his namesake, the first lord of Meath, by Thomas de Verdon between 1192 and 1199 (Orpen, *Normans*, II, 121–2). The 1211–12 Pipe Roll records the existence of a castle at Carlingford, although this may not be the existing structure: 'and for supplies and other things at the castle, 11 shillings'. The roll also records a gate there, possibly a town gate, but more likely the gate of the castle (Davies and Quinn, 1941, 65).

The early remains occupy the western half of the enclosure, which is some 30m (100 ft) across (Buckley and Sweetman, 1991, 320). The eastern half is occupied by buildings which abut the western curtain wall (see below, pp. 192–3). The curtain is built in short, straight sections; in plan it is divided about midway by a

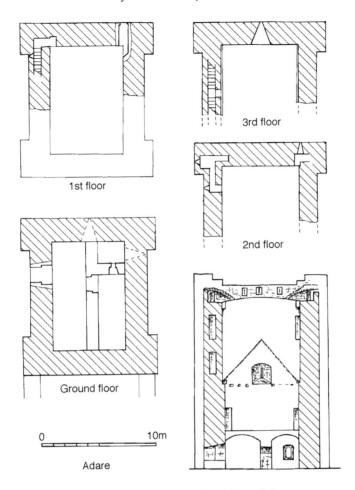

1st floor

3rd floor

2nd floor

Ground floor

0   10m

Adare

Figure 24 Adare castle: plan and section of the tower

tower projecting out to the west (fig. 26). Only the north wall of this tower and part of the west one survive, the rest being brought down presumably when the railway cutting was built just beyond it. Behind a modern wall are the remains of a rear wall and two east–west ones. These probably defined the gate passage, although it is only 1.7 m (5 ft 8 in) wide. As with the gate house of Dunamase, it is not clear whether we should look on the whole as a single tower, pierced by the gate passage, or a true double-towered gate house.

North of the gate tower, the curtain is built in short lengths, so that it bends round quite sharply. There are two tiers of loops in the existing walling: four at courtyard level and two at first floor, which are better preserved. At the point where the later wall abuts the early curtain, the stubs of two walls on the outside show that there was a tower here originally, reached by a first-floor door blocked by the later wall. This was probably then replaced by one adapted from an earlier loop.

Figure 25 Carlingford: view of the castle set above the harbour and town

CARLINGFORD

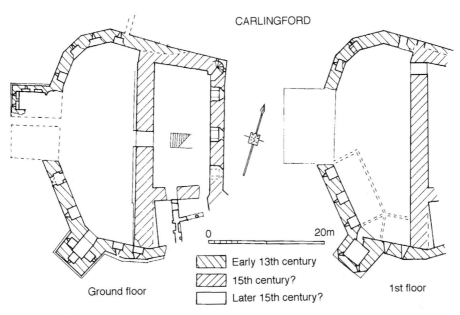

Early 13th century

15th century?

Later 15th century?

Ground floor

1st floor

0   20m

Figure 26 Carlingford castle: general plan of the ground floor, and the western half at first-floor level

The curtain south of the gate tower is in two sections, separated by the south-west tower. The section nearest the gate has two loops at courtyard level, three above them, and then the wall-walk. The section east of the south-west tower has a loop at the level (relative to the present courtyard) of a semi-basement, and then two levels above it before the wall-walk. The first floor of the south-west tower (which also has a basement) links with the first-floor loops of the curtain east of it; this floor is about 1.7 m (5 ft 8 in) above the first-floor level of the buildings to the north. They were joined by a lobby over the ground-floor entrance to the south-west tower, which presumably contained a stair. None of the buildings implied by the loops has left the stub or scar of a wall against the curtain wall and there is very little space between the first-floor doorway to the south-west tower and the first embrasure to its north. Presumably the buildings inside Carlingford were of timber.

Most of the loops were set in wide embrasures, square in plan, with bluntly pointed rear arches; none have seats. The first-floor ones have plunging loops. The parapet walls are pierced by square holes at wall-walk level which must be for true hoarding, not just, like Dundrum, to extend the wall-walk inwards, because the buildings on the inner side of the curtain would prevent that. The south-west tower changes in plan above the first floor from square to half octagonal, like the west gate of Trim; its likely builder, Hugh de Lacy, was Walter de Lacy's brother (fig. 27). With its cliff-top site, the two towers to the south and north, and the massive gate tower, Carlingford presented a formidable front to the world, but also timber buildings of some elaboration within.

Figure 27   Carlingford castle: south-west tower

EARLY ROYAL CASTLES

It is surprising to anyone accustomed to the study of castles in England that we have been able to proceed so far without much mention of the royal castles. This was one of the key elements of the polity of Ireland in the late twelfth century: the absence of real centres of English royal power in Ireland. The king had seized the ports of Dublin, Waterford and Wexford, and had demesne lands particularly in Munster, but he lacked either the equivalent of the baronial *capita*, or a close network of lesser castles in any region. The provision of the latter, as with the building of castles along the east side of the Shannon, is a topic which we will meet in the next chapter; here we must look at the question of the major castles.

There is no trace of what, if anything, served as Henry II's bases in Waterford or Wexford. Reginald's tower in the latter town was not a castle, but part of the town wall, stronger than most town towers because it was at the angle of the wall and the waterfront. He had a castle in Dublin, which he took from Strongbow, but it would appear to have been a motte and bailey structure (Orpen, *Normans*, II, 306). John seized Drogheda castle on the death of Hugh de Lacy in 1186, and never granted it to his son, although the king was still paying rent for it to the de Lacy heirs in the fourteenth century. Drogheda castle was also a motte and bailey, although it may have had stone walls added (Buckley and Sweetman, 1991, 289–91).

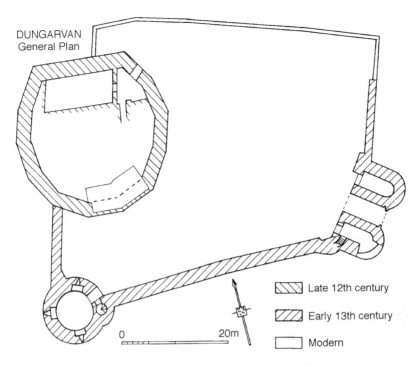

DUNGARVAN
General Plan

Late 12th century

Early 13th century

Modern

0   20m

Figure 28   Dungarvan castle: general plan

Dungarvan marked the south-western extremity of Henry II's demesne lands, as defined in the Treaty of Windsor in 1175 (Flanagan, 1989, appendix 3). The castle of Dungarvan is not at present an inspiring site: it became a British Army barracks, and then a Garda Siochana station after 1921, only to be deserted now. Its plan is in two parts: a twelve-sided enclosure, 21.6 m (71 ft) in internal diameter, with walls 2.4 m (8 ft) thick, and an outer courtyard with a large round angle tower and a twin-towered gate house (fig. 28). The walls have been much repointed and the crucial junctions are sometimes obscured, but it looks as though the outer curtain wall, angle tower and gate house of the outer ward were all built at the same time and added to the inner enclosure. This enclosure is now filled up with earth and vaulted structures to first-floor level; some of these latter are clearly later. It is possible, however, that the inner enclosure at Dungarvan, when stripped of modern accretions, may prove to have as its core the castle of Henry II or John.

Neither the mottes of Dublin or Drogheda nor the small enclosure at Dungarvan would do as royal *capita* after 1200. In 1204, John ordered the Justiciar to 'construct a strong castle there [at Dublin] with good ditches and strong walls'; the reason he gives is that 'you have no fit place for the custody of our treasure and for other purposes' (Orpen, *Normans*, II, 307–8). He commanded the Justiciar to start with a tower and then to proceed to build the '*castellum et baluum*'; as Orpen notes (*Normans*, II, 308), a good example of the distinction between a tower and enclosing walls. The castle itself has largely disappeared under the weight of post-medieval changes, although the south-eastern tower and the bases of the two western towers either survive in the core of later building or have been exposed by excavation.

The overall plan and the site of the great hall built by Henry III are known from eighteenth-century plans and descriptions (Maguire, 1974). The overall plan was roughly rectangular, with the main gate in the middle of one long side, the north wall. It was guarded by two quite small semicircular towers projecting forward on either side of the gate. The four angle towers were larger, internally circular, with widely splayed external plinths; there was a small semicircular tower more or less midway along the south wall. Interestingly, the plan has no such great tower as John's writ seems to demand, an indication perhaps of the small extent of his actual effect on the design, given that he was away in England when the plan was drawn up (fig. 29).

The Pipe Roll of 1211–12 records the massive total of £733–16–11 for works at Limerick castle. The only castle in England to receive such a sum in a single year in the reign of King John was Scarborough, also in 1211–12; Henry II exceeded £700 in four years at Dover, and Richard I in one year at the Tower of London, and, of course, at Château Gaillard (Brown, 1955). We can safely identify the existing castle at Limerick with King John (fig. 30). Excavation, already noted above for the discovery of the earlier fort on the site, has clarified greatly our knowledge of the castle plan (Wiggins, 1991). It was clearly intended to occupy an approximately square area between the Shannon river to the west and the road to the north, which led to the bridge over the Shannon. These two fronts were completed, but the curtain to the east, sheltered in part by the town, has now been shown never to have been finished; the south-east angle tower was never built, either, and it is not clear whether the southern curtain was. John's effort resulted in a tremendous masonry show front; round the back, the castle was enclosed by a ditch and timber. Since then, as elsewhere, the castle history has been chequered; it was converted to an infantry barrack in 1787, and the walls show many signs of rebuilding.

The curtain walls have all been more or less cut down and refaced in recent times. There were three large corner towers, circular inside; all have been cut down for artillery. The two western ones, fronting the river, have straightforward loops at ground level; the northern one has loops with seats, but they may be restorations of the 1930s. The north-eastern tower is the best preserved. At ground-floor level, there is a single embrasure serving two slightly plunging arrow loops facing out to the vulnerable salient angle (fig. 31).

The gate is the earliest in Ireland to be protected by two towers, although it, too, has suffered from later reconstruction (fig. 32). The entrance is barred by a gate with a high slot machicolation in front and a portcullis groove behind it. Recent excavation confirms that there was no structure behind the two towers beside the gate passage, but the gate passage was prolonged by a sort of reverse barbican. These towers now have ground floors entered only by recent doors from the courtyard; they may well have been reached originally only by ladders from above. The first floor had three elements joined together, the two tower rooms and the platform (now rebuilt) over the gate passage which supported the portcullis mechanism, and was reached by doors from either tower. Mural stairs linked the

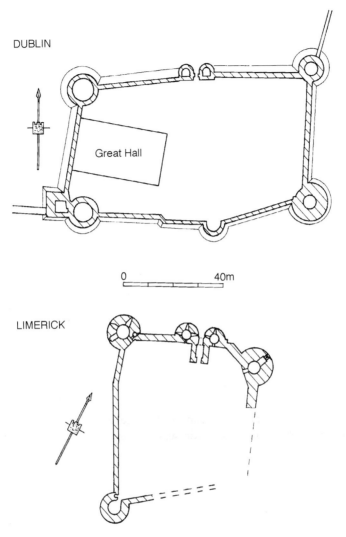

Figure 29 Dublin and Limerick: plans of the two main early royal castles in Ireland

first and second floors, which linked to the wall-walks on either side; the present doors at first-floor level were forced through in modern times when the curtain was lowered.

We may conclude this survey of early royal works with discussion of two lesser ones. The second largest sum recorded as spent on works at a castle is the £129–12–0 on Athlone (Davies and Quinn, 1941, 25). This must be connected with the decision of the Justiciar to build it in stone in 1210, and the recorded collapse of a tower there, which killed Richard Tuit (Orpen, 1907b, 262–5). Again, the position is confused by later rebuilding of the castle as a barracks, but there are the remains of a polygonal tower enclosing what is probably the base of a motte.

Figure 30 Limerick castle: general view from the Shannon bridge

Figure 31 Limerick castle: north-west tower and gate house

A writ of 1216 from King John ordered the Constable of Carrickfergus castle
to enclose an outer ward there, work which seems to have been completed by 1224
(McNeill, 1981, 4). This meant what is now the middle curtain at the castle, a wall
with two turrets and two wall towers, erected purely to reinforce the defences,
not to add significantly to the area enclosed. The main feature was the east tower,
guarding both a salient angle of the wall and the line of approach across the shore
exposed at low tide, but in dead ground from the great tower (fig. 33). This was
protected particularly by three triple arrow loops in the basement of the tower,
designed for the use of crossbowmen (McNeill, 1981, 29, 56). Although the central
section of this curtain and the central tower were knocked down to below ground
level around 1700, excavation showed the polygonal plan of the tower, and that
there was no gate house. The gate, which must have existed, was probably simply
sited beside the central tower.

DISCUSSION

We may pick out several themes for discussion among these castles. The first is
their actual existence in stone at all, at this date. The lords who caused them to be
built had come to a country where, as far as we know, there was no significant

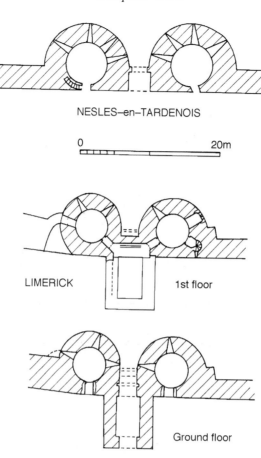

NESLES–en–TARDENOIS

0   20m

LIMERICK   1st floor

Ground floor

Figure 32   Plans of the gate houses of Nesles-en-Tardenois and Limerick castles

tradition of secular building in mortared stone. In the Church there had been round towers (which involved scaffolding and lifting gear) since the tenth century; complex mouldings and architectural carving in Irish Romanesque dated only from the early twelfth century; the elaborate planning of monastic complexes for Savignac or Cistercian houses dated from the same time. Organising the building of their castles must have needed a special effort, with at least the master masons brought into Ireland. Combined with the church building they patronised, they must have given a major boost to the building industry.

This effort they clearly found essential. John de Courcy had a castle to retreat to in Co. Antrim, surely Carrickfergus, in 1178, the year after his seizure of the lordship. Unless the great tower of Nenagh was built during the minority of Theobald Walter II, or he used remarkably old-fashioned masons after 1221, it must have been built by his father before 1206. Nenagh was granted to Theobald and Adare to Geoffrey de Marisco in about 1199. The window style Geoffrey's

Figure 33 Carrickfergus castle: east tower

masons used would have been outdated a decade or two later, so he must have started work soon after the grant. Here we see some of the organisation at work, for he employed men who had been working at the Cistercian abbey nearby to build his hall. Building in stone, rather than earth and timber, was neither cheap nor quick: these lords were sending a clear message of their intentions to commit themselves to Ireland.

A second theme is that they liked great towers in their castles. Of the baronial castles we have considered here, only Adare (which has a detached tower of uncertain date and status) and Carlingford (which has a dominant gate tower) do not have a clear great tower. At Carrickfergus, Trim, Dunamase and Maynooth, they are rectangular; at the others round. For the majority, it is clear that they were not built to accommodate halls. Trim and Carrickfergus have fine rooms on their third floors, but not only are they hopelessly remote for access by the general public for whom halls were intended, but there are halls in the courtyard. Like the round towers, these were towers for the accommodation of the lord and his household alone. Conversely, at Maynooth and Dunamase (in so far as we can say anything about the latter) the great towers were almost entirely taken up by the hall. The great towers were either for the lord's chamber or for the hall, but not for both. Nor can they be distinguished by size, but only by analysis of their internal plan in the context of the other buildings of the castle.

The traditional name for such towers, 'keeps', implies a military role for them: to be the strong point and place of ultimate resort for the whole castle. This role the great towers of castles in Ireland were ill suited to perform. The greatest, Trim, was weak enough to need to be reinforced later in the thirteenth century. Dividing the lord's accommodation off from the great hall meant that, if either was used as a place of strength, inevitably the other element was abandoned in the case of a serious attack. The price of giving up the great hall, the most expensive room in the castle and seat of the lord's prestige, to take the brunt of the damage seems a remarkable one, and the same applies to the lord's chamber. As 'keeps' they are inadequate. Nor were the curtain walls very much more consistently military in their design. The great hall windows of Adare, Trim and Carrickfergus were all obvious sources of weakness. Carlingford and Dunamase are strongly defended by nature and by construction. The two royal castles of Dublin and Limerick are strong, but Dungarvan was not. The second period of work significantly strengthened Carrickfergus, which illustrates the point: the first period placed comfort as high as defence in priority. The main purpose of these castles for the lords was to give a suitably impressive setting for their exercise of the new lordships they had acquired. This is seen at its most extreme at Carrickfergus, where the dominant tower with John de Courcy's lodging took up more than a quarter of the castle's area.

The deliberate nature of this choice is reinforced when we remember that the castles were all paid for and designed by men from outside Ireland. The lords had wide connections with the Angevin court and there was no native tradition of castle building to cause this pattern. These connections and a knowledge of ideas outside Ireland show freely in the designs. The most obvious is the popularity of the round great tower, which we must surely attribute to the prestige of the great tower of Pembroke castle (Renn, 1968; King, 1978). Its builder was William Marshal, lord of Leinster, and it was set at the main point of embarkation for Ireland. It is interesting to compare it with Nenagh. The latter takes the idea of the round great chamber tower from Pembroke, but its walls (themselves the thickest of the round towers of Ireland's castles) are some 70 cm (28 in) thinner than those of Pembroke, so that the windows give more light; Nenagh also has fine carving, which Pembroke lacks. There is nothing of Pembroke's elaborate fighting top at Nenagh: Theobald Walter asked for a more comfortable chamber tower than his model. A second general parallel is the use of the arrow loops with plunging loops which became popular in the early thirteenth century to control the base of walls, at Trim, Carlingford, Nenagh and Dunamase.

Two specific parallels are interesting. The first is the use of towers on the Lacy castles at Trim and at Carlingford, which go from square to semi-octagonal. This is surely a personal thing, recalling the north-east and north-west towers at the Lacy *caput* of Ludlow (Renn, 1987, fig. 8); we might almost talk of homesickness. The second is the round west gate tower at Trim, taken from the Poitevin castle of Coudray-Salbart (Curnow, 1980), but with an added barbican. This was clearly a question of de Lacy providing a suitably impressive parallel as the main element in the show front of his new castle. The town gate, with its square to polygonal plan, the parallel with his home castle, is almost a private matter, a personal reference; the west gate (the approach from Dublin) a design inviting comment and explanation to impress a guest.

Constructionally, round towers present the builder with one problem, that of flooring the space. In a rectangular building, it is easy to run joists between the two nearer sides, although there may be differing ways of securing them in to the walls. At three of the round towers of Ireland, the holes for the joists are still preserved enough to allow them to be measured and their pattern planned (fig. 34). Inchiquin and Clogh Oughter both have a very similar scheme, with a single central beam providing support to the beams running across it. The first floor at Dundrum is different, with three lower beams providing greater support; given the relative irregularity of the beams, however, this is as likely to be the result of a nervous carpenter giving more support in case of trouble as a careful assessment of the risks. The second floor is different: it uses half the number of beams, and the crossbeams are not set lower than the others, but must have been elaborately jointed where they met. This might reinforce the view (Jope, 1966, fig. 135) that the second floor is later than the rest of the tower. This view is based solely on the nature of the mural chamber vaults, and ignores the continuity of the stair, chimney flue and the absence of a change in masonry. What this information means is unclear: the ways used to floor the round towers of Wales would be the first point of comparison to see if there are different craft traditions at work here.

The royal castles compare interestingly with the baronial ones. Dublin and Limerick share the idea of the roughly polygonal plan with corner towers and a pair of smaller towers at the gate, but with no great tower. Again, as with round towers, this is a theme which links the castles of south Wales, the work of William Marshal or Hubert de Burgh (brother of William, lord of lands in Tipperary and Limerick), and then France (Knight, 1987; Curnow, 1980; Heliot 1965). The French ideas show most strongly in the design of the gates at Dublin and Limerick

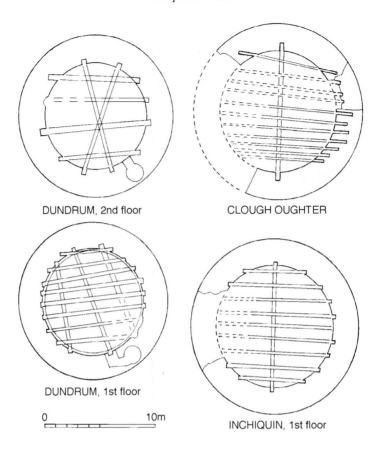

DUNDRUM, 2nd floor

CLOUGH OUGHTER

DUNDRUM, 1st floor

0   10m

INCHIQUIN, 1st floor

Figure 34 Plans of the floor joists in the great towers at Dundrum (Co. Down), Clogh Oughter and Inchiquin castles

(fig. 31). They do not have true gate houses in the sense of single buildings with towers on either side of the passage, bound together at first-floor level; instead there are two small towers set close together, with the gate between them. This is unlike the work of William Marshal at Chepstow or Usk, where there is no gate tower at all, although here we have the two similar gate houses of Dunamase and Carlingford. Nesles-en-Tardenois has the same design as Limerick, with the towers circular within (see fig. 32); Dourdan has similarly small towers, but projecting back behind the curtain to provide a second pair of rooms behind the towers, which leads, through Boulogne, Bolingbroke or Beeston, to the full gate houses of the later thirteenth century (Châtellain, 1981; Curnow, 1980).

    The royal work of 1215–23 at Carrickfergus was much less ambitious, although also putting general principles into practice. The aim was to strengthen the defences and the method was to deploy archery in the same way as in a number of late twelfth-century castles built by the Angevins in England, from the Avranches tower at Dover or the Bell tower at the Tower of London around 1190, to the Buttevant

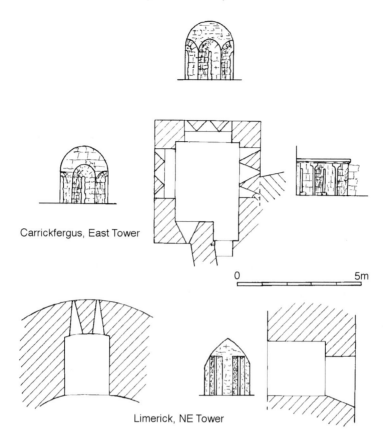

Carrickfergus, East Tower

0   5m

Limerick, NE Tower

Figure 35 Two examples of the royal works in Ireland: multiple arrow loops in the east
tower of Carrickfergus castle and the north-east tower at Limerick castle

tower at Corfe of 1202–4 (Renn, 1969; RCHM, 1970, 60), as well as in France. At
Carrickfergus, and in the north-east tower of Limerick castle, two or three arrow
loops were gathered into the one embrasure, giving the archer a choice of fields
to control (fig. 35). At Carrickfergus, a more specific idea was employed: to place
a strong tower, to be defended by archers firing through multiple loops, which
would control a weak point, typically a salient angle. Clearly the masons on the
royal works in Ireland were at least aware of the latest ideas of castle defence
design in England or France.

Defence was not the whole purpose of a castle, however: the administration of
the lordship depended on it, and the lord lived there in as much comfort as he
could. Below the major castles, which were the heads of lordships, stood the lord's
tenants. These take us to questions of the provision of lesser fortifications, not
meant to be the set pieces of design and major centres of power in the land: the
second line of castles. This matter of the proliferation of castles affected all the
lords, with their tenants and their lesser manors, and to this we must now turn.

CHAPTER THREE

EARLY CASTLES OF EARTH
AND TIMBER

———— •◆• ————

COMPARING EARTH AND TIMBER CASTLES WITH
STONE CASTLES

The castles which we now see as substantial earthworks must be approached in a different way from those which have left the remains of stone walls. This is not so much because the castles themselves were essentially different for being built in a different way, but because our knowledge of them is. Indeed, the very distinction between earthworks and stone may be shown to be wrong if excavation discovers the buried walls within what appeared as mounds of earth. To us they are earthworks, because that is how we see and recognise them now, but it is better to think of them as timber castles. Even if the builders used no stone, they were to the contemporary visitor's eye often predominately timber castles, either because much of the earthwork was revetted or concealed by timber, or because the buildings were of timber (Higham and Barker, 1992). Unless the earthwork sites have been excavated, we have little idea of much of their structure or development. Similarly, there are few, or no, documents that relate to many of the earthwork castles, unlike the stone castles, where normally we know the ownership and sometimes have dates of construction and use.

It is common to think of the timber and earth castles as being more 'primitive', and older; that somehow, timber castles were replaced by stone ones as time went on. Many were, but castles continued to use earthworks at all periods, while the use of timber for some of the buildings at least never ceased. Conversely, some of the earliest castles were of stone from the beginning. This said, it is equally true that there was a steady diminution over time in both the amount of timber work used in individual castles and in the number of wholly timber castles built. In particular, the commonest form of earthwork castle, the motte castle, does not seem to have been built beyond the thirteenth century, a matter to which we will return. Timber castles undoubtedly loom larger in the body of castles in Ireland before the mid-thirteenth century than they do later.

It would be convenient if we could equate stone castles with the high status of major *capita*, with the corollary that timber castles were the castles of the lesser lords and the major tenants. In part this may be true: all the lesser castles identified as such are earthworks now. However, it is also clear that some major castles in Ireland could be built of earth and timber. The castle of Drogheda is now marked by a large motte; the castle of Old Ross by a motte and bailey; a motte probably lies beneath the great tower of Athlone castle (Orpen, 1907b, 263–5); John de Courcy appears to have started to build a motte within the earlier earthwork at Downpatrick. Athlone may not have been a prime royal castle from the first (although it always takes a prominent position in the records), but the rest can be identified with major early *capita*. Elsewhere in these lordships, less important estates of the lord's demesne were also marked by earthworks. Clearly, the lords of the first lordships, Leinster, Meath and Ulster, were prepared to erect timber castles as *capita* of their demesnes in the first instance (fig. 36). However, they soon proceeded to select one as the *caput* of the whole lordship, and then build, or rebuild, it in stone. At Carrickfergus, Nenagh or Adare, the lords erected stone buildings from the first: perhaps an earthwork castle was acceptable only as some baronial *caput*, or perhaps only for a short time.

The nub of the difference between stone and timber castles is the difference in resources, time and commitment required to construct them. In 1212, the Justiciar, John de Gray, apparently conceived an elaborate strategic plan to enforce English control on Aedh Ua Neill, king of Cenel Eoghain in central Ulster. There were to be expeditions from Connacht, Meath and English Ulster, leading respectively to castles built at Narrow Water on the Erne, Clones, Co. Monaghan and Coleraine (Orpen, *Normans*, II, 288–94). The Pipe Roll of 1211–12 has preserved an account of the costs involved in the Clones effort. It has always been assumed that the motte and bailey earthwork at Clones represents the structure erected in 1212, and there seems no reason to doubt it. It is not possible to disentangle every item mentioned, between the costs of the castle and those of its garrison and of the army operating in the area, but we can get an approximate idea. The works of the castle itself account for £19–4–10½ of expenditure, as opposed to £15–4–7 on supplies or £21–11–0 on carriage of men and materials to Clones. The resources came mainly from Dublin and Meath, but some from elsewhere (fig. 37). The expenditure on the works may be tabulated as follows:

	£	s	d
Richard Dullard for work		13	4
Ranulf the carpenter		12	0
Carpenters	4	13	11
Smiths		12	0
Fine from Dublin for digging not done	4	13	4
Money spent in Westmeath in default of Irishmen to dig ditches	8	0	3½
Total	19	4	10½

What these figures show is that the costs of building the castle of Clones were not high. We may compare them with the £500–1,000 needed to erect a contemporary great tower of stone in Britain, or, indeed, with the £733 accounted for in the same Pipe Roll as being spent on Limerick castle. That only three kinds of workmen (including the unskilled diggers) are mentioned is significant: timber castles required

Figure 36 Knockgraffon motte

few skilled men to build them compared to stone ones. While a few of the earth-work castles which we now see were built by great lords on their own estates, the great majority were the castles of their tenants.

RECOGNITION AND DEFINITION

Before we can even start to study the remains of earthwork castles in the field, we must know what it is that we are considering, how we can recognise an earthwork castle. If the medieval field monuments of Ireland had been decently and tidily constructed according to modern archaeological norms, the answer would be easy because we would be faced with three basic types of sites. The first would be the rath or ringfort, a circular enclosure, defined by one or more rings of banks and ditches and dating to the period before the eleventh century. The second would be the motte, a high, round mound of earth with a flat top, acting as the strong point of an earthwork castle. The third would be the moated site, a rectangular enclo-sure, defined by a bank and ditch and to be equated with the similar sites in England, which are usually identified as the sites of manor houses or substantial farms. The briefest experience of fieldwork in Ireland is enough to show that, while this tidy classification may represent the classic types, it does not encompass the variety of sites which actually exist. The key question of what we recognise as a motte is

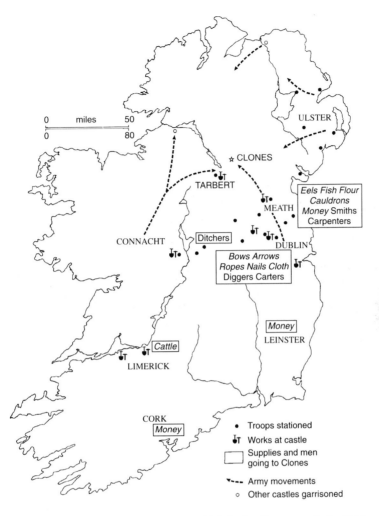

Figure 37 Map of the campaign which built Clones castle in 1211

illustrated by the definitions given in two reports of field survey of Leinster: O'Conor (1992) and McNeill (1990b). The first includes broad, low sites and rectangular ones, excluded by the latter. There is no absolute here, and with the best will in the world, a field worker will always make wrong identifications of monuments: he will miss a number of the sites he wants to list, and will include a number which he has wrongly identified as such. Not every spot or gap on a distribution map should be there.

The starting point for any consideration of the timber castles of Ireland must be with Orpen, when he was seeking to establish that mottes were castles in Ireland and not sites dating from a much earlier period (Orpen, 1907a, 133): 'As a result of the examination, already mentioned, of early castle sites, I found that out of eighty-four castles erected prior to 1216, the sites of which I thought could be approximately identified, in no fewer than sixty-six cases there are, or were, earthen mottes.' His method is still transparent and effective: comparison of two lists, one of mottes and one of documented castles. This is something we will have to cling to, for his conclusion, that overwhelmingly early castles were mottes, has been strongly questioned recently.

The problem is that the distribution of mottes on an all-Ireland scale does not correspond to that of the known distribution of the early English lordships: there are many mottes in Ulster, Oriel and Meath, fewer in Leinster, and very few in Munster (fig. 38).

> If the motte distribution map is re-examined it soon becomes clear that there are several surprising gaps in their distribution in areas that were known to have been settled by the Anglo-Normans. . . . It is in these areas that archaeologists like Twohig have suggested that we look for ringworks.
>
> (Barry, 1987, 45–6)

In other words, to fill up the perceived gap Twohig has thrown a spanner derived from the classification of earthwork castles in England during the 1960s, the so-called 'ringwork', and others have followed him. 'Ringwork' was a term coined to describe the earthwork castles which did not have the strong point of a motte but were identified as enclosures, defined by banks and ditches. In England, or Normandy, these were easy enough to recognise, even if the significance of the division between them and castles with mottes was disputed. In Ireland, however, it has proved impossible to produce a definition which might distinguish them from raths, the most ubiquitous field monument in the island.

The problems emerge with statements such as: 'The present total of 20 possible ringworks in Ireland should be increased to a figure of over 100, if the comparable proportion of 3.7 mottes to one ringwork in England and Wales is used as a guide' (Barry, 1983, 299; 1987, 50). Here we find an open invitation to 'hunt the ringwork' in a country where small, circular, embanked enclosures are common, but with no guidance as to how to tell a ringwork from a rath. Problems of identification may be illustrated by the question of the site of the small castle of Buninna in Co. Sligo (Lynn, 1986, 98). Graham (1988, 123) identified this with an 'earthwork, 40 m in diameter, with a bank averaging over 2 m (6 ft 6 in) in height, very possibly a ringwork' in an article where he argued that ringworks were the prevalent form of small castle in the west of Ireland. There appears to be no site in the actual townland of Buninna, but some 20 m (66 ft) over the boundary, in the next townland of Ballinphull, there is one. This is a mound with a polygonal mortared wall around its crest: the house nearest to it has been known since the 1830s as Castle Lodge (fig. 39). This is not the site identified by Graham, however. It seems to be one in the townland of Ballinlig, where there is a site which would, in other circumstances, be identified as a normal rath.

The main point is not so much that two people identified different sites as Buninna castle, but how the absence of clear criteria for identifying an earthwork castle in Ireland is bound to lead to trouble. In the absence of means of recognising ringworks, there is nothing to prevent anyone finding them anywhere. This

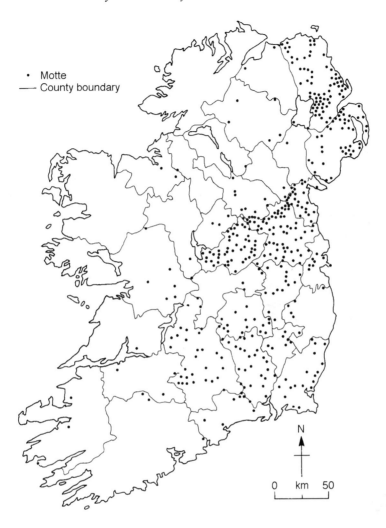

Figure 38 General map of mottes in Ireland

is not just a matter of the occasional individual misidentification. Much of our understanding of the lesser, earthwork castles is bound to be derived from analysis of overall patterns of their distribution in space or time, rather than from the study of individual examples. If we are not clear about how we define the sites, the patterns will be meaningless.

ENCLOSURES AND 'RINGWORKS'

An enclosure may have been better for some purposes than a motte, and vice versa. The restricted perimeter of a motte top, combined with the strength derived from

Figure 39 Buninna castle: view from the south-west

the height and steepness of the mound, provide a structure which is designed to be defended by a few men. An enclosure may accommodate many more men, just as it requires many more to defend its longer perimeter: crucially, too, it can accommodate horses, which cannot be taken to the top of a motte. An enclosure suits an army, or body of troops; a motte suits the defence of a small resident household.

There are a number of sites which must be identified as early enclosure castles, all promontories cut off by a bank and ditch. Orpen identified the promontory of Baginbun in Wexford as the site of the castle erected by Raymond le Gros on his arrival in Ireland with some 100 troops in 1170. There is a main promontory projecting south from the coast, which has a lesser one running off to the east from it. Both are cut off by lines of banks and ditches: the main promontory by one over 200 m (650 ft) long; the eastern by one less than 50 m (160 ft) long. In spite of Orpen's opinion, in view of the size of Raymond's force, which successfully defended the enclosure against attack by the men of Waterford, the eastern promontory must be identified as his castle. It enclosed an area at most about 200 m (650 ft) long and 50 m (160 ft) at its widest, sufficient to contain his small force and their booty, while the defensive line would have been short enough for them to defend. The site at Carrick, also in Wexford, differs from that of Baginbun in that, while it too was first built for the accommodation of troops in 1170–1, it continued in use after the need for campaigning armies had passed. Excavation there (Cotter, 1986, 1987) showed that the scale of the ditch which cut the promontory off was quite small: 2.0–5.4 m (6 ft 6 in–18 ft) wide and 2 m (6 ft 6 in) or less deep, but backed by a bank with a stone revetment. The enclosure at Mount Sandel near Coleraine (the Kilsantain of documents) has not been excavated, and the earthworks, again a promontory fort enclosed by a bank and ditch, may well have been altered during the rebellion of 1641.

Apart from these, the case for ringworks is circumstantial. Ringworks in Ireland are, in the present state of knowledge, impossible to define or identify. This effectively leaves us with, as Orpen pointed out, mottes as the typical earthwork castle in Ireland before 1225. Nor is this simply a counsel of despair, forcing us to admit that we can never recognise many of the early castles in Ireland. Again, we must return to Orpen's basic point. Wherever we know that an early castle existed, it is normal to find a motte now. Castles were not built everywhere, but in specific places for specific reasons, which we are trying to understand. In doing so we are looking both at the functions of the castles and at the structures of the lordships who built (or did not build) them. We can do so on the basis of two approaches: the results of the excavation of individual mottes, and the fieldwork observations and distribution of mottes within the various lordships

EXCAVATIONS OF MOTTES

Excavation of a motte might tell us about how the motte was constructed, the structures on its top, and something about buildings or defences of the bailey, if there is one. We will not be able to excavate all mottes, nor would we want to, for excavation destroys the site, but we would aim at building up a picture of mottes in general from the excavated examples, hoping that we have some sort of representative sample of all mottes. This we do not have, in any sense. There are maybe some 350 mottes in Ireland: some sort of excavation has taken place on at most 16, if we include sites such as Ballynarry and Piper's Fort in Co. Down or Doonmore in Co. Antrim: at best 5 per cent of the total. Our evidence from motte excavations is very biased geographically. Of the 16 excavated mottes, nine are in County Down, while four others are in the neighbouring counties of Antrim (two), Armagh and Louth. This is made worse when it is realised that the three southern sites involve only observations of sections through the mounds that have not been exposed as part of archaeological investigation, but by destruction or accidental collapse.

At Dunsilly, Co. Antrim (McNeill, 1991), the motte was totally excavated before its destruction for a farm improvement scheme. It was erected on remains of the platform of a house built against the bank of an abandoned rath, itself set at the edge of a low bluff over the small Dunsilly Burn (fig. 40). The first stage in building the motte was to give it a firm base on stones and clay. The next stage was the digging of the ditch at the base of the motte: spoil from it was piled along its inner edge to make a ring, which linked up with a portion of the old rath bank. The earth was piled to the intended height of the motte, and then the centre filled in and levelled off to give the flat top. We may term this method of construction 'ring and fill'. The motte of Rathmullan (Lynn, 1982) was built in the same manner, also over a former rath: the tip lines visible in the section through the motte at Lorrha, Co. Tipperary, looked like the same thing. It is possible that this is what lies behind the otherwise enigmatic mounds with deep central hollows. Excavation at Piper's Fort, Co. Down, showed that such a site was built in the medieval period, after the establishment of the Earldom of Ulster in 1177 (Waterman, 1959b); other sites, such as Pallis, Co. Wexford, also seem to relate to mottes.

The advantage of the method is that the ring acts as a stable base to the earthwork, with its potential lines of collapse acting counter to the general likelihood of the slumping of the whole mound. In the case of the small motte at Dunsilly, not only was it carefully built to counter slumping, but the stones at the base would have provided drainage for the earth above and prevented the sort of conditions which caused the tip at Aberfan to slide and collapse. Although we cannot parallel the practice of ring and fill construction in England, or elsewhere, there is evidence that builders of mottes there did not simply make a pile of earth and hope it would last (Kenyon, 1992, 9–12). While two sites which provided evidence from collapsed sections, at Kells, Co. Kilkenny (Barry, Culleton and Empey, 1984), and Old Ross, Co. Wexford (Culleton and Colfer, 1975), gave no indications of tip-lines and how the mounds were constructed, it is clear that many mottes were not casually erected.

Clough, Co. Down, as the first in the series of motte excavations in the county, is the natural starting point for considering our knowledge of the structures on the tops of mottes. The excavator (Waterman, 1954a) considered that the site saw five periods of activity, implying a long occupation, but it may not have been so lengthy. The excavator's suggestion of the replacement of a wooden palisade with a clay bank has since been very plausibly argued as two parts of the same thing, a clay wall reinforced by wood (Higham and Barker, 1992, 318–20). The central hollow of Waterman's first period, filled for later construction, may also be explained as the natural consequence of the settlement of the mound which would follow within months if it were built according to the ring-and-fill method. This would leave us with the important structures of the site as co-existent. The main one of these was a ground-floor hall (18 × 6 m; 59 × 20 ft), with mortared stone walls. Beside this, and constructionally later was a small stone and mortar tower, 5 m by 2 m (16 ft 6 in × 6 ft 6 in) internally, and entered at first-floor level, which might have acted as a chamber. Around the motte's perimeter was a defensive clay and timber wall, strengthened militarily by a least one arrow loop connected to a pit which allowed the archer to get down behind the wall for protection but still fire through it. While the hall was burned down quite soon after its construction, the tower survived for some centuries.

The other principal Co. Down sites of Lismahon (Waterman, 1959a) and Rathmullan (Lynn, 1982) also produced evidence of halls on the tops of their mottes. In the case of Lismahon, this came in a second phase, after the building of a smaller house and a second structure, interpreted by the excavator as a workshop. The hall (11.5 m by 5.5 m (38 × 18 ft) internally) was accompanied, as at Clough, by a small tower, but in this case it was timber-built, carried on four posts set in a square about 2 metres across, and built with the first house; unlike the Clough tower, it is not easy to see it as providing a chamber. In the first period,

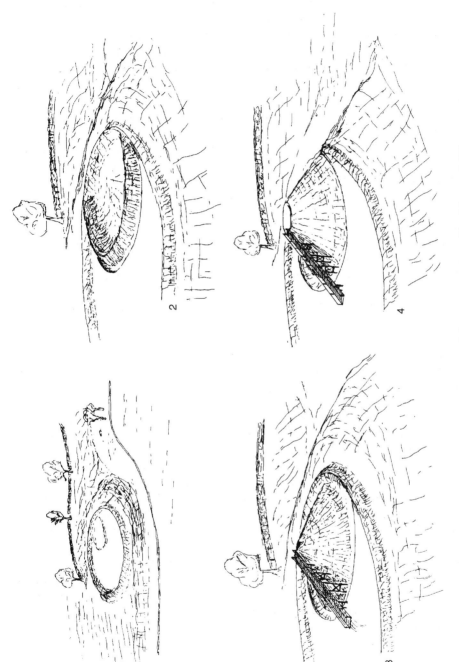

Figure 40 Phases in the construction of the motte at Dunsilly, 'ring and fill'

the perimeter defence was reinforced by a pit, similar to the archery pit at Clough. At Rathmullan, the primary phase of the motte was dominated by the dry-stone footings of three walls (a fourth was presumed to have been lost in the erosion of the east side of the motte). The stratigraphy of these walls is not easy to reconcile with what seems to be the obvious fact that they all relate to the one building, apparently a small 'hall' of timber carried on footings of stone and clay, 8 m by 5 m (26 ft × 16 ft 6 in) or more internally. There was a perimeter bank to the motte, with properly constructed entry through it to the west, opposite the door into the long wall of the building.

All three of these sites were dated to about 1200 by coins and gave evidence of the motte as the main living unit. Excavations of other motte tops have given different pictures. At the unpublished site of Lurgankeel, Co. Louth, the motte is reported as being surrounded by a palisade and to have supported a tower. The structure at Ballynarry (if we should indeed think of it as a motte) was, like those of the other Co. Down sites discussed, of timber-frame construction on top of dry-stone walls (Davison, 1962). It was square, with a raised floor, giving no sign of a hearth. Beside it was a pit, identified by the excavator as for storage and, indeed, the square building might have been a granary with a raised floor rather than a tower in any military sense.

It is quite conceivable that Dunsilly motte had no structure on its top. The top of the motte at Castleskreen, Co. Down, was fully excavated (Dickinson and Waterman, 1960), yet produced no evidence of structures. The motte at Dromore, and that at Ballyroney, both in Co. Down (Waterman, 1954b, 1955), saw too restricted excavation to tell us much, although we must note that a coin struck between 1177 and 1199 was found at Ballyroney. The motte top at Coney Island, Co. Armagh, was too disturbed for evidence to have survived. Between them, however, it is clear that we must be prepared to envisage the possibility that some mottes in Ireland were erected but then saw no structures on top. Why this should be one cannot but guess.

The excavations at Duneight, Co. Down (Waterman, 1963), have already been discussed because they involved an eleventh-century fortified site. It remains the only bailey excavation in Ireland (they are rarer than motte excavations elsewhere also); the baileys at Clough and Dromore were tested but proved to have been badly disturbed. The excavation report has problems of interpretation, but if the excavator is right to identify the second enlargement of the bank with the construction of the motte, the bailey was powerfully defended. It was also small: by the time the bank was widened inwards, the area enclosed was reduced to about 23 m by 14 m (75 × 46 ft), very similar to the area of the top of the motte at Clough. There were certainly no buildings found in the bailey to compare with the hall found at Clough, or even the smaller buildings of Lismahon or Rathmullan.

THE DISTRIBUTION OF MOTTES

We may turn from the excavation of a few mottes to consideration of the distribution (by class as well as geographically) of all those identified in the field within the various lordships. Leinster serves well as an entry into this discussion because in 1247 the lordship was surveyed in detail so that it could be divided among the five heiresses of the last Marshal lord (Brooks, 1950). The survey listed all the demesne lands farmed directly by the lord, and also each parcel of land held by military tenure, for the service of one knight, of more than one, or else for fractions of a knight. We have therefore a list of all the main estate centres in the lordship within three generations of its first organisation; it is possible to be quite confident of the identification of most of these place names on the modern map. If we combine this with field survey of the surviving monuments, we can begin to examine the social and geographical context of the mottes (McNeill, 1990b). We can then use Leinster as a yardstick by which to measure other lordships.

The first conclusion which emerges from such a study is that the social pattern of building mottes is not random. Of the 27 holdings, held in return for the service of half a knight, only four are now marked by mottes: none of the holdings held for less than half a knight have mottes now. On the other hand, of the 46 holdings held for a full knight's service or more, 19 are now marked by mottes. Put proportionally, 40 per cent of the higher holdings have mottes against 15 per cent of the half-fees. It is difficult to believe that this is a difference which reflects the resources available to the two groups. Full knight's fees were obviously larger than half-fees, but hardly so much so that the lesser tenants could not have erected mottes if they had wanted, or been encouraged, to do so. For example, if the new lords had been afraid of a rising by their Irish peasantry, is it likely that tenants of half-fees would have felt so much safer than those who held full fees? It seems odd that they would have thought the rebels would be so discriminating as to attack only one sort of tenant rather than the other. The result of this formal basis for the erection of mottes is that the lordship has a fairly even but rather sparse distribution of mottes over its area, a density which we may take as a norm for comparison for other lordships.

In the hinterland of the lordships of Meath and, less clearly, English Oriel, the same situation prevails. In the good lands of the plain of Meath (the bulk of the present county), the centres of the holdings of the major tenants are where the great majority of mottes are sited. The position is less clear partly because we have not got the sort of systematic contemporary survey that we have for Leinster. In Ulster, also, we have to try to make up such a list of major tenants' holdings from scattered sources, which are even less complete than for Meath. However, something of the same pattern emerges for the core area of the lordship in south-east Co. Antrim and in coastal Co. Down.

In the three last-named lordships, Meath, Oriel and Ulster, there is a contrast between the settled cores and their borders to the north-west and west. Mottes proliferate along the borders, at the most extreme in the north-western borders of Meath and Oriel, where some mottes are only one or two miles from their nearest neighbour (fig. 41). They make a dense line on the map along the strip of land where the plain gives way to the low hills and broken country of the present counties of Cavan and Monaghan. Interestingly, the line continues into the lordships of Oriel, in spite of the difference not only of lord but also of date: Meath was seized by Hugh de Lacy from the 1170s, but Oriel was not occupied by English

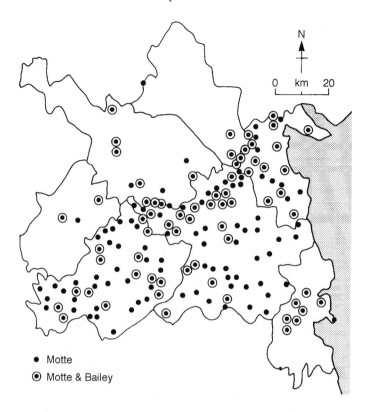

Figure 41 Map of mottes in the lordships of Meath and Oriel

lords until after the death of Murchad Ua Carbaill in 1189. In Ulster, the mottes are most densely distributed at the north-east corner of Lough Neagh and west of Dundrum Bay, the two points of easy entry into the lordship from the west.

The mottes in the border zones of these lordships are sufficiently densely distributed for the zones to be defined on a map. The borders concerned were not defined by lines of mottes spaced at intervals of ten or more miles, as has been proposed (Waterman, 1963, 77; Jope, 1966, 105; Graham, 1980, 52). To have an effective barrier of fortification for an Irish lordship it would have had to counter raids by small groups of mobile forces who might well enter the lordship at night. Ireland is a country with many small hills and valleys; in the twelfth century it was also well wooded. Intercepting a raiding force between bases ten miles apart would have needed constant patrolling by groups of men large enough to take on the raiding force themselves: sending five miles for help, without radios or helicopters, would be futile.

No medieval lordship could afford to keep permanent forces on the alert for long. The defence of a lordship depended essentially on rallying the tenants to fight on their own behalf: to gather them needs time and well-known meeting points. The best strategy is to intercept raiders on their way out, when they are burdened with loot and tired from the effects of rape and pillage, or have been mauled by a successful defence. Again, it is no use having bases ten miles apart. We see the system in action in the 1211–12 Pipe Roll, where there are accounts for groups of 20–50 men paid for guarding districts. They presumably acted as an immediate reaction force, but mainly to hold a base and act as a stiffening to the local tenants when they arrived. The bases these men occupied would have to be selected according to an assessment of the route that the raiders were likely to follow, and to be astride it. A successful defence plan would need many potential bases to cover all eventualities. It is likely that only one would be chosen on each occasion and many sites might be left empty at any one time: indeed, if there is no reason to expect a raid, all the frontier bases might be abandoned.

The second thing that we can note about these border mottes is that many more of them have baileys attached to them than do the mottes of the hinterland (fig. 42). In Ulster, one bailey (or two, counting the possible site at Downpatrick) still exists in the core area of the lordship, out of some 49 mottes. Nine baileys are found in the 19 mottes in the two key border areas noted above, or 47 per cent. In Meath and Oriel 55 per cent of the baileys are found attached to mottes along the border: only 31 per cent of the mottes in the hinterland have baileys. The latter figure drops to 25 per cent for the present Co. Meath alone. In the three Leinster counties of Kildare, Carlow and Wexford, nine out of 49 mottes (18 per cent) have baileys. Consistently in these lordships, some 50 per cent of the border mottes have baileys, twice as many as the mottes of the hinterland.

This difference between some areas and others in the frequency of baileys contrasts with the position elsewhere in the British Isles, where very few mottes lack baileys. Not only are they not almost automatic in Ireland, but the baileys are also smaller than elsewhere. It is not uncommon for a motte to have been added within an earlier rath, taking up a fair proportion of the enclosure, which may have been only 30 m (100 ft) in diameter to begin with. Why this should be is one of the real puzzles about these early castles in Ireland. Along the borders, it may be linked to the sort of use outlined above. The baileys could mark off those mottes where it was expected that forces might be stationed in times of tension and raids, protected within the bailey enclosure. This would certainly fit the results of the excavation of Duneight, itself one of the outer Co. Down sites, where the poor quality of the structures found would seem to be more what might be provided for troops. If the role of baileys along the borders may be explained thus, their small size and relative rarity in the core areas of the lordships cannot.

If the lordships north of Leinster present a contrast in their militarised borders, as evidenced by the density of their mottes, the lordships of Munster display a different contrast. Here we are faced with an extraordinary lack of mottes in the present counties of Waterford, Tipperary, Cork and Limerick. Between them, there are only about 22 mottes in these four counties. In part this may be due to a lack of field survey, but the counties of Tipperary and Cork have both been covered, and Limerick to some extent as well. It was this absence of mottes which prompted Twohig and others to postulate the existence of ringworks to fill up the gap, an argument criticised earlier in this chapter. The absence is almost certainly a real

Figure 42 Dromore, Co. Down: view of the motte and bailey from the south

one, not produced by differential destruction or the selective use of a different form of earthwork castle in these lordships. We are faced with a situation, not of a lack of castles as such in southern and eastern Munster, for there are stone castles and some earthwork ones, such as the royal mottes of Lismore or Tibberaghny and Philip of Worcester's Knockgraffon, but of a lack of the proliferation of castles, such as we can see in the lordships of the east and north.

EXPLANATIONS

We can put forward two explanations for this. The first would be to stress the complex but essentially political, as opposed to military, events which led to the replacement of the Irish kingdoms of Cork and Limerick by the various English lordships. Eastern Munster was an area securely controlled by none of the major kings before 1170, but disputed by all. It clear that there was no concerted campaign against the English by the kings of the three Irish kingdoms concerned: the Mac Carthaig of Desmond, the Ui Briain of Munster and the Ui Conchobair of Connacht. Kings of each of these families are to be found raiding each other, as often in alliance with English lords as against them. The occupation of the two kingdoms by the English followed the removal of strong kings of the neighbouring Irish: Ruadri Ua Conchobair's retirement in 1183, Diarmait Mac Carthaig's death in 1185, and Domnall Mor Ua Briain's in 1194. Their successors were in no position to provide strong action. By the later part of King John's reign, there were pro-English kings in place: Cathal Crobhderg Ua Conchobair in Connacht and Donough Ua Briain.

There is a strong case for regarding the establishment of the English lordships in eastern Munster as being accepted by the Irish kings whose power over the land was weak and disputed in any case. To an Ua Briain or a Mac Carthaig, faced with the potential military strength of the English king, the surrender of ambitions in Cork or Limerick seems to have been a price worth paying for secure tenure of their core lands of Thomond and Desmond. In these circumstances, the tenants of the new English lords may have felt so secure as not to feel the need for castles. This is the same period as that in which we saw, at the beginning of this chapter, the Justiciar making a major strategic effort along the southern borders of modern Ulster, with the establishment of the castle at Clones. In the years before 1216, he successfully established castles and royal organisation along the middle Shannon, with the help of Cathal Crobhdeg and Donough Ua Briain, but Clones castle was destroyed in 1213 by Aed Ua Neill of Cenel Eoghain in alliance with the men of Irish Oriel. Aed was the most powerful Irish king of the years after 1200, especially in alliance with the Irish of southern Ulster (in the modern sense). The English of Meath, Oriel and Ulster facing the power of the Cenel Eoghain and others needed border defences and other castles much more than the English of Munster.

An alternative explanation is to stress the large-scale and speculative nature of the grants of lordship in eastern Munster. Certainly King John felt able to play ducks and drakes with conflicting grants to William de Burgh, Philip of Worcester and William de Braose in the area. This might reflect a situation in which the lords had taken up positions in their lands themselves, as witnessed by their own castles, but not yet managed to settle many tenants on these lands. Castles did not proliferate because there were few or no tenants of the knightly class established to build them. What it reminds us is how little we know of the processes of the details of the establishing of the lordships of Munster in particular and of the rest of Ireland as well. This second explanation of the the absence of Munster mottes might suggest that the tenants did not erect them because they were no longer in fashion.

THE DATING OF MOTTES

We are led into a consideration of the chronology of motte building: effectively in Ireland this means how late mottes were still erected. There are three possible approaches to this question. The first involves the sort of argument just used, to find areas which were settled by the English at some known date but are now without mottes, and to argue from these a date when they went out of currency. The second works from the dates of individual mottes and extrapolates from them to the class of sites as a whole. The third is based on an empirical assessment of what seems to have been the probable circumstances at the time, a sort of common sense.

The argument from absence applies not only to Munster lordships but more powerfully to Connacht. In 1235 Richard de Burgh finally achieved the conquest and settlement by English tenants of a substantial part of the former Ua Conchobair kingdom. Numbers of the places which he granted to major tenants, as well as his own demesne estates, are now marked by castles of the thirteenth century, as we shall see in a later chapter, but there are no mottes among them (Lynn, 1986; Holland, 1988, 86). Counter to this lies the north of Co. Antrim where there are some dozen mottes in the area of the Earldom of Ulster known as the county of Twescard. In the records from the 1211–12 Pipe Roll to returns of seneschals of the Earldom before it was restored to Hugh de Lacy in 1227, it is clear that this area did not then form part of the Earldom (McNeill, 1980, 21–2). It would appear to have been settled under Hugh de Lacy, and the mottes to be associated with this settlement, although it is just possible that it was settled in the decades before but, being held by the Scottish lords of Galloway, excluded from the Earldom until seized by Hugh de Lacy.

The dates from excavation of mottes would need the precision of tree rings to bear effectively on this problem, but it is worth recalling the coins from Ballyroney, Clough, Lismahon and Rathmullan. When all the uncertainties of the date of deposition, as opposed to the date of striking, are admitted, the conclusion remains that both Rathmullan and Lismahon should have been erected before 1200 and Clough soon after. Some mottes are mentioned in documentary sources also. There is the weight of the general picture in eastern Ireland, that the sites of many of the castles mentioned in documents before 1216 are now occupied by mottes (Orpen, 1907a); after this there is a sharp drop in the number of references to the new building of castles. Clones is one of the latest of these, as is Roscrea, which a later inquisition shows was a motte and bailey erected in 1213 (Orpen, 1906, 426–7). In 1215 the Justiciar erected a castle at Clonmacnois (fig. 43). The present castle consists of a hall and courtyard of stone; the hall is raised up on what looks very much like a motte, with the courtyard occupying the bailey.

The most general argument would be from common sense. If castles are to articulate the new settlement, whether to defend the lords of it or to provide them with a suitably impressive centre for the administration of their lands, it seems perverse for a lord not to build one within a very few years of arriving in his land. We should expect the bulk of castles to have been substantially erected within a decade. This is particularly true of those castles of timber and earth where the main reason for choosing these materials was for speed and simplicity. Unlike the major stone castles, the materials were to be found throughout Ireland, as were men with the skills to work them. More importantly, however, this reminds us that the main effort of constructing castles will have varied from lordship to lordship, as each was settled and organised into estates. There can be no such thing as a date range for mottes throughout Ireland, for, even if they were being built in one area, there would be other parts where the stock of castles was complete.

MOTTES OF THE IRISH

It is one of the surprises of the period in Ireland that there is so little real evidence for the building of castles by Irish kings or lords, especially as there is some from

Figure 43 Clonmacnoise castle: aerial view of the earthworks

before the coming of the English, and we would expect it to be greatly reinforced after 1170. The evidence comes from the occurrence of sites in places or areas known to have been held by Irish and believed never to have been occupied, even temporarily, by English, and some direct accounts. We might expect that the Wicklow hill country, where the successors of Diarmait Mac Murchada continued to hold land under the lords of Leinster, would have seen the building of castles, but none have yet been identified. The only one suggested by O'Conor, for Leinster as a whole, is a small motte at Monally, Co. Laois, a place well away from known English settlement (O'Conor 1992, 9–10).

In Ulster in general, there are mottes far from the borders of the Earldom, even at their widest extent. One of them is the small motte at Coney Island in Lough Neagh (Addyman, 1965), which may possibly have been put up by one of the Irish archbishops of Armagh; it is certainly unlikely to be English. A second is the large motte and bailey of Managh Beg, Co. Londonderry, firmly in the lands of Ua Cathain. In 1220, as part of his efforts to regain his lands in Meath, Walter de Lacy attacked the crannog of Ua Ragallaig, which has been identified by Orpen with the tower on the artificial island of Lough Oughter, Co. Cavan (Orpen, *Normans*, III, 33; Manning, 1990). Island forts also appear in Connacht built and held by Irish a very little later: at Hen's Castle and Lough Key (Lynn, 1986, 102–4).

Figure 44 Harryville, Co. Antrim: a motte and bailey in the heart of the Irish kingdom of Ui Tuirtre

These are scattered examples, however; only one case has ever been put forward of an Irish kingdom being systematically equipped with castles and being able through them to hold off an English advance. This is the land of Ui Tuirtre in central Co. Antrim, which has a number of fine mottes (fig. 44), is attractive land which the English of the Earldom of Ulster might well have coveted, but which remained outside the Earldom in spite of being surrounded by it on three sides (McNeill, 1980, 103–4). Whether this is enough to make the case for Irish castle building before 1225 must be left to others to judge. It should be emphasised, however, that it would be peculiar if the Irish did not build castles. If they were useful to the English to hold on to land, surely they would also have been so for the Irish. It is also a curious society which will not adapt to save its land. Again, too, we must remember that there was some Irish fortification before the English came. None of this is really enough to overthrow the basic equation of castles, whether of stone and mortar, or of timber and earth, with the new lordships of the English.

CASTLES AND THE ESTABLISHING OF ENGLISH LORDSHIPS IN IRELAND

——— .•. ———

CASTLES AND THE QUESTION OF CONQUEST

There can be little doubt that the establishment of the new English lordships in Ireland saw a massive building programme of castles. Clearly the two things were connected, but exactly how is less obvious. It has often been assumed that castle building was part of the actual winning of the land, which is seen as a single act of military aggression ('conquest'), and the castles as inherently military in conception. One of the difficulties of writing about this period has been to avoid the two words 'conquest' and 'colonisation'. These are words loaded with nineteenth-century overtones, especially in the context of Ireland, which beg questions about the nature of the English lordship and the reaction of Irish kings and people to it.

These are words and ideas which go back a long way: they represent a view which starts with Giraldus Cambrensis, who wrote his account of the period very much as though it were a coherent conquest, to be approved of and extended. In chapter 38 of his *Expugnatio Hibernica*, Giraldus gives his prescription for 'how the Irish people are to be conquered' (Scott and Martin, 1978). He calls for special preparations for battle, emphasising archers and light cavalry, and also for castles to be built according to a strategic plan of advance:

> for it is far, far better to link together slowly at first castles set in suitable places and proceed to build them gradually, than to build many far apart in all sorts of places, unable to help each other in a systematic way or in times of necessity.

Castles would then provide one of the means of conquest and of holding down a rebellious native population.

In this view Giraldus has been generally followed: in his vision of the strategic plan of conquest, in the place of castles in it, and in the role of castles as protection against internal rebellion. It is, however, worth noting that his anonymous contemporary who composed the *chanson de geste* about the English in Ireland, the so-called *Song of Dermot and the Earl*, did not share his views. He mentions castles very rarely, nor does he give a picture of hostility between Irish and English as such; his fighting is between lords of different areas, irrespective of their place of birth, and, indeed, Diarmaid of Leinster is one of his heroes. Nor is Giraldus elsewhere a particularly sympathetic or reliable observer of the Irish scene. We should not follow his prescription blindly. We must look at castles to ask ourselves whether there is evidence from them of a strategic plan for a single conquest of the island or whether the fighting which accompanied the seizure of land (if it happened) was long-drawn-out, evidence of widespread resistance, or whether we should think of a war to displace one ruling aristocracy with another.

The first thing to strike us is the military weakness of the majority of the sites, compared to their Anglo-French contemporaries. The earthwork castle, in partic- ular the motte and bailey, while not actually obsolete in England and France, was certainly old-fashioned. It belonged essentially to the world of before 1150, yet we find it being used as the normal castle form in Ireland, even for castles on demesne manors of major magnates. Of the major stone castles, we have seen that there were serious military weaknesses in a number. Although Carlingford, Dunamase (in its second English phase) and the royal castles at Dublin and Limerick were strong, the rest were not. We cannot attribute this to being the reaction of the lords to Irish incompetence in siege warfare. Whether the Irish were good at it or not in the late twelfth century, there was nothing to say that they could not learn. The lords facing the Welsh, who had a similar social structure, certainly never underestimated their siege abilities. It would have been madness for the lords in Ireland simply to assume that any Irish weakness would continue. We must conclude that the magnates often felt quite confident of their future security.

If many of the individual castles show military weakness, there is little sign of an overall strategic pattern or plan. The sort of distribution that Giraldus called for is simply not visible in the record. The military aspect of castles is seen mainly in their proliferation along the borders of certain lordships. This cannot be the result of strategic planning and conquest, but follows the stabilising of the lord- ships; it happens at the end of the process, not during it. Castles here represent a shield which some lordships needed, but not others, depending on the situation outside their borders.

Behind the shield, Giraldus called for castles to be built, not only to a strategic plan of conquest, but also to hold down the countryside in the face of likely rebel- lion, or resistance from the bulk of the Irish population. We should see blanket coverage of a lordship with castles, acting together as Giraldus called for. This is most obviously breached in the lordships of eastern Munster, where either the lord- ships were very weak or else they saw little need for widespread defences. In the lordships of the east of Ireland, the areas behind their border shields fail to show the density of castellation we might expect. This is particularly so of Leinster, where we can actually see who built the castles. If they really faced the likelihood of widespread rebellion, it is difficult to see why the holders of less than half a knight's fee should have thought themselves immune. The Irish may have been snobs, but hardly to the extent of not attacking lesser tenants. Nor can we see the systematic building of castles at points which would be considered as strategic pressure points. In particular, the idea that we might see the lines of advance across a lordship in the distribution of chains of castles does not correspond to the evidence.

The two campaigns of the Justiciars between 1210 and 1216 are instructive here. Along the middle Shannon and south-western Meath, it was a question of the restoration or reinforcement of English control of the area in the face of attacks from disaffected Irish lords excluded from power by their kinsmen. In co-operation with the existing Irish lords, on either side of the Shannon, the Justiciar suppressed the 'rebellion' and asserted his control with the construction or restoration of castles. In 1212, the aggressive campaign to move into southern Ulster, spearheaded by the building of Clones castle, was a failure. The local Irish forces combined against the English and destroyed the castle. Constructing a castle alone would not ensure the establishing of power in an area.

A castle might serve to hold land already won, but that would be all. The land was won by battle, by a *coup de main*, or even by agreement. Opposition to the establishment of English lordships came from the Irish kings and aristocrats who had held the land before. The pattern of their castles does not indicate that there was any real fear of rebellion from the bulk of the Irish population in an area after the initial seizure of the land and displacement of the former lords. When there was a military threat to the English regime, it came from forces outside their lordship, as seen by the measures to reinforce the borders of Meath, Oriel and Ulster. The castles which were built to be militarily strong are equally instructive. Dunamase and Carlingford were built by English lords who were hoping to intrude into the established ranks of their contemporaries: William Marshal, inheritor of Leinster through his wife and royal patronage, and Hugh II de Lacy, Hugh I's younger son. Dublin and Limerick were the work of King John, part of his attempt to assert royal power in Ireland beyond the weak position established by his father. All may have been directed more at their fellow English than at Irish lords.

THE ROLE OF EARLY CASTLES IN ADMINISTRATION

The role of castles in the structuring of lordship is clear. From the first, we can see the main castles of the lordships being built in stone. The very fact of building in stone involved great resources, of both materials and men. Some of the latter must have been brought over to Ireland, because there was simply no tradition of designing such works there. Skilled masons had built churches in Ireland before, and we see them at work, making decorated features in Irish style, at Adare or Nenagh, but that is different from the overall planning of a castle. The programme of castle building must have joined that of the new church foundations of the new lords to give a major boost to the building industry. Both gave notice of the newcomers' commitment to their new lands, and their intention to stay and transform them.

They chose stone not for defence but for prestige and utility. These castles were there to provide the administrative headquarters of their lords in their lordships and it shows in their designs. This was not to be simply the exercise of the old Irish system under new masters but a new form of lordship. For this a hall was essential, to administer the formal justice of the English and to provide a suitable setting for the social organisation of lordship, meeting tenants or allies among other lords. The separation of this public side of castle life from the private one of the lord's chamber shows how the new men were determined to lead lives of at least as much pomp as their contemporaries. The extent of the accommodation provided for those not of the lord's immediate household, at Trim or Carlingford, shows clearly how the new regime meant new types of administration, with elaborate staffs of officials. The spirit of display was also expressed in military means, as witnessed by the show of mural towers, and gate towers at Trim, Dunamase or Carlingford, with their parallels outside Ireland.

The proliferation of castles, with the widespread building of lesser, earthwork castles, was part of the same new lordship. The building of the many lesser castles followed the organisation of the land into a hierarchy of tenancies and estates with fixed centres of power. The castles were of earth and timber, not because they were earlier than the major stone castles, but because they could be erected quickly and cheaply. This is where the question of the extent of castle building under the earlier Irish kings becomes crucial. If it had been widespread, then we would have good evidence that the land was organised into territorial lordships. Instead, the new castles of the Irish of the twelfth century seem to be the work of kings, part of the increase of royal military power of the period.

The final point to be made is that, from the beginning, there is a great variety among the castles. This is apparent not only between the individual castles, but also between types and between lordships. At any period there will be large castles, built with great expenditure of resources, and smaller ones. The earthwork castles were not earlier than stone ones, nor were they exclusively built for men with smaller purses: some were built by great magnates, but at their lesser centres. It was not only a matter of fashion and resources but also the intended use of the castle which dictated its form. Within a group of castles built by men of similar status, are differences of emphasis, for example on military or domestic aspects. It is also likely that the parallels which we can see were apparent then also, that the sources and quotations of the design were meant to convey messages to contemporaries as well. Finally, the variations between lordships, which we can see in the deployment of early castles, is not unique to the period. All these are aspects of castles which we will see in later times.

PART II

FROM THE EARLY THIRTEENTH TO THE MID-FOURTEENTH CENTURY

———— .•. ————

THE CENTRAL PERIOD OF ENGLISH LORDSHIP

— .◆. —

The century after about 1225 contrasts with the drama of the preceding 50 years. The only major conquest by the English was that of Connacht, in part seized by the king, but the greater part conquered by Richard de Burgh at the head of a federation of barons which saw success in 1235. There were other seizures, in Ulster and in Clare for example, but they were not on the same scale as that of Connacht or of the events of the preceding 50 years. The expedition of King John, and the subsequent dealings between the barons of Ireland with him and his son, resolved the question of who would be the dominant force in Ireland decisively in the king's favour. For most of the period the English supremacy was not seriously challenged, except on a local basis, by Irish lords, and within the English lordships the king was recognised as supreme. One of the features of the period, therefore, is the absence of fighting for long intervals, especially in the south-east, until the start of troubles around the Wicklow mountains towards the end of the thirteenth century.

The royal dominance was helped by the failure of heirs in the two largest of the early lordships. Walter de Lacy in 1241 left no single heir of Meath, while in 1245 Anselm, the last Marshal Earl of Leinster, also died without a male heir. In both cases the lordship was partitioned between heiresses and their husbands; neither Meath nor Leinster was ever reconstituted in its original form. Against the fragmentation of these two lordships we can put the grant of the Earldom of Ulster to Walter de Burgh in 1264, which combined it and the lordship of Connacht. For the following 69 years, until the death of the last resident Earl of Ulster in 1333, the de Burghs were the most powerful baronial family in Ireland. Connacht was never a Liberty in the way that Leinster, Meath and Ulster were; a further reinforcement of royal power over baronial.

As a whole, however, the baronial lordships went through a period of stability. Their territorial integrity was recognised and established, so that one can talk at this period of fixed boundaries both of the lordships themselves and of units, cantreds, manors or parishes within them. Within each lordship we have often the benefit of surveys by royal officials which allow us to see the structure of the tenancies. As a result it is often possible to assign a castle to an individual holding and to assign it to its position in the tenurial hierarchy, from the great tenants in chief, through the lesser ones to the honorial baronage and the lesser lords. Because the power of the king was at its height and it is royal documents which have survived most, this is the period of the middle ages about which we know most in terms of land holding.

It was this baronial stability which led Orpen, perhaps, to structure his general account of the period not chronologically but regionally, recognising that the lordships were the real units in the island, rather than presenting a unified history, either of the whole island or of the English part of it. This approach has not seen much favour since, but there is more than a grain of truth in it. The English barons seem to have recognised that their seizure of the whole island was an impossibility (the incomplete conquest regretted by Orpen), and that their task was to intensify the exploitation of their lordships internally. The economic boom over much of Europe may have faltered towards the end of the thirteenth century but, if its causes were over-exploitation of the land since the eleventh century, these should not have applied to Ireland. More to the point might have been a slackening in demand for the produce of Irish agriculture, but there is little serious sign of this before 1300.

It was also a period of continuing close personal contact with England. On the one hand the major barons continued to keep in close touch with the court of the English king and to contract marriages with the English aristocracy (Phillips, 1984). On the other, the royal bureaucracy was staffed in large part by clerks from England. There was a steady influx of new leaders from England or from France, like Geoffrey de Geneville, who married one of Walter de Lacy's heiresses. Ireland was closely tied at the top to England during the period, but that did not make Ireland into England. The estates had to be organised differently, because their origins were different. Even if they were aiming to introduce the pattern of agricultural settlement from England into Ireland, it was not fixed and organised. Equally, the nature of warfare in Ireland was different. The large, organised armies and the siege capacity which emerged in thirteenth-century England during Angevin kingship do not seem to have travelled to Ireland.

In church building we can see that English masons came over to work in Ireland during the thirteenth century and to train men who worked on there after them (Stalley, 1984). They brought with them new fashions of church design which reflected those of England closely: there is no sign of a 'time lag' in their work. As well as the designs of churches we can see the work of immigrant sculptors from England in Ireland, as at Kilfane, Co. Kilkenny (Stalley, 1987). Actual building stone was imported from England (Waterman, 1970). On the other hand, the work of such masons did not result in work on the scale of the great English or French churches. The parish churches remained very small and even the cathedrals and major abbeys were often not vaulted. Ireland remained poor in resources, whether money, trained men or building stone. By the end of the thirteenth century Edward I's reckless financial policy led to serious problems for the royal government in Ireland, which presaged its even more serious problems in the fourteenth century. The confidence of the first lordships must have ebbed away as the realisation of the limited wealth of Ireland gradually sank in to the barons: it was not just the lack of capital, technology and management which had kept Ireland from being a rich country.

If we want to compare the castles in Ireland with those of England or France during this period we have the advantage that this is a time, in England especially, when we can see a main stream of castle development, if such a thing exists. It is around the castles of the thirteenth century that many of our ideas of castles are built. Defensively, the emphasis was on the curtain wall, with mural towers and a great double-towered gate house dominating the trace. In a few, principally royal, castles this trend culminated in the concept of the concentric castle with two lines of defence working in concert. Great towers continued (if unusually) to be built but they were a facet of the status and display of the castles, not the point of ulti-mate defence. The builders used the space of the courtyards and the accommodation in the mural towers to expand the domestic provisions in castles. The great hall, of course, remained dominant as the venue for ceremonial and the most public events of the life of the castle, but increasingly as the pivot of a formal arrange-ment of the domestic rooms of the whole castle. At the 'low' end were the service rooms; at the other, the lord's. The lord had as a matter of course at least two rooms, an outer, great chamber for meeting his household, and an inner, private chamber for sleeping and confidential business. Important members of the house-hold were accommodated in single rooms or suites in the towers or else attached to the lord's chambers.

In England the increasing survival of baronial documentation, and in Ireland the growth of royal power and bureaucracy, has made the dating of castles less prob-lematical. In Ireland, of course, the destruction of the Public Records during the Civil War in 1922 deprived us of many documents, but thanks to the efforts of earlier scholars by no means all was lost. Many had been copied to London and the copies survived there but the Pipe and Justiciars' Rolls had been well calen-dared before the disaster; the documents in London have also been well calendared, so that, as well as surviving, much is easily accessible. This increasing documenta-tion also allows us to be much more confident about the ownership of the castles. This applies not only to the castles of the major tenants in chief but also increas-ingly to the principal men below them: just as we know more about the boundaries of the lordships, so we know more about their internal organisation.

This is the background to the questions which we may ask of the castles during this period. On the one hand, with a reasonable number of dated buildings and the knowledge that the patrons of the castles were closely in touch with England, we can expect to compare the castles in England and Ireland. On the other hand, if we can see local ways of doing things in the church buildings, we might expect the same among the castles. This might be simply a matter of whim or else a response to the genuinely different life in Ireland from that in England. Whether that was a matter of the organisation of estates or households, or of the nature of war, the result should show in their castles. We must also be aware of the hier-archy within the ranks of the castle builders: what applies to the higher tenants in chief may not apply to their men. This particularly applies to the Irish, of course. One of the key questions is to ask how they had reacted to two generations of the presence of English lords beside them. Castles offered them much in the way of defence of their lands, and they were by and large on the defensive during our period. In Wales the native lords took to castle building, with less enthusiasm perhaps than to the destruction of their enemies' castles, but systematically nevertheless. If the Irish felt as threatened as the Welsh, we should expect them to follow them in castellation of their lands.

CASTLES IN THE ENGLISH FASHION

——— •◦• ———

BARONIAL CASTLES OF THE MID-THIRTEENTH CENTURY

In 1236, Lady Rohesia de Verdon was reported to have built a castle in her lands in modern Co. Louth against the Irish (CDI, I, 2334): traditionally this new castle has been identified with the present Castle Roche, which was in existence by 1318 (42nd RDKPRI, 25). The castle is sited at the edge of an inland cliff, in effect a promontory (fig. 45). The end of the promontory is cut off by a rock-cut ditch to form the inner ward, the castle proper, with a large rectangular enclosure outside, surrounded by a stone wall and with the remains of at least one building visible in the grass: either the outer ward or a small borough settlement. The inner ward, behind the rock-cut ditch, is enclosed by a roughly triangular curtain wall, with a D-shaped tower at the northern angle (fig. 46). The existing buildings have been given different dates by different authorities. In particular, a tower around a deep pit approximately in the middle of the courtyard has been cited as evidence of a castle earlier than the bulk of the present visible remains (Stalley, 1971), but it has also been identified as evidence of a later structure (Buckley and Sweetman, 1991, 336). In fact, the remains are probably those of a well house, contemporary with the rest of the castle remains. Likewise, Leask (1936, 183) considered the tower at the north angle to be from a later period, because it is not bonded to the curtain wall behind it, a suggestion which is contradicted by the existence of doors in the curtain, leading to its upper floors. The straight joints visible here and at the junction of the curtain wall and the hall may be attributed to caution in building on a site close to the edge of a steep cliff. What we see are probably the remains of Rohesia's castle.

The principal feature of the castle now, and originally, is the gate house and great hall situated at the south end of the inner ward. There is a true gate house, unlike the gates at Dublin or Limerick, where the gate itself is set between two towers without any building behind to tie them together. At Castle Roche it is clear that the whole of the space above the gate passage behind the curtain wall and including the towers was treated as a whole. South of the gate house is a large rectangular building, entered through a secondary porch or lobby from the

Figure 45 Castle Roche: view of the castle site from the south-west

courtyard at the north-west corner. Its size and the three fine windows with seats in the southern wall at the ground floor show it to have been the great hall (fig. 47). The east wall rises to a gable, at whose south end is a small door leading into a passage in the thickness of the wall. This serves four arrow loops which face east, covering the approach to the gate, and leads up to a door in to the first-floor level of the gate house. There were two fine rooms in the gate house, at first- and second-floor levels, providing good chambers linked to the upper end of the great hall.

The design and siting of Castle Roche are very similar to those of Beeston castle in Cheshire (Ellis, 1994). Both are on inland rock promontories, and both have inner wards, cut off by rock-cut ditches, of very much the same shape and area. Entry to Beeston was by a gate house like that at Castle Roche, with side towers of the same shallow projection in plan, and also one which combined both towers and the passage together on the ground floor, although the space on the first floor is divided into two rooms. There are two main differences, which are as instructive as the similarities. The curtain wall at Beeston is equipped with three projecting towers for flanking fire, rather than the single, rather hesitant one at Castle Roche. At Beeston, the domestic accommodation seems never to have been finished: there is nothing of the integrated design of the great hall and the chambers in the gate house that we see at Castle Roche; the emphasis of Castle Roche is more domestic than military. Beeston was started about 1225 by Ranulf, Earl of

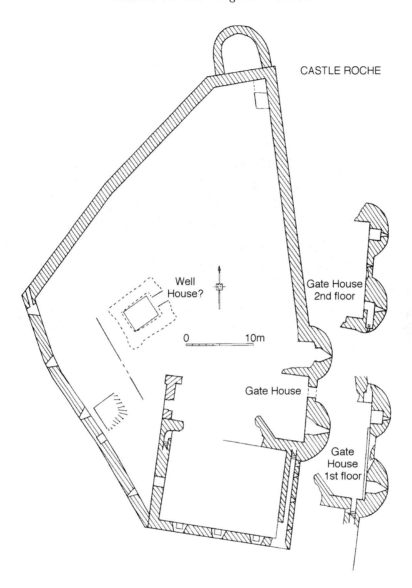

Figure 46 Castle Roche: general plan

Chester, after his return from the Holy Land in 1220; it was still unfinished at his death in 1232, and still so at his son's death in 1237, after which the castle reverted to the Crown and lost some of its importance. This was the year before the report that Rohesia de Verdon had built her castle in Louth. The design of Castle Roche must be based on that of Beeston, which was itself one of the first in England to rely on curtain wall, towers and true gate house for its strength. It seems most unlikely that Beeston would have been used as a model after 1237, when it

Figure 47 Castle Roche: view of the hall and the gate house from the south-east

continued unfinished and unoccupied by a lord; any imitation was probably started between 1225 and 1235.

After his return in 1226, but before his death in 1242, when his Earldom of Ulster reverted to the Crown, Hugh de Lacy II seems to have carried out two major castle-building projects. At his *caput*, Carrickfergus, he doubled the size of the castle by adding the present outer ward, taking in the whole of the rock peninsula on which the castle was built, eliminating the defensive weakness of the earlier castle when it occupied only the outer half of the rock (McNeill, 1981, 44–5). The new work culminated in a gate house, with towers built to be circular in plan (they were cut in half in the sixteenth century) but poorly linked, probably by a passage roofed in timber. This necessitated later work, vaulting the gate passage and constructing a new chamber over it. In their circularity, if not their poor articulation, the towers of the gate house recall those of the great gate house built by the last Marshal Earls at Chepstow in south Wales, during 1235–45 (Knight, 1991, 8–9).

To guard the southern approach to his Earldom from Dublin, and to link with his lordship of Carlingford, Hugh built a new castle at Greencastle in Co. Down (Jope, 1966, 211–19; Gaskell-Brown, 1979, 51–65; Hamlin and Lynn, 1988, 66–9). It consisted of a four-sided enclosure with corner towers, much of it reduced to ground level (fig. 48). Outside the curtain, excavation has uncovered the ditch cut into the rock. At the south-eastern angle a dam was built, remarkable for trying to retain water in a ditch cut through totally porous rock (fig. 49). The

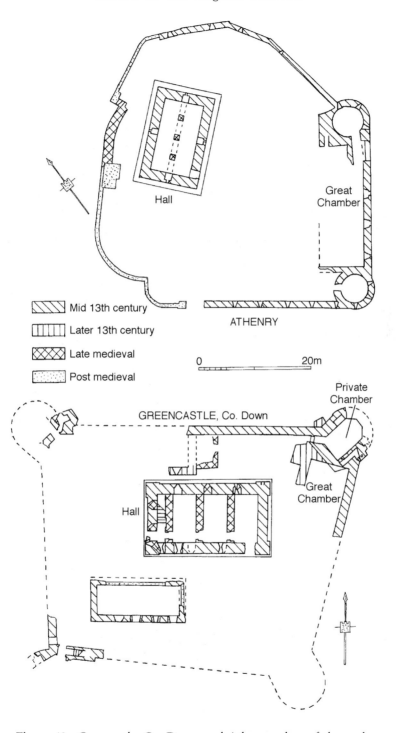

Figure 48 Greencastle, Co. Down, and Athenry: plans of the castles

Figure 49 Greencastle, Co. Down: general view from the south-east

south-western tower was more than a three-quarter round in plan, for it extended along the southern curtain with a second set of rooms; it may have been part of a gate house. Within the enclosure the castle is dominated by a first-floor great hall. The north-east tower contained private chambers at ground- and first-floor levels, with a large building attached to the south, which may have served as a great chamber. The plan of a central hall with lodgings in mural towers is standard for the thirteenth century, while the overall plan recalls that of Skenfrith in Gwent.

The standing remains of Greencastle have been described and it has been the site of several excavations; inevitably there are some points to be made about some of what has been published. There are two, interconnected, statements in Jope (1966) which need to be corrected (McNeill, 1980, 22–7). The date ascribed to the castle of 1260 is based on a misunderstanding of a document recording repairs in that year: there are references to it in the 1250s, such as of corn being sent to it in 1254–6. The second is the statement that the central block is an 'oblong keep of a type peculiar to Irish castle-building of the thirteenth century'. In fact it is a first-floor great hall, with an upper end at the opposite end to the entry, marked by a fireplace and a private latrine, while the presence of a dais at the same end is indicated by a raised window. This links to the remains of the tower at the north-east of the enclosure, with its great and private chambers; the hall and the chambers form a full domestic complex. As such it belongs in the mainstream of castle design, and is not peculiarly Irish, but provides a standard of living in line with contemporary castles elsewhere.

When it was excavated, the ditch along the east side was found to be half filled with masonry tumbled from the curtain wall. This lay directly on the bottom of the ditch and against the dam at the southern end of it. The sequence provides a classic conflict between interpretation from excavation and from documents. The destruction involved has been identified with that recorded in 1260 (Hamlin and Lynn, 1988, 68). Obviously this has the advantage of explaining the conclusion from the stratigraphy that the masonry was thrown into the ditch soon after the latter was dug and the dam built. The dam occupies a position where the ditch has been narrowed, apparently to accommodate it. It is also difficult to understand how anyone who had been long at the castle would fail to see that the rock was porous. Therefore, to the excavator, the dam looks as though it dates from early in the life of the castle and, because the debris lies against it, it too looks early.

This reasoning leaves us with a real historical problem. The ditch remained like this, partly filled by fallen masonry, for the rest of the castle's life. If the collapse dated to 1260, that would include the period under the succeeding de Burgh earls, notably Richard, who was an energetic castle builder, as we shall see. It is difficult to believe that he would have tolerated his castle, where he stayed on numbers of occasions and where two of his daughters were married, to remain with its ditch choked by memorials of its earlier destruction by his father's enemies. There are other captures and destructions noted for the castle, as in 1315, 1343, 1375 or 1381, and a historian would ask whether one of these dates might not be chosen instead of 1260.

Hugh de Lacy probably also added another, rather hesitant, gate house to an Ulster castle, Dundrum, Co. Down, for the same document which describes the

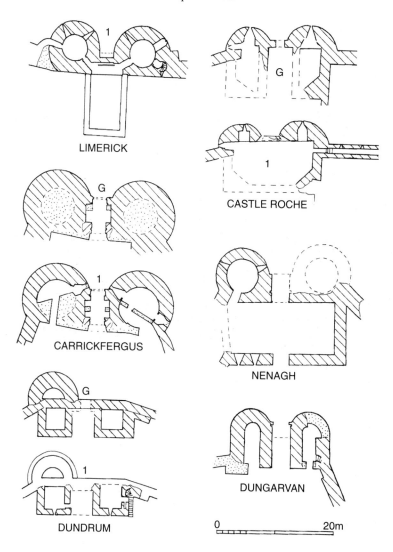

Figure 50 Plans of gate houses of the earlier thirteenth century

repairs to Greencastle in 1260 also records repairs to the doors of Dundrum castle. It is an asymmetrical structure, with only one tower projecting to enfilade the approach road, making it turn a right angle in to the gate (figs 15, 50). Within the castle courtyard are two rooms on either side of the gate passage. On the first floor there are three rooms: the western one is reached by an outside stair and does not communicate with the others; the other two are linked by a doorway. Although the asymmetrical design may be related to that of the great gate house of Pembroke castle (King, 1978, 40), just as the round great tower was, it was not used to provide a grand room or rooms as many gate houses are.

Figure 51 Nenagh castle: fireplace and window on the third floor of the great tower

That a later Theobald Walter added a third storey to the great tower at Nenagh, as evidenced by the change of window design (fig. 51) and the insertion of the corbels to carry the floor joists (fig. 52), shows how round chamber towers continued to be built into the thirteenth century. There was also a gate house. If the great tower has suffered at the hand of restorers, the gate house has suffered from neglect: modern buildings hem in its front, while the main walls crumble and most of the western tower has been destroyed. In plan it consists of a rectangular unit fronted by two towers which are nearly circular and which are poorly integrated into the main unit. They are neither the free-standing complete circles of Carrickfergus nor the individual towers without a uniting gate house of Dublin. On the ground floor, the stubs of walls show that the gate led into an unvaulted gate passage separated from rooms on either side: a fine room filled the first floor. It was reached by an external stair to a door in the rear, north, wall beside which are the remains of a good thirteenth-century window, flanked by the beginnings of another, and was presumably linked to rooms in the two towers. There may have been second floors, at least in the towers, as well: the gate house at Nenagh provided a good suite of rooms. In its overall plan (fig. 53) the gate house at Nenagh is reminiscent of that of the great castle at Montgomery, in particular the provision of towers which are circular in plan internally and more than semicircular to the field (Knight, 1992, fig. 14). There are differences: at Montgomery the towers are solid at ground-floor level; at first-floor, the passage

Figure 52 Nenagh castle: corbel inserted to support the third floor of the great tower

is prolonged there by a chapel, and the defensive apparatus at Montgomery is much better preserved at least.

As well as the additions to Nenagh, other round towers probably date from that time. Lough Mannin is likely to date from after the occupation of Connacht by William de Burgh, who granted it after 1235 to that John fitz Thomas who had held Dungarvan. The round tower of Kitinane castle in Co. Tipperary (see fig. 117) has a fine chamber equipped with wide embrasures, two for windows and two to a mural passage leading to the circular stair. The door in one of the latter has a segmental arch with a chamfer stopped at a delicate foliate carving of mid-thirteenth-century style. The round tower at Ardfinnan (fig. 18) in the same county has a pointed rear arch to its ground-floor loop and a crosslet loop on the first

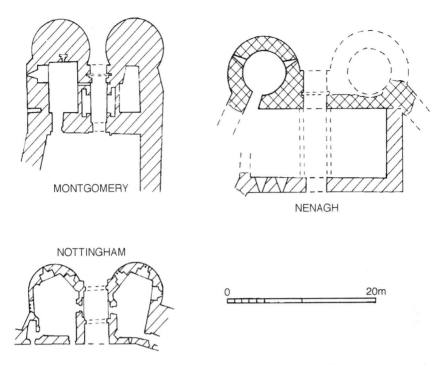

Figure 53   Plans of the gate houses of Montgomery, Nenagh and Nottingham castles

floor, both likely to be thirteenth century in date. The round chamber tower tradition continues, therefore, at least to the middle of the century. This is not surprising: Philip Augustus and his confidants in France continued to build such towers down to the 1220s at least (Châtellain, 1981). In England, the round tower at Barnard castle, added to the hall and chamber range to provide an inner chamber, may be the work of John de Baliol in the 1230s, although it may be earlier (Austin, 1988). In Wales in particular round chamber towers continued to be popular well into the thirteenth century.

ROYAL CASTLES

Henry III as king was never particularly involved in Ireland, unlike his father. However, in 1243, he did intend to visit the country. In advance of this proposed visit, he ordered that a new hall be constructed in Dublin castle, which was to have windows modelled on the great new hall at Canterbury, which the Archbishop had just built (Tatton-Brown, 1982). It was also to have a great rose window in the gable over the dais, and a fresco of the king with his barons behind it: a fine message for a country where the king was notable as much for his remoteness from the baronage as anything. The seventeenth-century plans of the castle show it dominating the castle ward, with one in particular showing how it was divided up internally for the four main courts, as Westminster Hall was (Maguire, 1974, fig. 2).

The royal castle of Dungarvan may have first consisted of a polygonal enclosure; if so, during the thirteenth century was added an outer courtyard with both a twin-towered gate house at the south-east angle and a round tower at the north-east. The tower is provided with fireplaces at ground- and first-floor levels, and a private latrine on the first floor. The gate house is not particularly large but its towers project boldly towards the field and it is equipped with a gate and portcullis at the outer end of the passage (see figs 28, 50). Although a royal castle, Dungarvan appears little in the thirteenth-century documentation. It was among the castles granted to Peter des Rivaux in 1232 and listed among the other important royal castles held by the Justiciar in 1233 (CDI, I, 1969, 1976, 2009): its royal constables are mentioned in the 1270s and early 1280s (CDI, II, 996, 1125, 1242, 1259, 1839, 1907). However, it seems to have become entangled with Thomas fitz Antony's lands from 1215 onwards, with the fitz Geralds constantly asserting their claim as Thomas' heirs. Perhaps as a result of this confusion as to its true status, in 1300 when it was surveyed with his other lands after Thomas fitz Maurice's death, the castle was stated to be in bad repair (CDI, IV, 727). It is likely that what we see now (still in bad repair) was built before that date.

In 1235, Richard de Burgh suceeded in occupying the majority of Connacht, leaving Felim Ua Conchobhair as king, confined to the so-called Five Cantreds, which he held directly from the Crown. Vacillations in royal policy, the rivalries of the English magnates, and the military aggression of Aedh, Felim's son, kept the position in the Five Cantreds, the east of the province, unstable. In 1269–70, the Treasurer of Ireland under the Justiciar, Robert d'Ufford, accounted for £98-0-0 which he spent on fortifying Roscommon against Aedh (CDI, II, 891). In 1270 and in 1272, Aedh burned Roscommon, along with other places, presumably bringing work to a halt. If so, it was resumed after his death in 1274. Between 1275 and 1285 there are records of some £3,500 being spent on the castle, in the Irish Pipe Rolls and elsewhere, the bulk of it being the £3,200 accounted for by the Justiciar in the roll for 1277–8 (36th DKPRI, 48). After 1285, there are records of repairs and of victualling, but no substantial sums expended, so we may attribute the present building to the decade before.

The castle is sited about a quarter of a mile north of the position of the market-place of Roscommon town in the nineteenth century, on flat ground to the east of a former lake (fig. 54). It consists of a formal rectangle enclosing an area of about 50 m by 40 m (160 × 140 ft) (fig. 55). Each corner has a D-shaped tower at the angle: midway along the east side is the great double-towered gate house, while there is a postern tower towards the south end of the west wall. The original castle is not well preserved. During the later sixteenth century, a large house was created out of the northern half of the castle, including the upper parts of the gate house; a ditch and platform north and west of the castle may belong to a garden attached to this house. The loss is considerable, for Roscommon was in its day one of the finest of castles in Ireland. The gate house was the largest in the island (fig. 56). It projects boldly both beyond the curtain, to the east, and into the courtyard, and

Figure 54 Roscommon castle: general view from the north-east

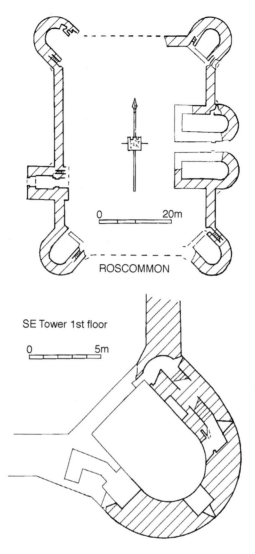

SE Tower 1st floor

0 _____ 5m

Figure 55 Roscommon castle: general plan, and first-floor plan of the south-east tower

was originally at least three stories high, although how these were arranged is now lost. All four angle towers provided individual lodgings at the first floor, with fireplaces and latrines ingeniously contrived in the angle of the tower and the curtain wall (figs. 55, 57).

A document of 1304 accounts for the vaulting of a tower south of the hall, whose steps were repaired at the same time; it also accounts for the roofing of an oriel; the hall was apparently along the west side. The castle well was refurbished and repairs made to the gates, which are described as having three turning bridges

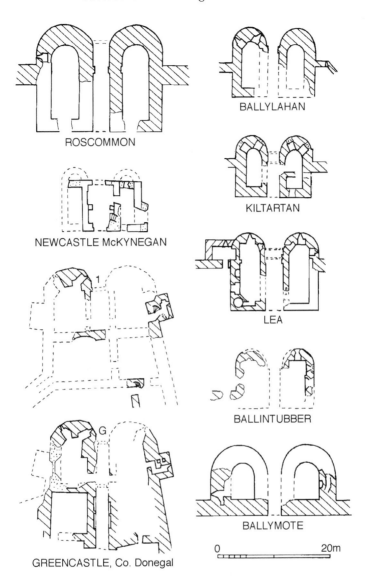

ROSCOMMON

NEWCASTLE McKYNEGAN

GREENCASTLE, Co. Donegal

BALLYLAHAN

KILTARTAN

LEA

BALLINTUBBER

BALLYMOTE

0   20m

Figure 56 Plans of gate houses of the later thirteenth century

('*pontes turnicios*'), presumably two in the main gate and one for the postern, and having two portcullises. There were outer bridges, one of which was equipped with two gates, presumably part of the outer works, such as the outer wall built in 1284 for £66–55–2½ (CDI, V, 306; PRO, E101/233/20).

In the size and rectangular plan of its courtyard, with the one big, twin-towered gate house, Roscommon castle recalls its almost exact contemporary in Wales,

Figure 57 Roscommon castle: view of the outside of the south-west tower

Harlech, built between 1283 and 1290 (Taylor, 1986, 67) for just about twice the price. The detail of the latrines in the angle of tower and curtain also recalls their siting at Harlech (Taylor, 1977, 267). Harlech is at the top of a cliff, with outer works linking it to the sea, but it is more elaborate in other ways. It is a fully concentric castle, with two lines of defences integrated together. The angle towers at Harlech are more circular than D-shaped, and enclose the rooms within more completely. Harlech was started in 1282, so it cannot have been the inspiration for Roscommon, started in 1275. It is clear, however, that the masons of the royal works were closely in touch with their counterparts in England as the latter embarked on one of the largest programmes of castle building in medieval Europe.

BARONIAL CASTLES OF ABOUT 1300: RICHARD DE BURGH

Richard de Burgh was the conqueror of Connacht and his son, Walter, was granted the Earldom of Ulster in 1264. Walter's son, Richard III de Burgh, the 'Red Earl', was the most powerful man in Ireland in his day, and closely linked to the court of Edward I where he was brought up. His children married into the great families of Ireland and England, in particular a double marriage with the Clares, Earls of Gloucester, the richest family in England and the builders of Caerphilly castle, one of the finest in Wales and a true rival to Edward I's castles. It was to be expected that he would show his power in the building of castles. Two reinforced his power in Connacht. At Ballymote he marked his seizure of the lordship of Corran, now southern Co. Sligo, from John fitz Thomas of Offaly, in 1299 by erecting a major castle. Like Roscommon, it is not well preserved, for, although its curtain wall is still existing, only the ground plan and inner wall of its great gate house survives. Again, like Roscommon, it is sited in a low-lying position, suitable for water defences, and is a formal, if markedly irregular, rectangle in plan approximately 40 m (130 ft) across, with a gate house in the north wall, a postern tower and angle towers, but also with towers midway along the east and west walls.

It is rather smaller in area than Roscommon, and differs in other ways. The gate house projects only to the north of the curtain, not into the courtyard. Excavation in the castle (Sweetman, 1986) produced two surprising results. On the south side, there was found to be virtually no moat, only a depression cut some 30 cm (1 ft) into the rock, which was, however, likely to have flooded and so appeared like a water-filled moat. It was also shown that the walls cutting the angle towers off from the courtyard were later additions, of the sixteenth or seventeenth centuries. In spite of this, the south-west tower, which is the best preserved, has a chase for the first floor and latrines at ground- and first-floor level, so there must have been a rear wall, presumably of timber. The two side towers also provided lodgings. The gate passage itself has now disappeared, with most of the front of the gate house, although the outer sides of the towers on either side survive at ground level. From these remains we can see that the chambers on the ground floor on either side of the passage were vaulted; the first floor was divided into two rooms, but the second floor provided a fine single chamber, communicating with the wall-walk.

Between Ballymote and Roscommon, and therefore between the English royal centre of the Five Cantreds, the remnant O'Connor lands and the John fitz Thomas' manor of Corran, lies the castle of Ballintubber. Leask (1977, 69) ascribes it to the O'Connors, although Orpen (*Normans*, III, 204–5) had pointed out that it was found to belong to the de Burghs in 1333, under the name of Toberbride. It was presumably built by Richard de Burgh at the end of the thirteenth century as part of the extension of his power in the area, perhaps before his successful seizure of fitz Thomas' lands. Like Ballymote, it is irregularly laid out, four-sided with angle towers, but with none of the sides parallel or of the same length: apart from north-west and south-west angle towers, it is in a poor state of preservation (fig. 58). It differs from Ballymote in a number of ways. It is almost four times the area with

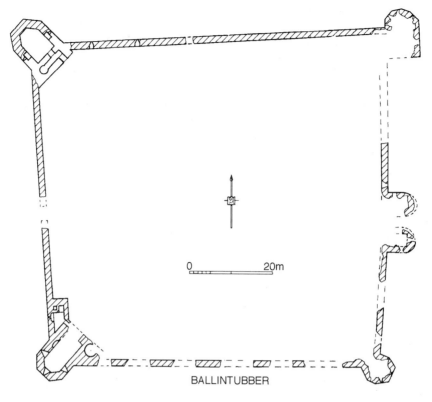

Figure 58 Ballintubber castle: general plan

sides around 75 m long, rather than 40 m. There are no towers along the sides and the gate house is definitely smaller than that of Ballymote, so that it is clearly weaker militarily. The angle towers are not rounded to the field but polygonal.

Curiously, the four angle towers are all different. The two eastern towers are now the more ruined, but were also the smallest. The north-eastern one is hexagonal to the north but squared off to the south, while the south-eastern one is a symmetrical hexagon in plan. The first was clearly a chamber tower, but the latter may not have been. The north-western tower is marked by punch-dressed dressings to the openings and the second-floor fireplace carries the date 1627. The rear wall dates entirely from this later period, as does the rest above the top of the ground floor. Not only is the gate house rather small (see fig. 56), but it is also poorly preserved, like the rest of the eastern side. It is curiously a little off-centre to the south in the east curtain wall. In the last century, the west wall was better preserved and, according to O'Conor Don (1889, 30), what is now a simple gap could be seen as a postern opposite the main gate, as in Ballymote.

The south-west tower was clearly a fine structure. Salter (1993, 28) seems to argue that its rear was rebuilt in the seventeenth century, but it is difficult to see the evidence for this. He may have been prompted by the fact that the rear embrasures of the northern and southern loops have wicker-work centring to their vaults, but this can occur at contemporary buildings, such as Greencastle, Donegal (Waterman, 1958, 77): the southern loop has been adapted for use with a hand-gun. The tower is extended back into the courtyard, while there is a small annexe to the north, against the curtain wall. The main chamber on the ground floor has a fireplace but is otherwise plain, with three simple loops and no direct access either to the upper floors or the northern annexe. The first, and presumably the second, floor were reached from the courtyard up a stair in the south-eastern angle of the tower. The first floor had windows with seats, a fireplace, and access to an inner chamber or latrine in the northern annexe. The second floor was arranged similarly, but with two more loops, and apparently no fireplace. The tower thus provided three self-contained chambers for members of the de Burgh household.

The third of Richard de Burgh's castles is Greencastle in Co. Donegal, known in medieval times as Northburgh; its construction in 1305 is noted in the Annals of Ulster. Like Ballymote, it was built to assert Richard's power in the area, where he was attempting to benefit from the disputes between the O'Donnells, allied to the O'Doherys on the one hand and the O'Neills, allied the MacLochlainns on the other. Although in a sad condition like Ballintubber, its remains were surveyed and published by Waterman (1958), and it has been somewhat reinterpreted in McNeill (1980, 73–6), so only its salient points need be discussed here. Its design reflects, not a general acquaintance with the current ideas of the time, but quite specifically Edward I's two castles in Wales, Caernarvon and Harlech. The first provided the inspiration for the overall plan, an oval with a gate house at one end and a great polygonal tower at the other (fig. 59); but more obviously for the use of polygonal towers, and for the use of two colours of stone emphasising the angles (fig. 60). The detailed planning of the first and second floors of the gate house reflects the layout of Harlech closely, not just in the general arrangement of the rooms, but in such details as the positioning of the fireplace midway along the long wall of the main chamber (fig. 61).

Domestically, there is evidence for the site of the great hall along the northern curtain, near the east tower. That tower provided rooms on at least two floors, each with access to what is probably a latrine tower attached to it. The gate house provided two suites, on the first and second floors, the second floor one being emphasised by the better quality of its windows. Each of the suites had a lobby or entrance room, a long great chamber and two private chambers in the projecting gate towers, with a small room between them. It is very tempting to see the gate house as providing accommodation for the Earl and his Countess on the second floor, and for an important visitor on the first. The east tower would accommodate his Steward, or the Constable, close to the hall. There is only one surprise in this fine castle, with its imagery and display of fashionable comfort, and that is with the actual gate house itself. The gate passage does not lead in to the main courtyard, but purely to a small space bounded by the rise of the rock. The courtyard was therefore inaccessible except by foot, up stairs in the rear of the gate house.

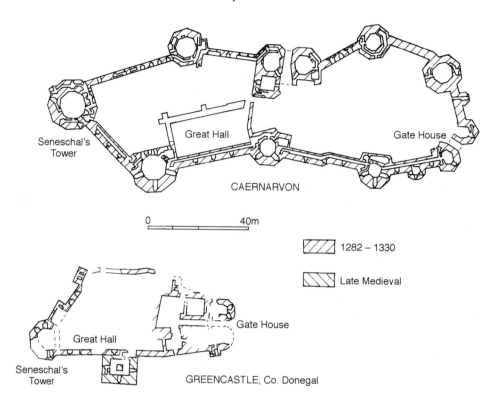

Figure 59 Greencastle, Co. Donegal: plan of the castle compared with that of Caernarvon

DOMESTIC DESIGNS

Three places in Ireland have buildings which are always called castles but which are better described in terms of country houses. They lack not only the gate houses which were the backbone of thirteenth-century English-style castle defences, but also the mural towers, at least as used primarily for defence. None of the three are well dated, relying purely on rather undiagnostic architectural features for their chronology. They should be considered here because their planning is directly comparable to that of the full range of domestic buildings of England. The first of these is Swords, in Co. Dublin, owned by the Archbishop. The site lies at the head of the market-place of the town, beside the River Ward, but otherwise in flat ground, not naturally defensive. It is surrounded by a single curtain wall enclosing an area about 75 m by 100 m (240 × 330 ft), with the simple entrance gate to the south, midway along one of the five stretches of wall and unprotected by any projecting tower (fig. 62).

There are four blocks of rooms in the castle: one on either side of the gate on the south, one at the south end of the east curtain, and the tower at the northern

Figure 60   Greencastle, Co. Donegal: the gate house from the exterior

apex of the enclosure (fig. 63). Leask (1914, 262) identified the northern part of the east side as the probable site of the great hall. It is likely that the fine east windows of the room east of the gate identify it as the chapel. The accommodation in the rest of the castle falls into two sets. There are two towers providing individual lodgings on each floor: the north tower and the tower attached to the chapel, between it and the gate. There are two suites of chambers: one west of the gate and one against the east curtain, south of the hall site. One of the ground-floor rooms in this latter suite proved on excavation to be paved with good tiles (Fanning, 1975), leading the excavator to identify it as a chapel, although it may well have been for the Archbishop's inner household, with his own apartments above.

An inquisition survives from 1326 (Leask, 1914, 259) which gives further evidence. Some of the buildings, such as the dairy, granary or workshop in the farmyard, have gone now. There was also a room and cloister for friars, which we might identify with the first- and second-floor rooms between the chapel and the gate, especially if there was a court to the north, represented now by the stump of walling. The suite to the west of the gate should be the lodgings of the Constable, stated to be by the gate, especially as they include the chamber actually over the gate passage. The inquisition is dated to 1326, and reports the building as being in poor condition, as so many inquisitions did. This has been put together with the fact that the Archbishop started another palace at Tallaght, south of Dublin,

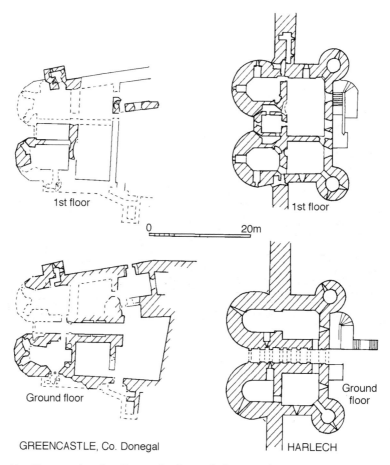

1st floor   1st floor

0   20m

Ground floor   Ground floor

GREENCASTLE, Co. Donegal   HARLECH

Figure 61 Greencastle, Co. Donegal: plans of the gate house compared with those of Harlech

and the conclusion drawn that Swords was abandoned then. The tiles of the paving are of fourteenth-century type, however, and seem to show that the building was repaired, or else that the inquisition drew too gloomy a picture of the state of the castle.

The castle of Clonmore in Co. Carlow consists of a rectangular enclosure with towers at the western angles, and a block of lodgings along the eastern wall (fig. 64). It presumably replaced the motte and bailey about quarter of a mile to the east. It lacks early documentation, but later belonged to the Butlers, builders of Nenagh: it may have been held from the lords of Leinster as part of the Butler fee of Tullowphelim (White, 1932, 2). The courtyard, measuring 43 m by 48 m (140 × 165 ft) internally, and the rectangular western angle towers may be quickly dealt with. The southern single tower has loops at ground-floor level; the domestic nature of the first floor (now largely ruined) is shown by a latrine chute in the

Figure 62 Swords castle: the south (entrance) front

west wall. The northern tower is vaulted over the ground floor and has a stair leading directly from the courtyard to the first floor. There is no sign of an entrance in the west curtain wall. There is a door in the north curtain, beside the north-west tower, which might be either a postern or have led to a building (a latrine perhaps) attached to the now ruined east side of the tower. The gate was probably in the south wall, which has been largely destroyed.

The eastern side is occupied by a line of buildings in three blocks, which may have been constructed in order from north to south: certainly the southern block is later than the central one. All are shrouded in ivy and in places ruined, so that no account can be complete at present. The northern and central blocks each have two floors, connected directly by doors at each level. Both provide large chambers at first-floor level: the one in the central block linked to a latrine in a turret at its south-east angle; the northern one probably connected to one in a turret at the north-west angle, apparently linked to a passage leading out along the north curtain wall-walk. The central block has a plank-centred vault over the ground floor.

The southern block is more complex. It consists of two parts: a long rectangular chamber, with a smaller tower attached to the south, which rises to four stories, one more than the main chamber. The ground floor has two doors from the courtyard, each guarded by a room in the thickness of the west wall, and each leading to a stair and into rooms in the building, two below the main chamber and one

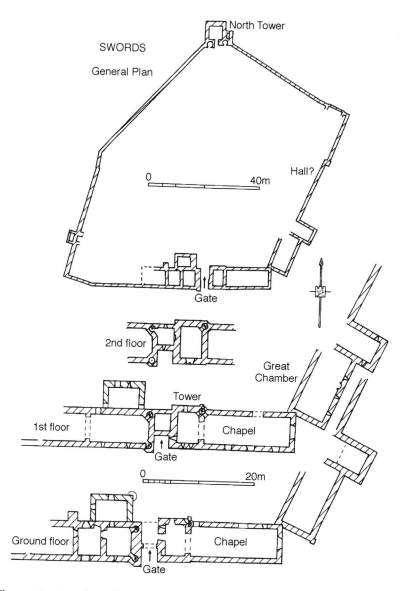

Figure 63 Swords castle: general plan and plans of the south-eastern range

below the south tower. Above this is a first floor, at a level intermediate between the floors of the two blocks to the north; the main part has a room with a fireplace and is linked to a room in the south tower; both have access to latrines in a turret east of the junction between the two parts. The main floor is the second floor, which connects with the first floor of the central block. The main part has a great chamber, with a fireplace in the west wall and two-light trefoil-headed

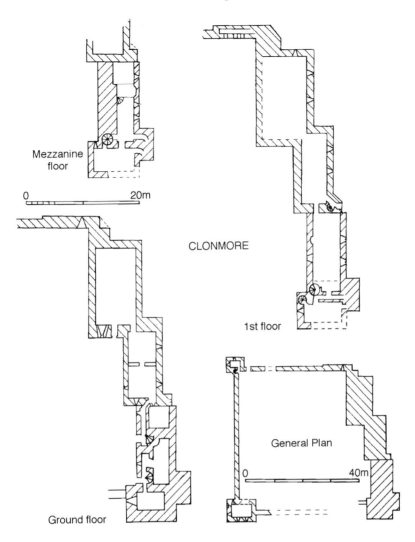

Figure 64 Clonmore castle: general plan and plans of the east range

windows both east and west. A door leads to a lobby and then the chamber in the south tower, from which a private stair leads up both to a balcony over the end of the great chamber and to the room in the third floor in the tower. This latter is marked out by a double-oillet arrow loop at the south-west angle, while above is a carved gargoyle, both adding to the display and showing that the south tower was roofed from east to west, not north to south like the rest of the three blocks.

What Clonmore offers is an example of a complex of domestic buildings of varying grades. That they were not all built at once is immaterial, for the interconnecting doors show that they were all eventually in use together: one did not replace the other. This must have been achieved by the middle of the fourteenth century, to judge from the trefoil windows and the oillets of the arrow loop in the latest work. The southern block provided a fine great chamber on the second floor with two attached private chambers, as well as accommodation on the first floor and rooms at ground level. The first-floor chamber of the northern block is 13 m by 7 m (43 × 23 ft) internally, rather larger than the Archbishop's chamber at Swords (if that is what the eastern chamber is). It is very tempting to see the central block as providing the first chamber attached to a hall in the northern block, only for it to be replaced as the principal lodging by the suite in the southern block. The combination of a great chamber, with two private chambers in a tower, and accommodation for the lord's inner household in the floor below, may be compared to the accommodation of the de Valence lords of Goodrich in Herefordshire around 1300 (Faulkner, 1963, 224–5).

Less than 20 miles south-west of Clonmore lies Ballymoon, one of the most challenging of castles in Ireland (fig. 65). It has four ranges built around a court-yard, making a (slightly irregular) square 41 m (135 ft) externally, but with towers projecting from three of the walls and one at the east angle (fig. 66). It is built of rough granite field stones with granite dressings, which hardly permit a high level of carving. Outside one entrance, to the south-west, are the remains of a quite extensive village or small town. While this entrance has only the remains of the toothing meant for the side walls of a tower to cover it, in the south-east wall is another entrance, which is through a tower. Apart from this last tower, which rises to the top of the second floor, all the outer walls stop at the level of the second floor, precisely. Within the outer walls are the remains of the inner walls of the four ranges which stood against them, much lower than the outer ones. The whole therefore looks as though it was never finished, for it is difficult to see why the inner walls should have eroded or been robbed so much more than the outer ones, while it seems also unlikely that any destruction would have left the outer walls so precisely at the level of the second floor. The only alternative is that it might have been saved and adapted, not as a dwelling, but as a cattle enclosure. A stair built into the inner wall of the north-east range runs down several steps before it is blocked by earth; it shows that what we are now seeing, at a little above ground level in this range, are the features of the first floor. The interior of Ballymoon must be choked with a considerable depth of rubble and debris, especially at the north and east.

Around the walls are windows and fireplaces, with latrines in the projecting towers. The windows along the north-east and south-east walls are loops with oillets, like the one at Clonmore, and with chamfered rear arches, which are carved with simple stops, as dictated by the nature of the granite. Those along the north-west wall and at the north-west end of the south-west wall are different. The north-west wall has an enormous double fireplace, at first-floor level, midway along it; to the north-east are the bases of the deep splays of two large, and presumably high, windows. These allow us to place the great hall on the first floor along the north-eastern two-thirds of the wall, served by the double latrine in the projecting tower: if so, it might have been at least 25 m long and almost 6 m wide

Figure 65 Ballymoon castle: general view from the south-west

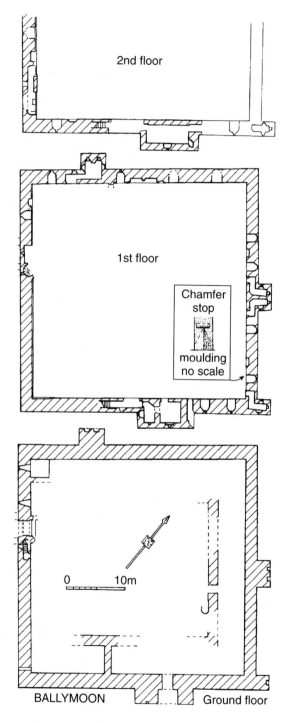

Figure 66　Ballymoon castle: general plans

(82 × 20 ft). To the south-west, between it and the gate, lay the best lodgings, marked out by larger windows, and linking to the accommodation over the gate out to the settlement.

The windows, fireplaces and latrines along the north-east wall, and that part of the south-east wall as far as the entrance tower, mark the provision of a series of individual lodgings. The one next to the hall has two windows on either side of the fireplace, and access to a latrine in the north-east tower. Next to it was a room with only one window and access to a latrine in the same tower. In the eastern angle was a room with windows in both outside walls, as well as a fireplace and a private latrine in the north tower. The space between it and the south-east entrance tower was occupied by a room, with only one window and a latrine, at the same, higher floor level as the rooms in the tower, the rise being dictated by the need to surmount the entrance. The south-eastern quarter of the castle shows few features at ground- or first-floor level, but there are the bases of a mural passage and a fire-place at the second floor. Presumably the lower levels were taken up with service rooms.

The dating and interpretation of Ballymoon are not easy. On the one hand we have a building with all the elaborate provision of great hall, private chambers and graded rooms for the principal men that would mark the household of a great magnate of the late middle ages in England. At any date before the middle of the fourteenth century, it would be very difficult to find an example of such careful and elaborate planning. On the other hand, the other striking thing about Ballymoon is its lack of defences. The gate to the settlement was left uncovered after work had proceeded a long way, and was only to be a single tower at best. The projecting towers provide few flanking loops at the existing levels, and corner towers are conspicuously absent: this is a building purely for domestic use. The later we date it, the more this becomes a problem, for Co. Carlow during the four-teenth and fifteenth century was the scene of many raids from the Irish in the Wicklow hills to the east. It would help if there were any documentary references to it, but there appear to be none, unless under some other name. It presumably lay within the lands of Dunleckny, held in 1247 with St Mullins by the Carews for the service of five knights (Brooks, 1950, 60): this was one of the largest hono-rial baronies of Leinster, and remained in the hands of the Carews, along with their lands in south Wales, down to the sixteenth century.

It is instructive to compare Ballymoon with the castle of Bodiam in Sussex, the work of an ambitious knight with the backing of the royal court. Both are built as formal squares although Ballymoon provides fewer suites, largely because it lacks the gate house and large towers at the angles of Bodiam. The lord at Bodiam had a larger suite of rooms, and the chapel is also prominent. The ideas and the standards which we may imagine at Ballymoon (fig. 67) are not far behind those of Bodiam in domestic comfort and display; they differ in quantity rather than in quality. Bodiam has been criticised as a castle for being less than adequate defen-sively, largely because of the size of some of the windows in the curtain walls, where the desire to light principal rooms takes precedence over defence. Its gate house, corner towers and wide moat, however, make it look formidable compared to Ballymoon.

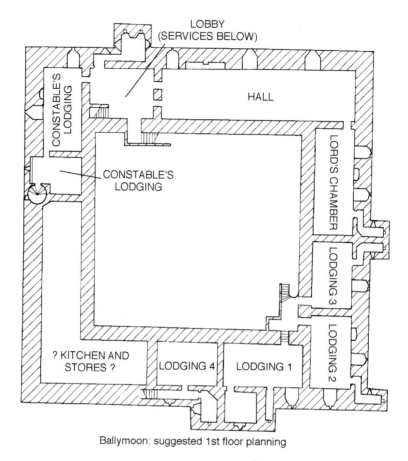

Ballymoon: suggested 1st floor planning

Figure 67   Ballymoon castle: reconstructed plan of the first floor

Close to Ballymoon lies the equally undocumented castle of Ballyloughan, which also presumably lay within the Carew manor of Dunleckny. It is less well preserved than Ballymoon, but enough survives to show that its basic plan was a courtyard some 45 m (150 ft) square (fig. 68). At the north-east and south-west corners there are now square towers; presumably there was one at each corner. Midway along the south curtain was a small double-towered gate house. The better preserved south-west tower has a good chamber on the first floor, reached directly from the courtyard and equipped with windows with seats (the one facing south has twin lights), a fireplace and a latrine. The gate house has been much rebuilt and it is difficult to analyse its original form. From the scar on the gate house and that on the south-western tower it can be seen that the curtain wall was quite low, only reaching to the first-floor levels of the two buildings; it is also only a little under 2 m (6 ft 6 in) wide. Excavation in 1955 around the north-eastern tower showed that the ditch outside the castle was under 3 m (10 ft) wide and only a little over

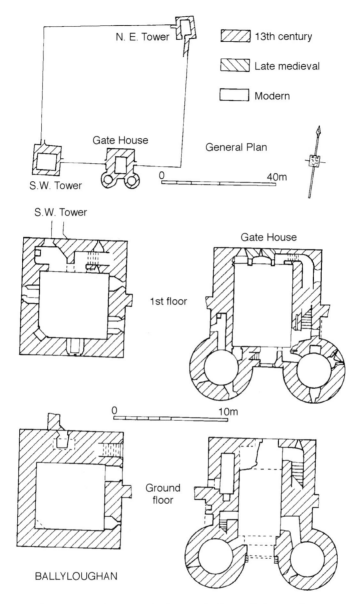

Figure 68 Ballyloughan castle: general plan, and plans of the south-west tower and gate house

1 m (3 ft 4 in) deep (De Paor, 1962, 7). Combined with the two-light window in the south-western tower, which faces out to the field of the castle, it is clear that defence was not a high priority at Ballyloughan any more than at Ballymoon.

There are no clear parallels for Ballyloughan: the gate house in particular is very small. However, the excavation did find that material dated broadly to the fourteenth century had accumulated against the curtain wall by the north-west tower (De Paor, 1962, 8). If we can take this as an indication, and the distinction between fourteenth- and fifteenth-century material in Ireland is still not well understood, then the general idea may be related to the north of England. In Northumbria, the castles of Etal and Ford both have quadrangular courtyards with square corner towers: as with Ballyloughan, these towers are self-sufficient chamber towers.

We can point to other examples of fragments of what became the standard domestic planning of the thirteenth century and later in England, of hall, twin service rooms (buttery and pantry) and chambers at the upper end, which were built in the period in Ireland. A new hall, on the ground floor and equipped with the twin service rooms which were made standard in the thirteenth century, can be seen at Adare (see fig. 23), where it replaced the first-floor hall put up when the castle was first built. Other ground-floor halls exist from the period. At Askeaton the fifteenth-century first-floor hall was built over an earlier one, which had a cross building attached, probably a classic example of Faulkner's end-hall type, where the cross building provides a great chamber (see fig. 109). At Newcastle West, there may have been another ground-floor hall, marked out by large windows equipped with good tracery, incorporating the curved triangles of early fourteenth-century English style; it may have been a chapel, but the style in either case is purely English Decorated (see fig. 107).

Wherever we are led to make direct comparisons with England, this is the message from the castles of the period. We may imagine Gilbert de Clare coming from his castle of Caerphilly, built by his father to assert his power in a lordship threatened by the Welsh king, Llewellyn, to visit his father-in-law, Richard de Burgh, Earl of Ulster, in one of his three new castles. Gilbert would have smiled at the defences, lacking any concept of concentricity, and in particular at Ballymote, which did have a plan with angle towers and a gate house, but which seems to have lacked a true moat. On the other hand, he must have been impressed with the ambition of Greencastle, Donegal: even if it was small in comparison with Edward I's castles, from which it drew its ideas, it provided the lord and his principal guest with accommodation of the highest standard. Had the Earl of Chester seen the changes that Rohesia de Verdon made to the plan of his castle of Beeston, when she built at Castle Roche, he must have acknowledged that she made it a much better castle to live in, if harder to defend.

It remains to define what such parallels may tell us of the men who built these castles: how did the ideas spread between England and Ireland in the period? In the case of Greencastle, Donegal, we can see the interest of the patron: Richard de Burgh was close to Edward I, and was himself knighted by the king at Rhuddlan castle. The architectural references, especially the external appearance derived from Caernarvon, must represent a deliberate choice by Richard, associating himself with the crowning castle of Edward's conquest, itself recalling the walls of Theodosius in Constantinople in just those ways: polygonal towers and two colours of stone. We may attribute to him the overall plan and the use of polygonal towers, with two colours of stone, because it would have been he who made the decisions about the political message contained in these architectural statements. On the other hand, it seems unlikely that he would have been concerned about the details of the internal arrangements, with their parallels in Harlech, and we may suspect that here we have a case of a mason directly recruited from the royal works in Wales to build Greencastle, at a time when the Welsh works were winding down. Similarly, the de Verdon lands in England were centred on Alton in Staffordshire: to reach them from Co. Louth, a traveller was almost bound to go through Chester, and near Beeston, so that the patron is likely to have been the direct means of transmitting the ideas or else recruiting a mason.

Little of the rest of the story of English ideas is so specific; it is more a matter of being in tune with the general run of ideas current at the time, whether of gate houses or the development of chamber suites. It is interesting to contrast this general awareness of style with times when we attribute awareness of style in a particular case to the arrival in Ireland of a particular mason or the experience of an individual patron. It shows that for these ideas to travel between the two countries, it is not necessary to invoke a specific incident. They were part of the general stock of ideas around at the time, on both sides of the Irish Sea. Patrons knew about them and masons understood how to translate them into buildings, if they were commissioned to do so. If they did not draw on this stock, that would not have been because of ignorance or incompetence, but through a deliberate choice to build something different.

CASTLES IN A DIVERGENT TRADITION

——— .◆. ———

If we take as the standard for important later thirteenth-century castles across Europe that they should deploy the defensive and domestic features outlined in the last chapter (the towered curtain, twin-towered gate house, great hall and one or more suites of chambers), then there are many castles in Ireland which do not fit the standard. There are some with good dating, either from documents or stylistic details, to show that they belong to the latter part of the thirteenth century, so that this cannot be the result of a time difference between the castles in the two countries. It cannot be that the builders of castles in Ireland were unaware of those features, for we have seen them in the last chapter systematically deployed through the period. That they do not belong to the English pattern must be a matter of deliberate choice. These divergent castles fall into two groups, based on physical criteria: a few with massive great towers or donjons, and a larger number which simply lack the expected gate house or mural towers along their enclosing curtain walls.

DONJONS

Leask first identified six castles which he called 'towered keeps' (Leask, 1977, 143). He linked them on the basis of their being rectangular blocks, with three-quarter-round towers at each angle and considered them all to be of the thirteenth century. Leask's use of the word 'keep' is unfortunate with its implications of gathering together under the one roof all the major elements of the castle in a military point of last resort. Yet they are tower blocks and we may follow Dixon and Lott (1993, 95) in referring to them as 'donjons'. The problem of relying on the plan alone is shown by Leask's inclusion in the group of Enniscorthy (Co. Wexford), which is a sixteenth-century structure, similar to other towers of the same period. To this one might add other examples which share the same plan but not the date: Dunmoe in Meath, or Delvin in Westmeath; the former is most probably of the fifteenth century. Another, Wexford, is only known from early drawings. The four remaining examples are: Carlow, Ferns, Lea and Terryglass. Three have good evidence that they were built in the thirteenth century or just after. Ferns has elaborate windows as well as capitals to the vault of the chapel (fig. 69), which may be placed in the

Figure 69 Ferns castle: interior of the chapel in the south-east tower

second half of the thirteenth century (Leask, 1977, fig. 34; Stalley, 1971, 26). Lea has a double trefoil pointed window, also of thirteenth-century style. An inquisition of 1333 refers to 'the good foundation of a castle with four towers, 12 feet in height' at Terryglass (Cunningham, 1987, 145), which is a good description of the present remains. Only Carlow is without independent evidence of date.

Ferns and Carlow were centres of the lordship of Leinster, both before and after its division in 1247. Lea was in the Fitzgerald barony of Offaly, while Terryglass was in the Butler lordship of Nenagh. The four castles were thus not particularly closely linked by ownership and none are particularly well preserved. Carlow had the eastern half demolished in the nineteenth century, along with the inner face of the western wall, leaving only half the two shorter north and south walls and the outer half of the western (fig. 70). Terryglass preserves its plan entire, but is still

Figure 70   Carlow castle: the great tower from the west

no higher than it was in 1333; it was presumably never finished and we can say little or nothing about its first floor, which we can assume would have been the most important one. The basic plan of Lea survives, but only one corner tower and one wall and a half of the main block survive above the first, entry-floor level. Two towers exist at Ferns, with the foundations of a third, along with the two walls between them, and part of a third. Only at Lea are there significant remains of what surrounded, or was attached to, the structures.

Lea is the best introduction to these buildings. The donjon occupies most of an inner enclosure, which is surrounded by a wall pierced by plunging arrow loops. The donjon was reached through a simple doorway at the level of the ground floor, guarded by a forework and a machicolation in the angle of the wall and the north tower. The details of the openings, where they survive, are of fine masonry, especially the round-headed rear arch of the opening in the north-east wall at second-floor level (fig. 71). The arrangement of internal access in the building is interesting, although it must be borne in mind that more than half is missing (fig. 72). There is a straight mural stair within the north-west wall up from the first-floor entry, which bypasses the second floor and leads only to the third. It is not that the third floor contained an unimportant room, or rooms, directly accessible from the outside because it was for servants, for it has two double-light windows, one in each surviving wall, and both are set in fine embrasures. The wall-walk may be reached by a stair from the third floor, but it is carried past

Figure 71 Lea castle: interior of the great tower from the south-west

the inner side of the tower on a squinch over the third-floor room: how this affected the roof is difficult to imagine, but it is all part of the careful provision for circulation in the tower.

Lea is notable as being the only one of these four castles where there are remains of more than the donjon. Not only is there an inner ward, but a large outer ward, entered by a gate house of standard twin D-shaped tower pattern. This shares with Kiltartan and Ballylahan the feature of having the walls towards the gate passage thinner than the other walls of the towers (fig. 73). It was later blocked and converted into a self-contained residential tower, while a new gate was opened beside it. The rest of the circuit of the outer curtain is notable for its absence of mural towers, particularly as there are a number of angles which needed them.

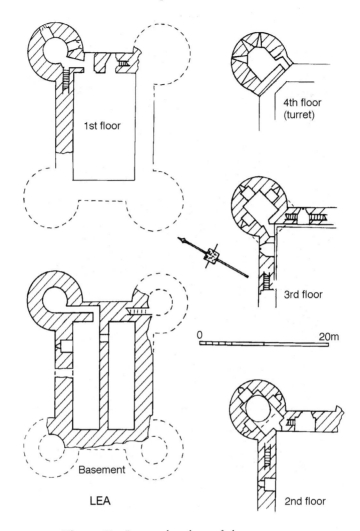

Figure 72   Lea castle: plans of the great tower

The great tower at Carlow is of similar size to that at Lea (see fig. 70). Both are entered by doors in one of the shorter walls, close to the angle of a tower, and the stairs linking the floors both run within the length of the longer wall. At Carlow, however, the door is at first-floor level, with only the one floor above this. The entry floor seems also to have been divided, for there are two latrines on it, one at either end of the surviving long wall. Terryglass is again of similar dimensions, with a door in the same position, while the ground floor is divided into two spaces, though not vaulted. Although only the ground floor exists, two differences may be noted from Lea: the stairs are circular and occupy one tower, while the two southern towers are provided with thicker walls and more arrow

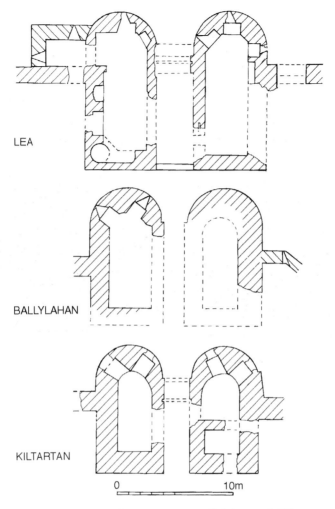

LEA

BALLYLAHAN

KILTARTAN

0   10m

Figure 73 Plans of the gate houses at Lea, Ballylahan and Kiltartan castles

loops. This last is probably connected with the remains of a gate attached to the southern end of one long wall; it may have led into the castle enclosure, leaving the two southern towers projecting beyond the curtain, guarding the angle and the entrance.

Ferns is different (fig. 74). It is larger but, more significantly, nearly square, 18 m by about 20 m (59 × 66 ft) internally, and rather irregularly laid out, with the east wall clearly not square to the south. The internal south-eastern angle is canted to accommodate the tower, while the northern part of the east wall is stepped out at the junction with the tower. As Leask recognised in 1936 (1936, 171), the interior of the building cannot have been a single space. At the very least, the 18 m (59 ft) span from north to south cannot have been crossed by unsupported floor beams;

Figure 74 Ferns castle: exterior view of the 'donjon'

there would have to have been an east–west line of supporting posts. In the centre of the east wall, at first-floor level, is a large fireplace, now much restored, which would sit across the line of any formal arcade: while it is possible that the restoration of the fireplace hood has destroyed the socket for an east–west beam, there is simply not enough room vertically between the top of the hood and the second floor above for any emplacement of a brace or arch in timber. Although the southeast tower floor levels integrate with those of the east wall of the main block, the second and third floors of the south-west one do not (fig. 75). Also, on excavation (Sweetman, 1979, 218–20), it was found that the ground-floor level of the southern half was some 2 m (6 ft 6 in) higher than that of the northern.

The remains are clearly those of a magnificent castle which we should perhaps consider to have been four ranges around a narrow light well, rather than a building under a single roof. The windows on the first and second floors are finely carved, with good fireplaces at both levels. The south-east tower contains a chapel with rib vaulting, at a time when such things were rare even in Irish cathedrals, with foliage capitals (see fig. 69). Excavation showed that it was surrounded by a rock-cut ditch, at least on the southern and eastern sides, with the entry guarded by a movable bridge of some kind. This provision for defence was nullified, however, by the windows to east and south at first-floor level, two-light with trefoil heads.

Figure 75 Ferns castle: interior of the 'donjon', showing the different floor levels on the east and south sides

ROYAL CASTLES

The efforts of the Justiciars under King John had left the area where Munster, Leinster and Connacht met, along the middle Shannon eastwards to Co. Laois, still lying between securely organised lordships. Here the Crown made a real effort to assert detailed control on the ground, through the construction of castles. Whether this was because of a real grasp of the strategy of Ireland or simply because it was a vacuum between the English lordships which inherited Irish boundaries is not the point here. The effort started with the English-style castle of Limerick in the 1210s; to the north it culminated in Roscommon in the 1280s. Geographically, chronologically and in the scale of building, however, there were other royal castles in between.

Although it is now overgrown, substantial remains survive at the castle of Rinndown to the north of Athlone, sited towards the end of a peninsula jutting out from its western shore into Lough Ree (fig. 76). Work on it was started in 1227, and masonry work on it was suspended so that the money could be diverted to building a bridge at Athlone (CDI, I, 2043). The castle is very simple in plan (fig. 77). A ditch cuts off part of the peninsula, where it is naturally narrow; within this is an oval enclosure surrounded by a simple curtain wall, without mural towers and with only a single, and very simple, gate tower, containing just the

Figure 76   Rinndown castle: general view

gate and a portcullis (fig. 78). A later building projects to the south. The castle is dominated by a first-floor hall, built beside the entrance; the ground floor is vaulted and there were two good windows facing north over the ditch and a door communicated with the gate tower.

The remarkable document describing the construction of a motte and bailey at Roscrea in north Tipperary has already beeen referred to. Between 1278 and 1285, £875, along with unspecified sums, were accounted for to pay for works at Roscrea, under the direction of John de Lydyard (CDI, II, 1570; III, 169; 36th RDKPRI, 40, 41, 44, 47, 59). To this we may attribute the core of the present structure (Stout, 1984, 116–17), an irregular oval courtyard, some 40 m (130 ft) across, enclosed by a wall and ditch (fig. 79). Along the curtain are three towers: a gate tower to the north and two to the south. The south-western tower is curious in that it flanks the western curtain but not the southern one. Within it there is a first-floor chamber with a fireplace, itself later, but probably replacing an earlier one. The south-eastern tower is larger and provided rooms on three levels. The gate tower is a single rectangular block, divided into gate passage and flanking rooms at ground level. Although recent excavation has shown that the gate was defended by a turning bridge over the ditch, the tower projects very little from the line of the curtain. It belongs with the single gate tower as seen at Carlingford or Dunamase just after 1200, rather than with the gate house with twin projecting towers of the normal later thirteenth-century type. At both first and second floors (the latter showing

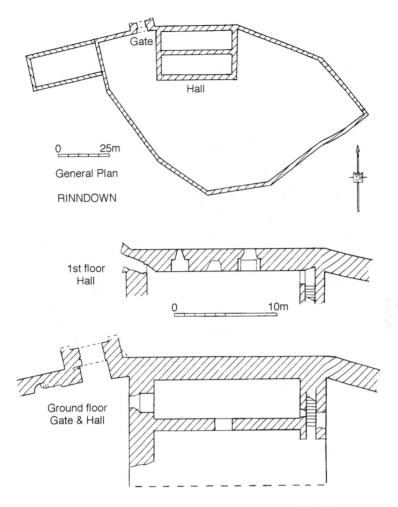

Figure 77 Rinndown castle: general plan and plans of the hall and gate

signs of considerable later adaptations) were two fine rooms, occupying the whole area of the tower.

From the beginning of the thirteenth century, there was a royal castle and manor at Newcastle McKynegan (Orpen, 1908, 129). During the 1270s trouble broke out between the Irish of the Wicklow hills and the English Crown, which was to continue to the end of the sixteenth century. The trouble took the form of Irish raids on the lowland settlements, followed by counter-raids by the English up into the hills. For the latter, the Crown needed bases, the chief one of which on the eastern side of the hills seems to have been Newcastle. It was not chosen for its particular suitability, but because it was already a royal manor: it has good views to the east over the coastal lands, but not to the west from where danger

Figure 78 Rinndown castle: the gate seen from the castle courtyard

threatened. The site consists of a broad, low earthwork platform about 40 m (130 ft) across, at the end of a ridge. At the same time as the work was proceeding at Roscrea, between 1274 and 1295, £284 were accounted for works at Newcastle McKynegan (CDI, II, 309–10, 317, 440–1; 36th RDKPRI, 35, 44, 53, 59, 61, 68; 38th RDKPRI, 47). It is worth comparing this with the £3,500 spent on Roscommon or the £875 on Roscrea: Newcastle was not high on the royal agenda. The documents record the existence of an enclosing wall, a hall and a tower. The tower was probably the lower parts of the present standing building, which was rebuilt from first-floor level upwards, and substantially at ground-floor level as well, during the sixteenth century (figs. 80, 81). Originally, however, it was a gate house with twin D-shaped towers projecting well beyond the line of the curtain wall.

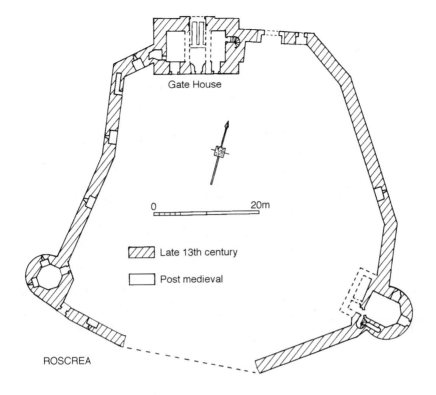

Figure 79 Roscrea castle: general plan

To these three castles we may add two others. An early key to the area of the middle Shannon was the castle of Athlone (fig. 82). Here there was a motte and bailey of around 1210; the motte was later encased in a polygonal tower which still survives, much rebuilt, at the core of the castle, itself now largely shaped by its use as a barrack in the nineteenth century. Along the frontage of the Shannon are the bases of two round angle towers, which are the only remnants of the later thirteenth-century work at the castle (see fig. 81). South of Athlone lies Clonmacnoise, where John de Gray, the Justiciar, also erected an earthwork castle in 1213 (see fig. 43). The remains now consist of three parts: the ditch and earth bank; a rectangular curtain wall set within the eastern half of the earthwork; and a hall set on a raised area against the east curtain wall. Although it has been described as a ringwork (Barry, 1983, 301), the raised area is almost certainly the remains of a partially levelled motte. The stone castle, which was royal at least as late as the 1230s, consists of a courtyard about 16 m (50 ft) square internally, with the gate set in a single tower at the south-west corner. This was entered, at first-floor level, through a later stone forework, containing latrines serving first and second floors; a circular stair in the south-west corner led down to the ground floor and up to the second (fig. 83).

Figure 80 Newcastle McKynegan castle: gate house seen from the outside

CASTLES IN THE LORDSHIP OF CONNACHT

The conquest of Connacht in 1235 by Richard de Burgh called for a whole series of castles, both for his own family and for his tenants. Later, as we saw in the last chapter, his grandson Richard put up castles of English design, but the de Burghs did not always follow English design. The principal de Burgh castles of Galway and Loughrea have been destroyed, but they marked their holding of the manor of Kiltartan with a surviving castle, sometimes known as Ballinamantaine. The site is an irregular triangle, some 60 m (200 ft) from north to south, set with the east side against a ravine in otherwise fairly flat country (fig. 84). The apex of the triangle is to the south: midway along the north front is the gate house, approached across the level limestone plateau. It is ruined below first-floor level, but the ground floor shows twin D-shaped towers which are markedly asymmetrical in plan; the inner walls against the gate passage are only two-thirds the thickness of the outer ones (see fig. 73). In contrast to the tower at the south and the gate house to the north, the west side of the courtyard is enclosed by a wall without any trace of mural towers, in spite of having one projecting angle, and there being no natural defences on the west, like the ravine along the east side.

In terms of surviving castles, the principal barons of Connacht, under the de Burghs, were the de Berminghams. At Athenry, they founded a town with their castle at the north-east corner, sited with the Clarinbridge river to the south-east.

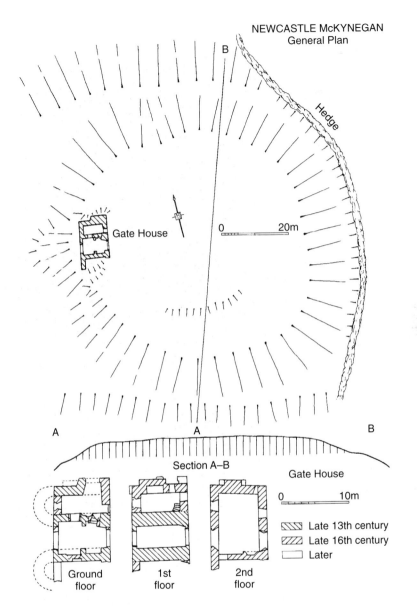

Figure 81 Newcastle McKynegan castle: general plan and plans of the gate house

The existing curtain wall has been much rebuilt in later times, although probably along the same lines. The river frontage has the remains of two towers along it, the southern being less reconstructed (fig. 85). Both are notable in that, like the south-western tower at Roscrea, they do not project from the line of the curtain walls on either side. There is no sign of an entrance tower of any sort: excavation

Figure 82 Athlone castle: general view from across the Shannon

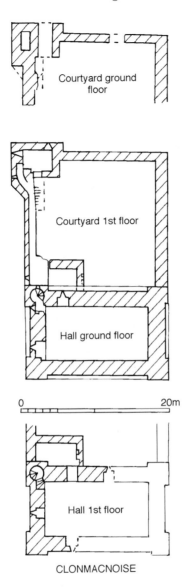

Courtyard ground floor

Courtyard 1st floor

Hall ground floor

0   20m

Hall 1st floor

CLONMACNOISE

Figure 83 Clonmacnoise castle: plans of the stone castle

to find one in 1989 failed to trace it, although the trenches were sited well away from the modern entrance in the south-western curtain (see fig. 48).

The castle is, and probably always was, dominated by the great hall. This is a free-standing tower, with a vaulted basement or ground-floor level (Leask, 1977, 36–9). The hall is entered by a doorway with a moulded arch carried on attached shafts with well-carved capitals. Inside, the windows also have carved capitals to

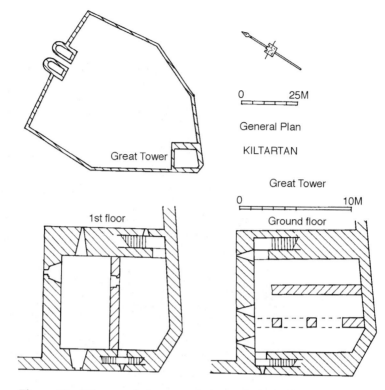

0 ⸻ 25M

General Plan

KILTARTAN

Great Tower

0 ⸻ 10M

1st floor

Ground floor

Great Tower

Figure 84 Kiltartan castle: general plan and plans of the great tower

their rear arches. There is a latrine at the northern corner, the one furthest from the door. With no fireplace on the first floor, indicating that there had to be a central fire in the hall, and with only one window at second-floor level, it is likely that the building was originally open from the first floor to the roof. The south-eastern curtain along the river has three large windows at first-floor level, showing that there was once a large chamber attached to the curtain and to the southern tower.

Athenry has often been compared to Greencastle, Co. Down, and the comparison is a useful one, though as much for the contrasts as for the similarities. In both cases the enclosure is dominated by the bulk of the great tower (rather larger at Greencastle) which contains the great hall on the first floor, over a later vault. In both cases there is evidence of a chamber block, with great and private chambers at first floor, set against the curtain wall. Defensively, however, there is a contrast between the strongly projecting corner towers of Greencastle and those of Athenry. This is particularly strong when one considers the size of the south-western tower at Greencastle, which may also have guarded the entrance; at Athenry the gate was apparently just that. Athenry provides the same standard of domestic comfort as Greencastle, but not the same standard of defence. This is not to be explained by the protection given by the town beside it, for the castle projects out from the line of the town wall, and is not set within it.

Figure 85 Athenry castle: general view from the south-west

The other major de Bermingham castle in Connacht was Dunmore, Co. Galway. It is sited on a rock outcrop, surrounded on the north, east and south by a bog and the Sinking river. The remains of the enclosing curtain wall are now mostly lost, although at the east end there are the shattered and overgrown remains of what is apparently a double-towered gate house. A circular structure at the west end appears to be modern, and not to be a mural tower. The enclosure is dominated, like Athenry, by a rectangular block. This was raised to a four-storey structure in the later middle ages, but was originally simply a two-storey one (fig. 86). It was entered at first-floor level through a door in the east wall, one of the short walls, which is different from the position at Athenry. However, there is a latrine in the diagonally opposite corner (later partially blocked up), just as at Athenry, while there is a fireplace midway along the north wall, and the window in the west wall shows signs of having had seats in the embrasure. The line of the roof is clearly visible in the east and west gable walls, with the eaves at the level of an offset in the south and north walls meant to carry a wall plate. This was clearly originally a building put up to accommodate purely a first-floor hall.

There are remains of a similar hall building at the centre of the enclosure of the de Bermingham castle at Castle Conor in Co. Sligo, the *caput* of their lands in north Connacht. Other honorial barons in Connacht built similar castles. The Templar manor at Templehouse, Co. Roscommon, also had a hall in a rectangular enclosure (Lynn, 1986, 105–7). The fitz Gerald castle of Ardrahan, Co. Galway, had the remains of a similar rectangular block in the south-western part of the castle enclosure (much of this collapsed in 1983, but it was described by Holland, 1987, 219–26). The de Stauntons erected a similar hall block, like so many with a ground-floor vault later inserted, within the enclosure at Castle Carra, Co. Galway; the enclosure was later rebuilt, and the whole castle has suffered from heavy-handed restoration work. The castle of Castle More in Roscommon is now marked only by foundations in the grass (Lynn, 1986, 98–9): within a rectangular enclosure are the remains of a rectangular building of similar dimensions to the rest of these halls. There may be a distinctly smaller example at the fitz Gerald castle of Lough Mannin, again visible as foundations in the grass south-west of the base of the round great tower.

By contrast, there are two castles which survive, not as halls within enclosures but as stone-walled enclosures with simple gate towers. At Rathgorgin, held by the Dolfins under the de Burghs, the courtyard is rectangular, some 30 m by 20 m (100 × 65 ft) in dimensions: a motte and bailey some 200 m (650 ft) to the south-east is presumably its predecessor. Midway along the north wall are the remains of a gate tower very like that of Roscrea, a rectangular block with a gate passage and two side towers contained within it (fig. 87). Tooloobaun, built on a lesser de Burgh manor, has a much larger walled courtyard, with a single tower pierced by the gate passage midway along the south wall. The tower has a side room visible in the grass but, unlike Rathgorgin and Roscrea, the passage takes up the whole ground-floor area. As far as can be seen from the fragmentary remains, neither curtain has towers apart from at the gate; none at the angles, for example.

The last of the castles associated with the conquest of Connacht, and datable to the middle of the thirteenth century, which we must consider here, is the d'Exeter

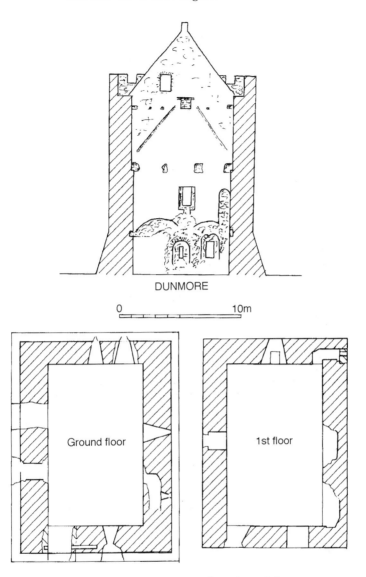

DUNMORE

0   10m

Ground floor

1st floor

Figure 86   Dunmore castle: plans and section of the great tower

castle of Ballylahan. This consists now of an irregular enclosure, roughly circular and approximately 40 m (130 ft) across. Part of the circuit has been destroyed, while loops for hand-guns show that part, at least, of the north-western curtain is late, although presumably it was built on roughly similar lines originally. To the east is a small, double-towered gate house; in plan it is markedly asymmetrical, with thin inner walls like those of Kiltartan (see fig. 73). Visible as foundations in the grass are the remains of two buildings of unknown date, while a fireplace in the north wall marks the site of a building attached to the wall.

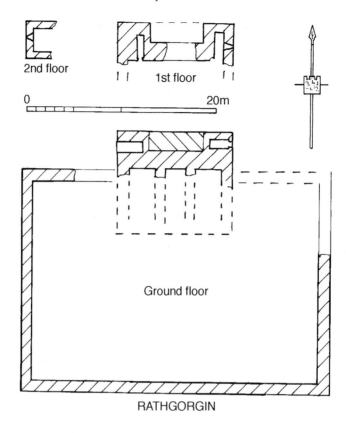

2nd floor

1st floor

0   20m

Ground floor

RATHGORGIN

Figure 87 Rathgorgin castle: general plan

CASTLES IN MUNSTER AND LEINSTER

There are other castles, elsewhere in Ireland, which we may associate with the smaller royal castles, or those in Connacht. Glanworth in Co. Cork is set on a promontory with steep drops to the east and south. Excavations in 1982–4 (Manning, 1987) showed that the earliest form of the castle had an enclosing wall, apparently without mural towers. Within this was a free-standing, roughly square building of three stories (Waterman, 1968). The entrance was on the first floor, which was also equipped with a latrine. Midway along the western curtain was a gate house. This may be compared with the one at Roscrea, for it was also a rectangular block, projecting only a little beyond the line of the curtain. It was divided into a gate passage and two rooms on either side, but the latter were not developed into projecting towers, let alone in the classic D-shaped form.

The present appearance of Cahir castle, Co. Tipperary, owes much to nineteenth-century restoration and to late medieval adaptation and expansion. At its core, however, at the north end of the island in the River Suir on which it stands, are the remains of the earlier castle, now the inner ward. The early remains consist of three elements: the quadrangular curtain wall; the gate house; and the hall and chamber block. The curtain has a round tower at the south-east angle, but the small towers at the two northern angles are square and do not project beyond the line of the curtain. The gate house was blocked (another gate being opened through the curtain beside it) in the late middle ages, but the signs of the former gate arches can be seen both on the inside and the out (Wheeler, n.d., 16). Both in its plan and in its history of later blocking and Butler occupation, it resembles the gate house of Roscrea. The present hall is a nineteenth-century restoration of the late medieval one. At its north end is a chamber tower, with remains at ground-floor level of an earlier building. The east wall of this has a window and a mural stair with plank centring used for the vault, rather than the wickerwork used for the vault over the ground floor as a whole (Wheeler, n.d., 15). The south wall also has a plank-centred arch over the doorway through it, which may well show that there was a building on the site of the hall to the south at the same time; there is a latrine projection to the west as well.

The remaining enclosure castles of the period in Munster need not detain us long. Liscarrol, Co. Cork, consists of a very large rectangular courtyard, some 61 m by 44 m (108 × 145 ft), with three-quarter-round towers at each corner (Leask, 1936, 189). Otherwise the only towers are the two midway along the (shorter) north and south walls. The southern is the rectangular gate tower which stands over the gate passage; it was rebuilt in the later middle ages above the passage. The only sign of internal buildings is the northern tower, which consists solely of a large latrine at first-floor level. Also in Co. Cork is Kilbolane castle, now much ruined but with most of the south-western curtain and the two towers, south and west, at its end still surviving (fig. 88). The rest of the enclosure, some 31 m by 43 m (110 × 140 ft), is defined by a wet ditch, continuing the line of the stubs of the south-east and north-west curtains. The towers have both been vaulted, using wickerwork centring. In the southern one, however, at first-floor level in partic- ular, this can be seen to be associated with the rebuilding of the junction with the south-eastern curtain and the insertion of a spiral stair there. Facing west is a window with a plank-centred rear arch, which allows us to suggest that the core of what we see now is a thirteenth-century castle. At Castle Mora (known also as Castle Barrett, but see Orpen, *Normans*, III, 118, 139) the de Cogans cut off an inland promontory with a ditch to create an enclosure some 30 m (100 ft) across (fig. 89). Within it are the remains of a first-floor hall with a four-storied chamber tower added to it between 1350 and 1550.

Castle Grace in Co. Tipperary looks by contrast to the layout of the stone castle of Clonmacnoise, with a residential building taking up one end of a quadrangular courtyard (fig. 90). The latter is badly preserved, for its stones have been reused to make a walled garden, but its presence can be deduced from the existence of the remains of the rectangular north-east tower. At the corners of the west side are two round towers which link up to the main building between them (fig. 91). At the south end this clearly provided living accommodation at ground level, for there is a blocked fireplace and loop in the south wall. At the south end of the first floor was apparently a hall, linking to a chamber in the angle tower. To

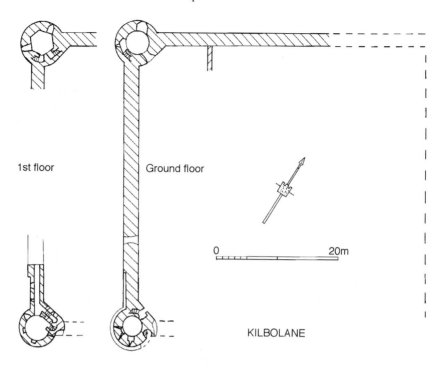

Figure 88 Kilbolane castle: general plan, and plans of the towers

the north there is a straight joint in the masonry, showing that it and the north tower were at least constructionally later. The northern tower is reached along a mural passage, which might indicate that there was a separate room to the north.

In Leinster are three castles which we may consider here. One marks the Archbishop of Dublin's manor of Castle Kevin, near Glendalough, on the eastern slopes of the Wicklow mountains. During the later thirteenth century, at the same time as the nearby royal Newcastle McKynegan was being rebuilt, Castle Kevin was in the king's hands, and it was also used as a base against the Wicklow Irish. In 1276 nearly £500 were spent on wages, provisions and materials for the castle's fortification (CDI, II, 1412); in 1278–9 the Justiciar accounted for nearly £70 on works there (36th RDKPRI, 44); it was repaired after being damaged by the Irish in 1308 (PRO, E101/235/13). The site is a rectangular platform, some 35 m by 40 m (115 × 130 ft), now defined by deep, heavily overgrown ditches (fig. 92). On the inner sides of these can be seen the traces of masonry revetment, while there is the corner of a rectangular tower at the north-east angle and a bridge revetment midway along the eastern side. It is perhaps best thought of as a strongly defended moated site.

Grenan castle is set beside the river Nore and now appears as an isolated hall building within a ditched enclosure (fig. 93), but we know that the enclosure was once surrounded by a stone wall (Waterman, 1968, 69). The ground floor has the

Figure 89 Castle Mora: general view of the enclosure, tower and hall

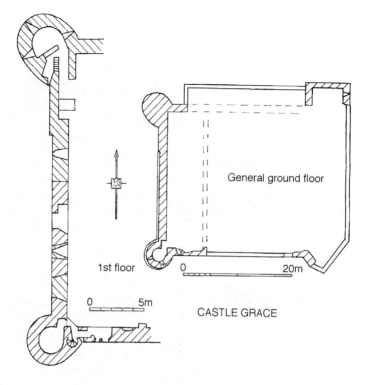

1st floor

0   5m

General ground floor

0   20m

CASTLE GRACE

Figure 90 Castle Grace: general plan and first-floor plan of the north range

entry and later was divided into three rooms with vaults showing the signs of wicker centring. The first floor was probably divided into a hall, occupying two-thirds of the space, and a chamber in the remainder. Waterman suggests that a second floor was added, on the basis of a change in the nature of the masonry, but the change is not visible in the south wall or in the quoins, while a latrine shaft in the first floor, but coming from above, shows that there was likely always to have been a second floor. It has several indications of expense: the use of Dundry stone from Bristol and a small chapel with a nicely cut quatrefoil window in it. Its builder is unknown, presumably one of the descendants of Thomas fitz Anthony, Steward of the Earl Marshal in Ireland, who died in 1229, leaving only heiresses. Recent excavation has added the castle of Dundrum, Co. Dublin, to the list of those with Roscrea-type gate blocks (O'Brien, 1989).

DISCUSSION

The castles considered in this chapter are not uniform but cover a range of quality. To start with the donjon castles, Leask may have been wrong to base his description of 'towered keeps' on their plan alone, and he was certainly wrong to identify

Figure 91   Castle Grace: view of the west front from outside the castle

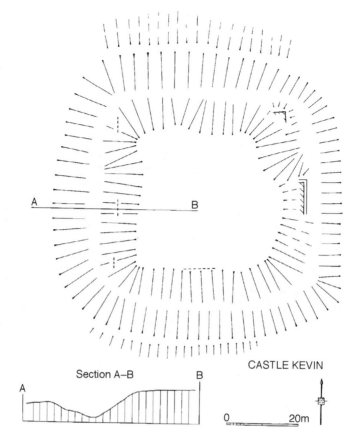

Figure 92 Castle Kevin: plan

them as keeps, but his instinct was not out of place. The grandest is Ferns, which appears to be a set of four ranges, in a single tradition, looking perhaps to the idea of the so-called 'shell keep'. In the thirteenth century, Richard of Cornwall at Launceston, or Edward I more spectacularly at Flint in the 1270s, erected lodgings on a similar plan, arranged around a narrow light well. These two were round (as Castel del Monte was octagonal) but the idea may be the same. We should attribute Ferns to William de Valence, Henry I's half-brother, lord of part of Leinster between 1247 and 1296, or his son Aymer, who died in 1324.

Lea, Carlow and Terryglass were also castles of major magnates of Ireland, fitz Gerald of Offaly, Bigod and Butler. The great tower of Lea in particular was clearly a very interesting building, much more than a simple first-floor hall structure. Interestingly, although it has a fine outer gate house, the defences of Lea are not very impressive: the money went into the domestic side. Even if we reject the idea of these three buildings being connected by anything more than a rectangular plan with corner towers, they remain unparalleled elsewhere, and are of fine quality as buildings. They are variants on the first-floor hall theme, which we have seen

Figure 93 Grenan castle: view of the enclosure and hall of the castle

at Maynooth, earlier, or Greencastle, Co. Down, later, but with angle towers being used to accommodate chambers.

The bulk of the other castles in this chapter may be considered as stripped-down castles. This is most apparent in their provision for defence. The relatively small size of many of the enclosures may not have been a source of weakness in itself, but it does imply fewer men inside. The enclosures are all defended either by curtain walls with mural towers or by a twin-towered gate house, but not with both. This makes little sense militarily, for both were necessary, and one without the other was rendered much weaker. Nor was the weakness of the perimeter compensated for by siting the castle on high rocks or in inaccessible marshes, both situations which are not rare in Ireland. Only Cahir on its island in the river was difficult to approach. It was obviously important to the builders that they had towers, whether at the gate or along the wall, but not perhaps for strictly military reasons. There is a large element of display here.

Simplicity is also evident in the domestic provision of these castles, but less so than in their military aspect. The two are connected, for towers provided not only defence but accommodation. The emphasis here is clearly on the free-standing hall. In all the castles considered, the hall was on the first floor, unlike the ground-floor halls of Dublin, Adare or Greencastle, Donegal. The halls were located in buildings normally free-standing or connected only to the curtain, not set in a range of buildings like Clonmore or Ballymoon, for example: the sole exception might be

145

Table 1 Features and owners of castles in a local tradition

Castle	Donjon	Gate house	Gate block	Angle tower	Hall size (m)	Owner
Ferns	Yes				20+ x 18	de Valence
Carlow	Yes				16 x 9.2	Bigod
Lea	Yes	Yes		No	14 x 9.7	fitz Gerald
Terryglass	Yes				14.6 x 10.5	Butler
Rinndown		No	No	No	14.8 x 7.2	Royal
Ardrahan					16 x 8	fitz Gerald
Athenry		No		Yes	13 x 7.4	de Bermingham
Castle Connor		No		No	14.6 x 7+	de Bermingham
Dunmore		Yes		No	12.7 x 7.8	de Bermingham
Castle Carra		No	No	Yes	14 x 7.5	Staunton
Castle Mora		No (?)		No (?)	14.2 x 6.8	de Cogan
Castlemore		No (?)		No (?)	15 x 9	de Nangle
Castle Grace		No	No	Yes	14(?) x 7.2	de Paor
Clonmacnoise		No	No	Yes	14.2 x 8	Royal (?)
Templehouse						Templars
Grenan		No (?)		No (?)	15/10 x 8.5	fitz Anthony heir
Roscrea			Yes	Yes		Royal
Cahir			Yes	Yes	13.6 x 7.7	de Worcester ?
Glanworth			Yes	No (?)	8.5 x 7.3	Roche
Kiltartan		Yes		No		de Burgh

Note: Blanks = no surviving evidence

Castle Grace after the addition of the northern part of the block. The result was an overtly dominating hall block, harking back to the sort of structure found at Maynooth or Dunamase. This must reflect a love of towers or gate houses for their own sake, expressions of the pride of their owners in their castles and lands. That there was something of a consensus as to the size of such a hall may be seen from table 1 of the internal dimensions of surviving first-floor halls considered in this chapter.

As well as the evidence of the physical traits, this table also shows us social patterns. It is worth recalling that the criteria for selection of these castles were physical. The first four were donjons; Ferns should be detached from these because of its size and because it was probably not a single space but a courtyard building. Then come the castles with mural towers, gate blocks or twin-towered gate houses. When we look at their builders, they cohere as a group. Most belong to the second rank of Irish barons, men who were not the major players within the Ireland of their time, although there were men like John fitz Thomas of Offaly (Lea) who was on his way up. There are major names here, most obviously the king, but also de Burgh. These castles, however, are not their major ones: Kiltartan was subordinate to Loughrea or Galway, just as Ardrahan was subordinate to Lea.

The magnates, men who normally built castles on the English pattern discussed in the last chapter, figure here in two ways. They might build the elaborate donjons in their major centres, diverging from the English pattern without a loss of quality, or they might put up lesser buildings at their lesser centres. When they did that they joined the men whom they would have seen as occupying a rank below theirs. They retained most of the comforts they were used to for themselves, derived from English or French standards, but there was less provision for a large household. In this way, the importance of the hall continued, rather than being overshadowed by their own chamber suite, pivoting on a great chamber and linked to subsidary lodgings. Castles were simpler because life was simpler among the second rank of barons. There was also, apparently, not much threat of attack.

CHAPTER EIGHT

LESSER STONE CASTLES

The point below which, socially, a building cannot be considered a castle is not one which confronts writers in England or France so much after the twelfth century. Earthwork enclosures and small mottes pose the question, but it does not much arise with stone buildings. Into the breach steps the idea of manor houses as separate buildings from castles, often of timber, and not well preserved until the fifteenth century. The commonest remains from the thirteenth century are the moats surrounding the courtyard of the building, but they overlap clearly with the similar moats from around the houses of assarting free men. Moated sites are also to be

Figure 94 Witches castle: view of the small hall-house from the north-west

found in Ireland, mainly in the south-east, but they are not usually to be found at sites of the *capita* of manors (Barry, 1977, 175). Because of this, we are probably justified in equating them in Ireland with the moats of assarting freemen that are found in similar peripheral sites in England and elsewhere. They do not represent castles, or even manor houses, in Ireland. There are, however, stone castles which are clearly less elaborate than the ones discussed in the last chapter. They are castles which have left either a single stone building, the hall-houses, or else those which consist only of an enclosure.

HALL-HOUSES

Stell (1981, 23–4; 1985, 203) has rightly warned against too casual an assumption either that hall-houses are a separate group of buildings in their own right or that they need to be dated to before 1350. Nevertheless, it is worth trying to isolate such structures in Ireland, because they may answer part of the question concerning the lowest end of castle building, and because their relationship to the later tower-houses needs to be examined. The first feature that we would be looking for is that they should be clearly rectangular, for, although 'the distinction between a hall and a tower is a fine matter of degree, if not wholly imperceptible' (Stell, 1985, 203), it is a distinction which we must explore (fig. 95). We may pick out a number of buildings and present some of their characteristics to test the possibility of there being such a thing in Ireland as the hall-house, and then to suggest its date range and use. In table 2, the first eight buildings are reasonable candidates for thirteenth-century hall-houses. Ballisnihiney, Delvin and Dunmoe have features which might lead us to consider them as later, while Clough and Lismahon are included as excavated examples of thirteenth-century halls.

The table of details of candidates for inclusion as hall-houses, and others for comparison, includes 11 buildings whose interior dimensions may be obtained: they all approach proportions of 2:1 of length to breadth (fig. 95). The first nine buildings all have first-floor doorways, marked by the presence on the outside of two large beam holes below the door jambs, to support a timber platform reached by an external timber stair (fig. 96). This links with two other features. The first is that the windows of the first floor are always clearly larger, in height and in breadth, than those of the ground floor. None of the buildings have a stone division of the first floor: although a timber division might have existed and left no trace of its fixing, it does seem as though we are dealing with a single room, a hall. If we compare the buildings with later tower-houses, we can note that there is a contrast between them and the towers, which have lesser rooms on most floors. Similarly, most tower-houses have spiral stairs, but only Moylough among the candidates for hall-houses has a stair which is not straight: it makes a half-turn before carrying on straight.

The most obvious difference between them and the tower-houses lies in the presence of a vault: this is almost universal among tower-houses, except for overtly late (i.e. seventeenth-century) ones. Not only is it usually absent among the halls but where it is present, it can be seen to be an insertion. Ballisnihiney, Co. Galway,

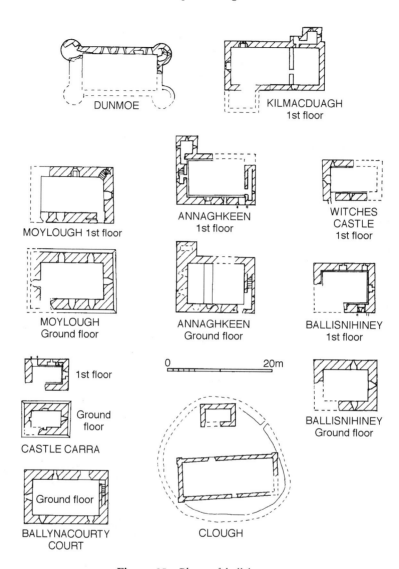

Figure 95 Plans of hall-houses

is the exception here, with a wicker-centred vault over the first floor (fig. 97). The use of wicker centring is normally thought of as belonging to the fifteenth rather than the thirteenth century, although this is not a rigid rule, for examples of its earlier use are found. Similarly, the corner turrets of Delvin and Dunmoe should probably be seen as indicating a link to tower-houses in date: the surviving window of the principal floor at Dunmoe has double lights surmounted by a square hood mould, which must be late in date. This contrasts with the others in the table, where late details, such as loops finely carved from limestone or box machicolations, which are so typical of tower-houses in Ireland, are noticeably absent.

Table 2 Halls and hall-houses

Site		Internal dimensions (m)	Enclosure ?	Added vault ?	Other features
1	Annaghkeen (Galway)	11.0 x 7.5	No		Later division of ground floor. Turret vault wicker centred
2	Ballynacourty Court (Galway)	6.5 x 3.5	No		
3	Cargin (Galway)	10.7? x 7.4	?	Wicker centre	
4	Castle Carra (Antrim)	6.0 x 3.2	No	No	
5	Kilmacduagh (Galway)	11.3 x 7.0	No		
6	Moylough (Galway)	12.0 x 6.5	No	No	Spiral stair to second floor?
7	Shrule (Mayo)	9.5 x 6.7			Rebuilt above ground floor
8	Witches Castle (Galway)	c. 9.0 x 4.5	No?	No	
9	Ballisnihiney (Mayo)	8.5 x 6.6	No	Original	
10	Delvin (Westmeath)	14? x 6.7		Modern	East end lost. Turrets at west angles. 2nd floor added?
11	Dunmore (Meath)	14.6 x 6.4		Original	Angle turrets
12	Clough (Down)	17.5 x 5.4	Bailey		Ground-floor hall on motte
13	Lismahon (Down)	12.0 x 6.0	No		Ground-floor hall on motte

Note: Blanks = no surviving evidence

Finally, we should note that none of these buildings shows signs of being originally set within an enclosure, which distinguishes them from some of the lesser castles discussed in the last chapter. Moylough is also set on an inland promontory, cut off by a ditch, but here there is no room for subsidiary buildings apart from the stone hall (fig. 98). As with a hall such as that at Lismahon, set on a motte without an accompanying bailey, if there were subsidiary buildings, either chambers or farm buildings, they do not seem to have been much valued if they were built outside the ditch. They are noticeably smaller than the halls listed in the last chapter, as well as having no indications of subsidiary rooms. It is therefore possible to distinguish the first eight buildings of table 2 above as a group, on

Figure 96   Ballisnihiney castle: first-floor door from the outside

physical criteria, and to identify them as being what are described elsewhere (Cruden, 1960, 91–9) as hall-houses, probably dating from before 1350.

It is notable that these hall-houses are also set apart in terms of their distribution, socially and geographically. Socially, half of them cannot be associated with any documentation. Ballynacourty Court was on one of the demesne manors of the de Burgh lords of Connacht, but not one where they are recorded as having a castle. Shrule was one of the manors granted by Richard de Burgh to his son John in 1308 (Orpen, *Normans*, III, 208); again, it was not apparently a place where the de Burghs lived. Kilmacduagh lies within the cathedral precinct, and presumably was built by an official of the Church, possibly the Bishop. It was a small diocese, whose bishops were normally Irish, which covered the south-western parts

Figure 97   Ballisnihiney castle: the remains of the vault over the first floor

Figure 98   Moylough castle: general view of the hall-house with ditch close to it

Figure 99 Map of hall-houses, polygonal enclosure castles and Irish stone castles of the thirteenth and fourteenth centuries

of the de Burgh lordship, occupied through the thirteenth and fourteenth centuries by the O'Heynes and O'Shaughnessies. Moylough may be associated with the grant of the land to Robert de Coterel (Holland, 1988, 77). These stand in contrast to the halls set in enclosures, which were discussed in the last chapter, such as Grenan or Castle Mora, which can be associated with the lesser baronage: these are apparently one step down from that.

They are, however, clearly residential in nature. Their main purpose is to provide a well-built and impressive hall. Defence seems to have been of limited importance, confined to placing the door at the first floor, possibly up a stair which could be removed if necessary. Seven of the eight are to be found in north Co. Galway, indeed (apart from Kilmacduagh) within a tract of land less than 20 miles square (fig. 99). This immediately raises the suspicion that this is a product of the academic work done, in this case the field survey of Holland in that county. However, it is odd that no other examples, apart from Castle Carra in Antrim, have come to light: we might expect Holland's work to have produced a preponderance of sites in his area, but not so exclusively. These look like being associated with the de Burgh lordship of Connacht. It is worth remembering the relative absence of mottes in Connacht. The land with the small hall-houses is an area where the drift deposits over the limestone are thin: digging earthworks may have been harder than building in rubble, with stone and lime locally plentiful.

POLYGONAL ENCLOSURES

The second group of minor castles consists of enclosures surrounded by polygonal stone walls (fig. 100). They, or some of them (for it may well be that their relatively inconspicuous remains have led to their having been missed in the field), have been described elsewhere (McNeill, forthcoming) and can be quickly summarised. With the exception of Seafin castle, Co. Down, they seem to lack any towers, and consist simply of a stone wall. They enclose areas of about 30 m (100 ft) or less across. The walls are neither thick nor well built, so that they do not look capable of supporting much in the way of wall-walks. They are not to be found at manorial centres but are associated with the frontiers of lordship and areas of military tension, rather like the mottes with baileys (see fig. 99).

For dates, we rely on the evidence from two Ulster examples: Seafin (Waterman, 1955) and Doonbought in Co. Antrim. Seafin may be identified with the castle of Maycove from Magh Cobha (Lawlor, 1938). It was built first (replacing Ballyroney motte) in 1252 (CDI, I, 32, 124; Annals of Ulster, 1252) by the Justiciar, when the Earldom of Ulster was in the king's hands. It was destroyed in 1253, but rebuilt again in 1254–5 (Annals of Loch Key, 1253; *Analecta Hibernica*, II, 262). The dating of Doonbought to the thirteenth century is based on the finds of artefacts from an immediately preceding phase of the site; indeed, the stone wall of the enclosure was probably never finished (McNeill, 1977). The function of these small castles was to provide a base for troops stationed during times of tension. They were there to defend the area from raids by Irish while forces were prepared for counter-raids by the English.

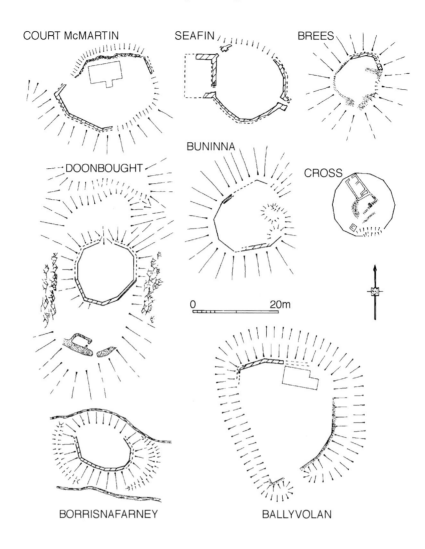

Figure 100   Plans of polygonal enclosure castles

CHAPTER NINE

CASTLES OF THE IRISH

— •◦• —

It is one of the oddities of the subject that the question of whether the Irish constructed castles before 1350 has been very little discussed. Intuitively we would expect them to do so. In Wales, faced by determined assaults by the English barons, the native lords did so to protect their lands. In Gaelic Scotland, without the same pressing need to resist conquest, the lords also built castles during the thirteenth century. By 1250 it would have been quite difficult for an Irish lord to have found a lord outside Ireland who neither occupied a castle himself nor had a neighbour who did. Orpen was not inclined to address the question: the main thrust of his work on castles was to show that mottes were not early Irish mounds, while his historical work was aimed at recounting the actions of the English lords, with whom he identified unashamedly. On the other side, there has been perhaps a curious idea that it would somehow have contaminated the Irish if they were to indulge in such an English activity as building castles. This not only demeans the intelligence of Irish lords – if castles were effective tools for their lordship, only a fool and a bigot would eschew them – but prevents us from examining a potential source of information about the nature of Irish lordship under the impact of the new ideas from England. We have seen something of these issues in considering the possibility of Irish lords constructing castles before 1169.

One of the difficulties with trying to grapple with the problem is that of agreeing how we might recognise an Irish castle. To be identified at all as a castle the site must obviously be different from earlier Irish ones. If it is, and thus relates to English castles, how are we to tell if it was Irish-owned or built? There are no contemporary surveys of Irish lands or estates, which would name castles for us, while the Annals name few places; arguing from such silence is clearly no good. It usually comes down to making a statement as to where the boundaries of English and Irish lordships lay, and then arguing that sites within the Irish lands were Irish.

It is easy to illustrate the snares in this argument. The motte at Clones was built on land which any map of medieval Ireland, except one for the year 1212, would identify as Irish: it was built as part of an unsuccessful attempt to expand the borders of English lordship. In the 1211–12 Pipe Roll, the castles of Dromore (fig. 42) and Moycove in Ulster are recorded as being supplied and repaired by the Justiciar; they were clearly English castles but they lie in land which was then the small Irish kingdom of Iveagh. We assume that they were outposts built by the English, but they could have been Irish castles captured in that year: there was war between the English and Iveagh then. A further dimension to the problem comes with other mottes in the same county, especially Duneight or Crown Mound, near Newry. They might be similar English outposts which just happen not to have generated expenses accounted for in the Pipe Roll. On the other hand, Duneight was built on the site of an earlier fort and township of the Dal Fiatach (see chapter 1) and that part of the county (ecclesiastically the deanery of Dalboyn) may have been reserved for the Mac Dunleavy kings who continued in the area as 'Kings of the Irish of Ulster' under the English earls. Crown Mound lies close to the Cistercian abbey, and possibly the town, of Newry; if the Magennis kings of Iveagh had a fixed, fortified centre, Crown Mound would be a likely candidate. Outpost or Irish castle, simply arguing from location will not decide the question in any individual case.

IRISH KINGDOMS LINKED TO THE EARLDOM OF ULSTER

A parallel case to that of Crown Mound is found to the north-west, at Managh Beg in Co. Londonderry. This is a very large motte, although constructed rather by reshaping a gravel spur than by heaping up much earth. It lies on the right bank of the Faughan river about two miles upstream from Lough Enagh, where there was a crannog, and has been identified as the 'town of O'Cahan' visited by Archbishop Colton in 1397 (Reeves, 1850, 28–9). It seems very far from the land held by the English in Ulster before the middle of the thirteenth century, and the general association with O'Cahan power might support the case for it being an Irish motte.

The case for the systematic use of castles by Irish in Ulster is best made with the small kingdom of Ui Tuirtre, ruled by the O'Flynn family. It occupied central Co. Antrim from the Clough Water river to the north almost to the town of Antrim in the south. Within this area are a number of mottes, including such fine examples as Harryville in the modern outskirts of Ballymena town (see fig. 44). On the northern border of Ui Tuirtre, on a spur overlooking the Clough Water, lies the fort of Doonbought (McNeill, 1977). It saw the construction, in its second phase, of a small polygonal enclosure castle of the English border type discussed in the last chapter. In the first phase it had three parts: an inner enclosure and two outer areas. The inner enclosure was set on the rocky crest of the spur defined by a dry-stone wall, while the northern line of approach was cut off by a ditch and bank, retained in the front by another dry-stone wall. In its plan it is a motte with two baileys, but the use of dry-stone walling does not look like the work of English castle builders. The date of the artefacts in the soil dumped directly on top of the first-phase levels was clearly of the thirteenth century. It is difficult to see this as being other than a fort or castle of the Irish of that date.

In 1259–60 O'Flynn, king of Ui Tuirtre, signed a general letter about an agreement he had made with Hugh Byset and the Earl of Ulster 'apud Conoriam', i.e.

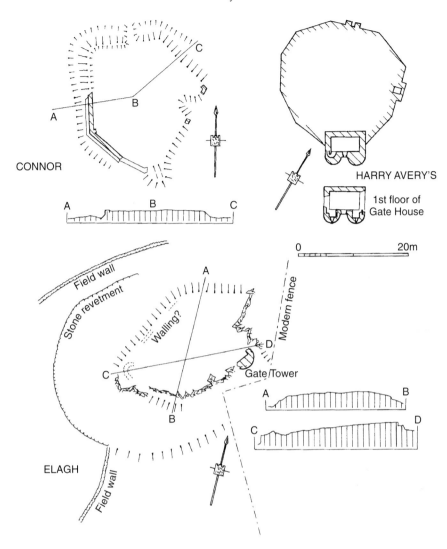

CONNOR

HARRY AVERY'S

1st floor of
Gate House

0   20m

Field wall

Stone revetment

Walling?

Modern fence

D

Gate Tower

ELAGH

Field wall

Figure 101 Plans of Irish castles of stone in Ulster

at Connor, Co. Antrim, in the centre of his kingdom (McNeill, 1980, 102–3). This was the traditional seat of the bishop, but it also has preserved the remains of a stone castle. These are not very impressive, consisting of a basically pentagonal curtain wall mostly reduced to a little above ground level, and with a ditch outside it (fig. 101). There are no signs of towers along it, or any elaboration for an entrance, which may have been at the southern angle: the only feature it has is a base batter and the stub of a wall at the south-west. This has a good claim to be the site where O'Flynn lived and where he signed documents issued in his name.

The survival of the kingdom of Ui Tuirtre does need explanation, for it was surrounded on three sides by the Earldom of Ulster during the thirteenth century when the Earldom was expanding. The land of mid-Antrim is good for agriculture and it would seem an obvious target for the English, yet it survived until the collapse of the Earldom in the fourteenth century. One of the reasons for its success may have been because the O'Flynns deployed castles: mottes, a border fort and a stone castle for themselves, the whole acting as a deterrent to English land hunger.

THE WEST OF IRELAND

The strongest individual case is that of Carrigogunnell in Co. Limerick, granted to Donough O'Brien in 1210 (Empey, 1981, 14; Warren, 1981, 29). The site is a strong one, on an isolated rock on the southern shore of the Shannon estuary, but the castle is both ruined and overgrown. This makes its study the more difficult, for it is clearly a castle of several periods. It is interesting to note how the grant of this castle has been seen by historians as part of a demonstration of how Donough O'Brien was one of the most anglicised of Irish kings at the time, integrated into the English polity. Be that as it may, it is also significant that the castle remained in O'Brien hands for the rest of the century.

The English attacks north-west of Meath and in Connacht are well documented in the Irish Annals, notably those of Lough Key and Connacht. Lynn (1985; 1986) has drawn attention in particular to the information on castles in Connacht for a rather different purpose. There are a number of references to Irish use of sites, all of them on islands in lakes, fortified in some way and therefore to be considered in the context of the possible use of castles. In 1220 the Annals of Lough Key record William de Lacy's attack on O'Reilly's crannog, identified with the island in Lough Oughter (Orpen, *Normans*, III, 33). On this rocky island, which may have been extended artificially with piles (Kirker, 1890, 295), there is now a large circular tower, badly damaged by gunpowder during or following the siege of 1653 (Manning, 1990). In spite of the loss of a quarter of its circumference, this tower does not look like other round great towers of the period: it notably lacks windows or fireplace. It could be the work of O'Reilly, but the castle was apparently used by William de Lacy in 1224 as a refuge (Orpen, *Normans*, III, 43), and he may have built the tower. Unfortunately, excavation in 1987 shed no light on the earlier history of the tower (Manning, 1990).

Islands were apparently important in Connacht; as a sign of his defeat in 1225, O'Flaherty yielded up island forts in Lough Corrib, including Castle Kirke, to Richard de Burgh. In 1235, the forces of Richard de Burgh, engaged in the conquest of Connacht, attacked McDermot's castle on one of the Lough Key islands. As well as bombarding it with stones from perriers mounted on the shore and on boats, they threatened to burn it using combustible rafts towed against it (Annals of Lough Key and Connacht; Orpen, *Normans*, II, 183–4). This might imply that the structure was fundamentally of wood, but the Annals of Connacht record that after its recapture by treachery, in 1235 McDermot threw it down and scattered its stones.

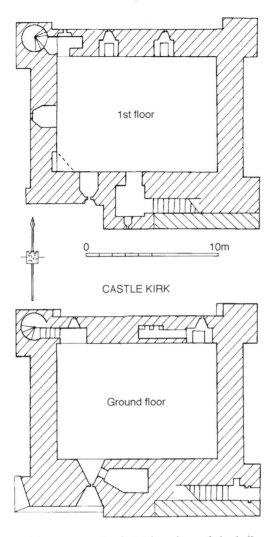

Figure 102 Castle Kirke: plans of the hall

In 1233 the Annals of Connacht record that Fedhlim Ua Conchobair destroyed four castles (Galway, Dunamon, Hag's Castle and Castle Kirke) which had been built by de Burgh and his Irish allies, the sons of Ruadhri Ua Conchobair: in 1232 the same Annals record that Galway and Dunamon castles were built by de Burgh and Adam de Staunton. The sons of Ruadhri may be credited, by implication, with building the other two. Hag's Castle is a simple circular enclosure about 31–33 m (100 ft) across, surrounded by a wall up to 5 m (16 ft 6 in) high, built of massive stone blocks with some mortar: there are no features to it.

Castle Kirke is different. It is a rectangular building (fig. 102), with pointed lancets and rear arches to the embrasures of the windows, undoubtedly of the

Figure 103 Harry Avery's castle: general view from the south

thirteenth century. It is entered by a door in the first floor, from a stone stair which has been added to the southern side; it was guarded by a portcullis, whose slot survives at the base of the stairs. All this relates to the first-floor halls typical of the thirteenth-century English castles, but it shows variations. The angles are marked by turrets with base batter on the west. These do not provide extra space for rooms (except the north-western one, which accommodates a circular stair), nor do they project equally to be effective buttresses. This is especially noticeable on the northern side, closest to the lake where it most needs support; here the projection is least. The wicker-centred vault over the little room on the ground floor below the doorway may mark the presence of Irish workmen, but we have seen this elsewhere. It is on the rather anomalous plan of the hall and the presumed identification of this building with the one mentioned in the Annals, that we might identify Castle Kirke as an Irish version of an English hall-house castle.

TIR EOGHAIN AND TIR CONNAILL

We may conclude this discussion with the consideration of two more castles in the Irish west of Ulster. The only references to a castle at Elagh, Co. Donegal, come from long after 1350, but the physical remains indicate a longer history. It is possible that it was this site, not the Grianan of Ailech, so called in modern times, which was the ancient capital of the northern Ui Neill. There appears to have been a larger enclosure around the rock outcrop which was the site of the castle. The inner core of the castle consists of traces of a low, ruined curtain wall around the edge of the rock, with a tower at one end (see fig. 101). This is solid at ground-floor level but there are traces of a wall running back from its northern angle. In the north side, also, is a portcullis slot, with a rebate for a gate and a draw-bar hole behind it. The tower was clearly therefore one of two gate towers, with a room behind the projecting tower, making a true gate house. In the absence of documentation and diagnostic architectural details, little can be said of its date, but it is clearly not a tower-house, and relates much better to a thirteenth- or fourteenth-century castle of English type. Without a date, it is difficult to attribute the castle to any particular lord, but later it was the seat of the O'Dohertys who replaced the Mac Lochlainns as lords of Inishowen in the thirteenth century.

South of Elagh, in western Tyrone, lies Harry Avery's castle (Jope et al., 1950; Rees-Jones and Waterman, 1967). It consists of a nine-sided mortared wall surrounding the scarped top of a low hill with fine views over the land to the north and west (fig. 103). In front of this is a twin-towered building, looking like a gate house of English type, but unable to function other than as an entry for people on foot; no horses or carts could reach the courtyard through it. Like Greencastle, Co. Donegal, the entrance leads, not to the courtyard which lies at first-floor level, but simply into the rear of the tower, from which a narrow mural stair leads up to the floor above. The ground floors of the two projecting towers are solid, like Elagh, but above them were two levels of chambers, while behind ran a large rectangular room. The ideas of the castle can be traced to contemporary castles of the English in Ireland: a combination of a standard gate house, modifed like Greencastle in its entry arrangements, and one of the polygonal border enclosure castles for the courtyard.

The interpretation of the castle depends on the name, an anglicisation of Henry Aimredh Ua Neill, who died in 1385. He was not such a glamorous or mythical figure as to make us suspect that his name was applied to the castle later by popular distortion. He was the brother of Niall Og O'Neill, king of Cenel Eoghain and the father of a fraction of the O'Neill family which was able to have members who were kings too. The castle is sited in a part of the country in dispute during the thirteenth and earlier fourteenth centuries between Cenel Eoghain and Cenel Connaill to the west. Henry Aimredh and his family, by establishing themselves firmly in it, made sure that the dispute went the way of Cenel Eoghain. Apparently, as part of his efforts, Henry constructed a castle of English ancestry.

With Harry Avery's castle, we have probably crossed the notional boundary of 1350 for this section. We can draw two conclusions about the Irish use of castles before this date. The first is that some Irish lords did see fit to apply the techniques of English castle building in their lordships. The second is that it was not a common occurrence. The cases which we can point to are all of lords who were under pressure to retain their lands, or, with the last two, perhaps to conquer them. In this there are echoes of the period before 1169. The kingdoms around the Earldom of Ulster were threatened by its expansion, or else by the power of Cenel Eoghain, or, indeed, by both. The island sites of Connacht tell something of the same story: they appear more as refuges or purely military strongholds than as castles in the sense of being the normal residences of their lords. The exception here would be Castle Kirke, which makes the same sort of provision for domestic life as English castles. Equally, it would clearly be crucial here to excavate and see what buildings were provided within the enclosure of Connor castle.

CHAPTER TEN

SUMMARY

———— •◆• ————

The first lesson when we consider the period as a whole, which we must empha-
sise and use as the basis for the whole discussion, is the clear evidence of the close
acquaintance shown by the builders of castles in Ireland with contemporary work
elsewhere. This is visible, not surprisingly, in the royal works, whether at the new
hall for Dublin castle, overtly to be modelled on an English one, or the strongly
defended castle at Roscommon. It also applies to baronial castles, from Castle
Roche at the start of the period to the castles of Richard de Burgh around 1300.
We can attribute this both to the knowledge of the patrons, and to the masons
themselves. The use at Greencastle, Co. Donegal, of polygonal towers and two
colours of masonry was a political message, recalling Caernarvon castle, which
must surely imply that this was Richard de Burgh's idea. On the other hand, the
details of the layout of the rooms in the gate house, paralleled at Harlech, must
have come from the mason. Likewise, the decision to build Roscommon castle on
such a scale must have been Robert d'Ufford's. Details, such as the integration of
the tower rooms and the latrines in the angles between them and the curtains,
would then have been the decision of the mason.

In itself, such a close acquaintance is no surprise, when we consider the close
relations of the officials and the aristocracy with their counterparts in England.
This said, the main impression is not that of the bulk of castles conforming to the
Anglo-French standard, but of differences from that. The castles in Ireland differ
in simplification and formality. The simplification is partly a matter of scale: Ferns
and Lea are the only really first-rate castles of the period; even then, we do not
know the surroundings of Ferns, while the outer gate house of Lea is relatively
unimpressive. The simplicity is particularly seen in the provision of defences.
Roscommon is a fine castle, but it is notable that it seems to lack any outer enve-
lope of defence, even along the line of approach from the east. The enclosure to
the north looks more like a garden, perhaps of the sixteenth or seventeenth
centuries, than a defence; because it has survived, it makes the absence of any
remains visible to the east in front of the gate more likely to be genuine. At
Ballymote and Ballintober outer works appear to have been conspicuous by their
absence. The individual gate houses are poorly preserved but it would appear that
Carrickfergus, after its reinforcement of around 1300, was the only one with a gate

passage closed at both ends with a gate and portcullis, and commanded from above with a murder hole. The rest seem to have relied on a single closure of gate and portcullis. The builders of even the royal castle of Roscrea were satisfied with a gate house whose gate passage ran through a rectangular tower, in the manner of the twelfth or earlier thirteenth century, rather than between two projecting towers.

In the provision for domestic life, the contrast is less clear than for defence. Castle Roche takes the defensive design of Beeston and scales it down in terms of mural towers, but the integration of the hall and the lodgings in the gate house is a sophisticated improvement. Assessment of many of the castles is hampered by the lack of preservation, and also of excavation of the courtyards. Ferns castle may be a remarkable design of a compressed courtyard castle, but that interpretation requires us to know what lay around the central tower. Likewise, judging the position of Ballymoon, without knowing the century to which it belongs, is difficult. The surviving structures at Swords hint at elaborate domestic provision within the courtyard, but only excavation of the area will take the argument further. All that said, it is likely that the provision of domestic accommodation for the lords in castles built in Ireland in this period was directly comparable to that in England.

We can also see the simplification of the castles in the provision of lodgings for the wider household, which is associated with the simplification of the defences. The obvious place for providing lodgings was in the mural towers, which were so easy to adapt as individual rooms. When, as in Ireland, castles are not built with an array of mural towers, but tend to provide either towers or a gate house, it is obvious that the designers had a problem with providing chambers. The organisation of Roscommon, with the rooms in the four corner towers and the lesser gate house as well as whatever was provided in the great gate house stands out by contrast. Greencastle, Co. Donegal, had fine lodgings in the gate house, presumably for the Earl and his Countess or a principal official or guest, and accommodation in the east tower at the other end of the courtyard for the Constable or similar official: apart from these, there is only the evidence of the south-east latrine tower for further accommodation. Clonmore provides a fine range of lodgings for the lord, but there is little evidence from the poorly preserved other three sides of the courtyard. Even Ballymoon, as has been pointed out, provides a less full range of accommodation for the larger household than Bodiam. This last is significant, for Dalyngrigge, the builder of Bodiam, was not a magnate who might be expected to have had a large and elaborate household. In Ireland, apparently baronial households were smaller and simpler than in England.

The castles of this period present us with a series of gradations from the major ones through to the distinctly minor ones. It is expressed most clearly in the group where the builders seem to have had to make the choice between mural towers and a double-towered gate house. There is a strong element here of formality, almost of sumptuary laws. Towers and gate houses were being used as much for their formal statements of the power and status of their owner as for the practicalities of defence. In this context, it is interesting to note the one positively different type of castle found in Ireland: the small polygonal enclosure. This is associated with the borders of lordships but is far from elaborate. These enclosures were developed to serve in the small-scale border raids which were the normal form of warfare in Ireland, not the widespread movement of armies.

Throughout the documentation of the south-east of Ireland in the later thirteenth and fourteenth centuries, there are accounts of the manorial establishments found on the estates (e.g. CDI, V, 1302–7, 175–6, 190, 195, 197; White, 1932, 37; Abraham, 1991, 330–2). They refer to enclosures, sometimes defined by stone walls, containing a hall and other buildings, often a chamber, a barn and other agricultural buildings, as one would expect. There were towers at a number of places, sometimes specifically stated to be of stone, sometimes to be understood from the term *bretagium*. In Meath particularly, a number of the sites in the extents are now marked by mottes which must have existed at the time of the account. These records provide, therefore, a background against which we can place the discovery by excavation of the halls on the tops of the Ulster mottes at Clough and Lismahon (Waterman, 1954a; 1959a). These showed the continued use of the site of a motte by someone who lived in something recognisable as a hall.

What we do not know was whether the last two sites also featured the sort of ancillary buildings noted in the manorial extents, just as we do not know whether the hall-houses of Connacht were the centrepieces of complexes of farm buildings. Nowhere in Europe is there a greater lack of evidence for the courtyards of castles than in Ireland. Neither at the lesser sites nor in the outer courts of the greater castles has the necessary excavation taken place. We cannot say how extensive they were; when they might have been established, at the first occupation or grafted on later; or how widespread they were, for it is possible that they were more a feature of the corn-rich south-east than of Ulster or Connacht. The nature of the enclosure, whether it should be seen as a measure of enclosure against theft rather than a defensive feature, would also tell us much of the nature of the life in the period. These manorial sites should not be routinely identified with the widespread moated sites, for they are not usually to be found at the centres of the documented manors. They belong to the phase of colonisation marked by expansion into the periphery away from the initial settlement, like the moats of the assarting free men in England.

The other massive area of missing evidence concerns, notoriously, the Irish lords. Here, while there is a case that some built castles, they are the exceptions. Not only are they few, but they are also not typical. The examples which we may point to come from unusual situations: not caused so much by imitation resulting from close cultural relations with the English but by the fact that their lords felt under pressure. The pressure could be of isolation among the English, as with Ui Tuirtre. It might be that of an uncertain conquest, as with Henry Aimredh O'Neill. Here we apparently have a member of the ruling family being established in a border district, disputed with the neighbouring lord, and building a castle as part of his successful attempt to ensure that the area remained O'Neill, not O'Donnell: nothing is more like the linking of castles and the early feudal lordship as this case. This contrasts with the position in both Wales and Scotland. In Wales, the lords were driven to build castles in order to hold on to their lands in the face of the determined advance of the English lords and the frequency of war. This was not the situation in Highland Scotland. Here the lords of the southern Highlands built castles from the late twelfth century onwards, but their fellows to the north did not (Dunbar, 1981).

Investing in a castle, particularly one of mortared stone, may well have had considerable implications for traditional Gaelic kingship or lordship, particularly with the problem of inheritance. Gaelic lordship, unlike English feudal lordship, did not practise primogeniture, but the lordship passed to a close adult relation of the king or lord, often by some balancing act between the various lineages of the royal kin. A castle would complicate this process. If the kingship is associated with a castle, on the death of a king his successor would have to move into it, displacing any son of the previous king. Alternatively, each lineage would have to build a castle, in the hope that, in the event of the kingship passing to their line, their candidate would not be disparaged by other unsuccessful candidates who already possessed castles. A castle above all locked lordship to a locality, and more especially centred it in a particular place in the area of the lordship. Again this could be said to conflict with traditional Gaelic lordship, which valued the allegiance of men over acres, but this was always a false contrast (what use are men without land to support them, or land without men to work it?).

The lack of castles among the Irish seems to tell us two things. One is that, in contrast with the Welsh, only a few Irish lords felt sufficiently threatened or unsure in their lordship to need to build a castle. This links to the lower level of defence among the English castles of Ireland, compared to the English castles in Wales. On both sides of the hill, Welsh castles were built more with war in mind than those of Ireland. The Irish lordships of the thirteenth and earlier fourteenth centuries remained like the northern Highlands, not like the southern, in not building castles as part of their equipment of lordship. Just as they did not feel as threatened as the Welsh lords, so their lordship was apparently more similar to the northern Highlands, in this respect at least, than to the southern.

PART III

CASTLES OF THE
LATER MIDDLE AGES

CHAPTER ELEVEN

THE FOURTEENTH CENTURY

—— ·◆· ——

For a long time the fourteenth century, however precisely defined, has been seen as a major horizon in the study of the medieval history of Ireland. This is usually presented in terms of political or military events, typically starting with the invasion of Ireland by Edward Bruce in 1315, and finishing with Richard II's expeditions to Ireland in 1395 and 1399. Elsewhere in Europe historians see the outstanding problems of the century as economic in their roots, not political. It is true that there are few direct sources for the demography or economic processes of the period in Ireland, such as taxation records or continuous series of manorial accounts. The main phenomenon of the Black Death did, however, strike in Ireland; notoriously so in the case of Friar Clyn, who left parchment for the continuation of his chronicle after his death, should anyone survive. It is reasonable, therefore, to assume that the main trends applied in Ireland as over the rest of Europe.

The basic assumption must be of population decline. Elsewhere this had profound results for the agricultural market, which was the main economic engine of the middle ages. The decline in population resulted in a rise in the price of labour and a decline in the price of food, so that some agriculture moved from a position of low profitability to one of loss and so was abandoned. Typically this involved cereal farming being changed to pastoral, which employed fewer people, the effects of which were most to be seen on the margins of the core areas of arable agriculture. In this European context, Ireland as a whole was marginal land, and so would have seen a decline in or cessation of the immigration of land-hungry peasants from England or elsewhere. Within Ireland, there were also areas, whether upland or because of poorer soil or wetter climate, which would have been marginal compared to the good, drier lands of the south-east, which are still more likely to be farmed for corn. Pastoralism in Ireland overwhelmingly meant rearing cattle, for which Ireland is ideally suited; they were exported principally as hides. Indeed, if the main emphasis is on cattle rather than arable farming, much more of Ireland can be considered good land.

Politically, the century did see major change. South of a line from Dublin to Limerick the land was dominated by three great new lordships which arose from English families established among the thirteenth-century baronage. The descendants of Theobald Walter, now known as the Butlers from their hereditary office,

171

moved their centre from Nenagh in north Tipperary southwards and eastwards to the valley of the Suir and to Co. Kilkenny, culminating in their purchase of the castle and barony of Kilkenny itself in 1393. The two Geraldine lineages founded the Earldoms of Kildare, to the east, and Desmond, in Limerick and the west. North of Dublin, the area of the modern counties of Meath and Louth was under the control of lords of lesser lordships, at least one of which, that of the Prestons, was a creation of the fourteenth century. In the west, the O'Brians were resurgent in Clare, following their victory over Richard de Clare in 1318. North of this the descendants of the de Burgh lords of Connacht and Ulster formed themselves into the lineages of the Burkes, in the eyes of the English government the most spectacular case of gaelicisation. The murder of William de Burgh, the last resident Earl of Ulster, in 1333 left a power vacuum in Ulster. The lands of the former Earldom were mostly seized by the Clandeboy line of the O'Neills, with a small area in the south-east remaining nominally part of the English polity. The Earls' position of dominant lord in the North was increasingly assumed by the main line of the O'Neills.

The principal loser in this process was the royal government in Dublin. The rise of the new lordships in the English areas ushered in a cycle of decline for the power of Dublin. The new Earldoms were constituted as Liberties, where the royal power was significantly weaker than in the shires. The loss of power meant the loss of revenue, which in turn led to further loss of power. To the lesser lords and towns of the south-east, the result was increasingly a choice between competing powers, those of the royal government and those of local lords. Both aimed to raise revenue and both offered protection against the other competing powers. Not surprisingly, it was often the local lords who were able to provide the better deal in fact. This simply reinforced the cycle of decline of royal power, so that it shrank steadily both in terms of the area of Ireland which it controlled and even in its power within that area. By the end of the fourteenth century, Ireland was more than ever a land of competing local lordships.

When we combine the economic changes in settlement which we may postulate with some certainty and the changes in lordship which also took place in the fourteenth century, it is clear that the period was one of massive change. To the civil servants of the royal government, whose documents dominate our view of events, this was all disastrous, and they used such words as 'decline' and 'degeneracy' liberally to describe what was happening. In this they have been followed by many historians. However, as Frame points out (1982, 335), the structure of society and government created in the fourteenth century was very durable. Inevitably in the middle ages (as in other periods), competing lordships meant violence between them, taking the form of raids and devastation of territory. This appears in the Annals as war, as indeed it appeared to the people who were killed and whose crops and herds were stolen or destroyed. It was, however, a particular form of war, which could also be seen as being distinctly limited in its scope, in the numbers of men involved and in the duration of individual campaigns. Whether we should really think of fourteenth- or fifteenth-century Ireland as especially dominated by war, compared to the England or France of the Hundred Years' War and the Wars of the Roses, is a moot point.

Some writers have linked the impression of war and the complaints of degeneracy together and have associated them with the cultural changes of the period, as did, indeed, contemporaries. To them the changes in speech, from French to Irish among the aristocracy, and the measures taken to enforce local law, often using measures borrowed from Irish practice, such as making the kin responsible for bringing malefactors to justice, or billeting troops on communities, rather than taxing them in money, all seemed part of a cultural decline. To men like Eoin MacNeill this was a 'Gaelic Revival', the stirrings of nineteenth-century nationalism, while to Orpen it was the abandonment of good, royal government for Celtic chaos. Leask picked up the basic message of both, that the fourteenth century was one of war and collapse which saw a halt to building, both of churches and of castles. To him, the years around 1400 then saw a new start, with new styles and new types of building, not a continuation from the thirteenth century.

Irrespective of the validity of the idea of the new start, Leask, like Champneys before him, picked out the main identifying traits of the late medieval building style in Ireland. Primarily they derived this from the study of churches, but the style applies to castles as well. Some of the features associated with it are indeed derived from English Decorated style: window tracery, ogee-headed openings or low, four-centred arches, and the use of shallow 'wave-like' mouldings. There are other particularly Irish traits, however. The use of sandstone for dressings disappears, to be replaced over much of the country by the use of the hard, Carboniferous limestone: extremely durable, it may be that the use of better chisels is implied in the change. Commonly the stones are decorated with shallow punched dressing, and occasionally with the sort of leaf decoration more commonly found on late churches. The arches of doors especially were often built, not of many voussoirs, but of only two or three long curved stones. While we have seen the occasional use of wicker centring for vaults in the earlier period, after 1350 this appears to be universal, so that, when we find it, there is a presumption that the vault is late. Roof lines were also distinctive, marked by stepped merlons on the battlements and corbelled machicolations and turrets, the latter again reflecting French or north British ideas.

Leask's idea of a hiatus in building followed by a new start has been challenged for church building and style (Stalley, 1984; McNeill, 1986): late Irish Gothic should now be seen as arising from early fourteenth-century English Decorated style, modified to accommodate Irish resources. Leask in fact put forward two ideas on castles of the late middle ages. The first was that, with secular buildings as with the churches, there was also a gap in work. The second, which he never overtly stated, was that castles after 1350 were almost exclusively tower-houses. This last is conveyed in the layout of his book on Irish castles (Leask, 1977). The chapters (9–11) which follow his account of the enclosure castles of the later thirteenth century concern tower-houses, while only the last two pages of chapter 12 ('The larger castles of the fifteenth, sixteenth and seventeenth centuries') consider castles other than tower-houses, and then only three: Cahir, Askeaton and Newcastle West. The question of continuity through the fourteenth century has been challenged in considering the origins of Irish tower-houses, as we shall see.

When it comes to dating, it is worth emphasising that no scheme has yet been produced to discriminate within the work of the late middle ages, to distinguish work of 1350–1450 from that of 1450–1550, for example. In part this is because, if the early 70 years were removed from this range, it did not seem worth distinguishing, of producing dating schemes of half a century or so. Mainly, however, it is because the masons at the end of the period seem to have been quite as likely to use any individual feature as those at the beginning, that the style was uniform throughout. At present, therefore, we must treat the period as a unity, with all the problems which that must bring.

The argument is more than this point of dating, however. Inherent in Leask's view were two assumptions, or conclusions. The first is that there was a dislocation in the way of life from the thirteenth to fifteenth centuries. The second was that the pattern of life of the later period, which could not be traced back to the earlier, was distinctively Irish, that it was a part of the Gaelic Revival, or gaelicisation of Irish society, which he was told by historians had taken place. Even from those who have challenged Leask's views on the dating of late medieval castles, his view of the period as one of change in the way of life has survived.

> I would rather view this period as a time of major change, indeed almost of a revolution in castle construction in Ireland when the great feudal fortresses were largely made obsolete by the smaller scale but generally endemic warfare of the later middle ages.
>
> (Barry, 1993, 216)

This quote links together Leask's idea of a shift in the castles (from enclosures to tower-houses) to the idea of endemic warfare in the period.

Just as the present generation of historians has challenged this view of collapse and a great social upheaval, so too we can challenge such views on castles. Although they are all connected, we can try to examine separately three issues. The first is how far evidence from the study of castles might shed light on the question of the extent and nature of the changes of the fourteenth century and later. The second is whether tower-houses did really replace enclosure castles. The third is the extent and nature of warfare in late medieval Ireland, as seen from the perspective of the castles. These three questions run through the whole period but cannot, unfortunately perhaps, be isolated and dealt with separately.

CHAPTER TWELVE

ENCLOSURE CASTLES OF THE LATER MIDDLE AGES

——— ·✦· ———

THE THREE EARLDOMS IN THE SOUTH

We may start with the castles which were the centres of the power of the new Earls of the fourteenth century. In Co. Limerick the Earldom of Desmond, as it was after 1329, was based on two fine castles: Newcastle West and Askeaton. In both cases they represent the expansion of Geraldine power from its original modest holding at Shanid (Empey, 1981) and both saw the construction in the fifteenth century of first-rate first-floor halls, in each case over earlier structures. The halls are linked by their windows: both employ paired lights with cinque-foiled ogee heads and a squared hood mould externally (fig. 104). The ends of both halls are marked by blank arcades carried on corbels, although the one at Askeaton is finely decorated, while both corbels and arch at Newcastle are plain (fig. 105). The upper end of the Askeaton hall, away from the entrance and leading to a chamber, is clearly demarcated by a window lighting it and overlooking the court-yard, which has the remains of good tracery which was of the same design as one of the windows at Askeaton Friary, founded by 1420, if not by 1400 (Gwynn and Hadcock, 1988, 242). The earlier (probably thirteenth-century) chamber attached to the earlier ground-floor hall at Askeaton was also refurbished when the first-floor hall was built. There are two small chambers attached to the hall at Newcastle (in the first and second floors of a small turret), but they lack fireplaces and latrines, and are too small to be considered as proper chambers for a lord.

The castle at Newcastle is now divided up between different properties, since Westropp's account of 1909 (fig. 106). The eastern half of the area, containing the two halls, is now in the hands of the state; the Office of Public Works is engaged in a programme of vigorous, not to say drastic, restoration of the buildings. Surprisingly, the disengagement of the castle buildings to the east has not revealed the remains of any curtain wall, although we would expect any thick wall to have been reused along the backs of the properties further to the east. To the west, the house of the Devonshire estates' agents, which was built among the medieval remains, has now been demolished; the area has reverted to jungle with the Devonshire house ruins adding to the general air of confusion.

Figure 104 Askeaton castle: the great hall from the Desmond tower

Figure 105   Askeaton castle: the blank arcade on the dais end wall of the great hall

The earliest remains are those of a fine ground-floor building of several phases (fig. 107). The second phase saw the insertion of fine windows with classic fourteenth-century Decorated tracery; this Westropp identified as the first hall of the castle. It may have been but it lacks any indications of service rooms at either end and could just as easily have been a chapel. It was remodelled at the west end at a later date, as shown by the later style of the doors, and by the ogee-headed loop, framed in a rectangular hood mould, in the west wall (this is now difficult to see but it was recorded by Westropp, 1909, 362). South and west of the two halls, and close to the only remaining parts of the curtain wall which runs along the River Arra, are the remains, much overgrown, of a two-part building (see fig. 106). To the east is a vaulted ground floor with a first-floor chamber, some 13 m by 7.5 m (43 × 25 ft). Attached to the west end of this is a tower, with a ground-floor vault: the two rooms communicate at ground-floor and first-floor level, but the floors do not communicate directly with each other. The tower contains two further chambers above the first floor. At the east end of the large chamber is a first-floor door leading to a room in the circular tower on the curtain. Oddly called a keep by Westropp, this mural tower was much mutilated when it was incorporated into the Devonshire house. Within the castle as a whole, however, there are remains within its presumed enclosure of two public buildings and a block providing a great chamber with two towers of subsidiary chambers.

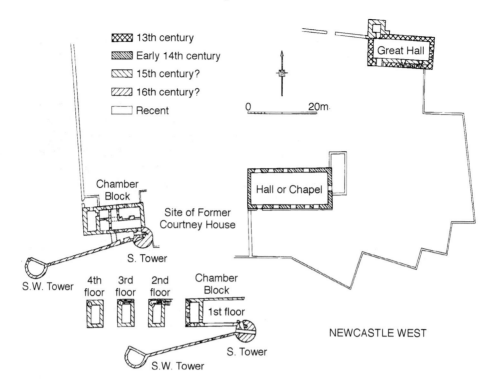

Figure 106 Newcastle West castle: general plan

The island in the River Deel which accommodates Askeaton castle (fig. 108) has a raised central rock platform, which forms an inner ward for the castle: the first-floor hall lies in the outer ward (fig. 109). The outer curtain is equipped with key-hole loops for guns and small square holes for hand-guns: curiously, it does not enclose the whole island, but leaves about a third outside, acting as a garden, to judge from a view of *c.* 1580. The site is made strong by the river defences, but it is totally overlooked by higher ground a few hundred metres to the west. The inner ward, enclosed by a wall with a small gate tower, contains three other structures. One is known as the Constable's tower, now very ruinous, but originally of three stories. The ground floor, with the door, is vaulted while the first and second floors are both marked by fireplaces; the second floor has a latrine in the south-west corner above the one at first-floor level, which is, however, linked to the wall-walk outside, and not, apparently, to the chamber. At the west of the inner ward is the stump of a latrine tower, presumably serving a building beside it which has now vanished.

The principal building of the inner ward is the so-called Desmond tower. This is a two-part structure (fig. 110). To the south are the truncated remains of three superimposed large rooms, some 11 m by 6 m (34 × 20 ft). The ground floor of these was vaulted but otherwise marked only by two loops. Only parts of the west

Figure 107 Newcastle West castle: the fourteenth-century hall or chapel

Figure 108 Askeaton castle: general view from the north

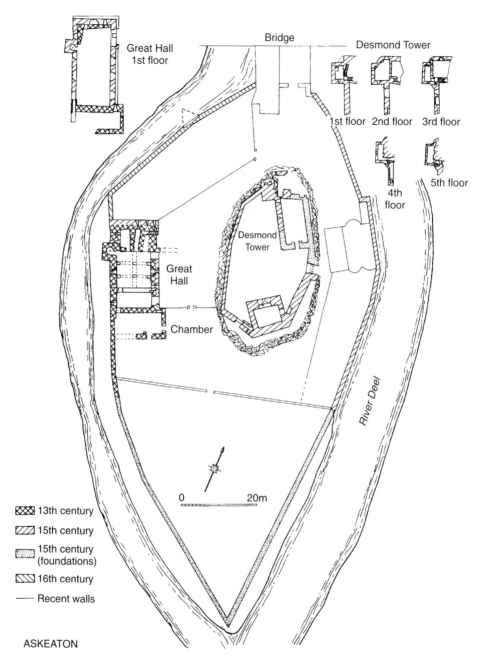

Great Hall
1st floor

Bridge

Desmond Tower

1st floor 2nd floor 3rd floor

4th
floor

5th floor

Desmond
Tower

Great
Hall

Chamber

River Deel

0   20m

13th century
15th century
15th century
(foundations)
16th century
Recent walls

ASKEATON

Figure 109   Askeaton castle: general plan and plans of the hall and Desmond tower

Figure 110 Askeaton castle: Desmond tower from the east

and north walls survive above this. The first floor has a large transomed two-light window with stepped heads to the lights (fig. 111) and the truncated flue of a massive fireplace. Above is a smaller window, decorated on the external mullion like the east door of the cloister in the nearby Friary or, indeed, the later door in the ground-floor hall at Newcastle West. The second floor also has a finely decorated fireplace like the first floor, but rather smaller. Attached to the north side of this three-storied building is a five-storied tower containing superimposed chambers to the north, with latrines or inner chambers in a projection to the south. All have well-cut details of doors and windows and a carefully contrived quarter-round projection for the latrine chute (fig. 112). One noteworthy detail is the use, in the second-floor chamber, of contemporary vaults centred on both planks and wickerwork. The whole inner ward complex provided a range of great and private

Figure 111   Askeaton castle: second-floor window in the Desmond tower

chambers to complement the first-floor great hall in the outer ward; the Earl's household in the Desmond tower, with officials in the Constable's tower. The date of both buildings is uncertain, whether of the fifteenth or earlier sixteenth century.

The Earls of Desmond also had extensive lands in Co. Waterford. Although they had been granted the royal castle of Dungarvan, they appear to have done little work there, while the castle of Inchiquin similarly shows no trace of late work, although its ruinous condition makes this less significant. By contrast, the castle of Mocollop, in spite of being seriously overgrown, was the scene of considerable work in this period. The entry is guarded by a tower with a drawbridge and a portcullis. Behind it lies the principal surviving feature, a round chamber tower accommodating four floors of rooms: the third-floor room has a single light window with a scalloped or stepped head comparable to that on the Desmond tower at

Figure 112 Askeaton castle: Desmond tower from the north-west

Askeaton. Buried in the vegetation is a further, square tower whose base carries over the base batter of the round tower beside it.

The other line of Geraldine earls, the Earls of Kildare, is represented by the castles of Adare and Maynooth, both with remains from the beginning of the thirteenth century. The castle of Adare in Co. Limerick was remote from the Earl's main power (see fig. 23); it is now very overgrown, in spite of Lord Dunraven's clearance and conservation of the last century. Two buildings show evidence of adaptation in the period. The east, ground-floor hall in the outer ward had a window with ogee-headed lights inserted (Dunraven, 1865, 121). The present tower in the inner ward is a result of increasing the height of the earlier building from two stories to four (fig. 24). At the same time presumably, vaults were inserted into the ground floor and doorways, with punch-dressed limestone jambs inserted in the west wall of the ground floor and the north wall of the first floor. The tower is now cut off from the outer ward by an inner wall and ditch, entered through a single gate tower. This last has a recess and loop through the front wall for the chain of a lifting bridge, and there are rebates for a gate at either end of the gate passage; it also has small loops, indications of a later medieval date. The outer curtain on the western side bends where the inner ditch meets it; north of the bend (i.e. where it forms the inner curtain as well) the wall has a plinth which disappears south of the bend, but the actual junction is obscured on the exterior by the addition of small stones. On the interior side, the inner curtain appears to have been added to the outer: it is quite possible that the creation of the inner ward was a part of the late work at the castle.

Maynooth castle is even less rewarding (see fig. 21). Not only was it damaged during the famous siege of 1534, but the Earl of Cork converted it into a house in the early seventeenth century, and it has been ruthlessly restored over the last century (FitzGerald, 1914). It is dominated by the early great tower on the western side of the enclosure. This was a first-floor hall from the first, but it had a vault, carried on a spine wall and wickerwork centring, inserted to carry a central pier (with a late medieval octagonal base) dividing the first-floor hall into two areas with an arcade. Above this, and quite possibly in post-medieval times, there were floors inserted which never had windows associated with them. The Earl of Cork inserted windows into the gate tower and the south-eastern tower; north of this he may have built the arches which link buttresses in front of the eastern curtain, to carry a gallery attached to the hall. The south-western tower looks late medieval, and may be so; at the least, the Kildare Earls continued to use Maynooth as a courtyard castle.

Seventeenth-century extensions and a massive rebuilding in the nineteenth have meant that it is very difficult now to assess how much, if at all, the Butlers carried out work at Kilkenny castle after they had bought it in 1393. The most conspicuous monument nowadays to the extension of their power east and south is the castle of Granny, set on a bluff on the north bank of the River Suir about three miles upstream of Waterford city, just short of a ford across the river, which is still navigable for small oil tankers to a terminal near the castle (McFadden, 1990). Three round towers along the low cliff command the river, with loops for guns set down at high-tide level: they have cross-slits and bases expanded into an oval (fig. 113). The westernmost of the three towers is linked to the central one by a curtain wall which is thinner than the rest of the enclosing walls, but it shows no sign of being an addition. The main enclosure is a rough square, some 30 m across (fig. 114). Only the south, river front has projecting towers. The entrance in the east wall is a simple opening closed by a gate, marked by a rebate and draw-bar hole; it may have been commanded by a box machicolation over it reached from the upper parts of the curtain wall, which have fallen, but it is otherwise undefended.

The main buildings lie against the north curtain (fig. 115). The central part is occupied by a first-floor hall which was equipped with at least two fine windows opening through the curtain wall. One is reduced to one side of the splay but the other is complete, with three lights with ogee heads: the splays are decorated with

Figure 113   Granny castle: the river front

angels, one holding the sword and scales of justice, the other the arms of the Butlers, while the rear arch is also decorated with twisted arris mouldings (fig. 116). The hall roof-line is preserved on the wall of a five-storey chamber tower to the east, whose north-west quarter has unfortunately fallen. While its ground floor is occupied by two narrow, vaulted rooms, each of the four upper floors provides a room with fireplace and latrine. The stairs in the north-east angle give access, not directly into the chambers (except on the top, fourth, floor), but to passages, to preserve the rooms' privacy: the first-floor chamber also communicates with the end of the first-floor hall. The chambers of the first floor and above all have two or three light windows to the east, while the fourth floor is equipped with a fine oriel corbelled out of the south wall. Leask states that this oriel is inserted, but the evidence is not now visible. The central tower along the river front provided two rooms with fireplaces and latrines at ground- and first-floor levels.

The castle must be treated as a whole. The tower and the hall were clearly a single unit, while a gunloop of the distinctive type found in the river towers is also found in the north-east angle of the chamber tower. Defensively, it was designed with a single purpose in mind: control of the river. The landward sides are barely more than enclosed. Domestically, it is dominated by the hall and chamber tower, which acted as a single unit: until a modern door was inserted into the ground floor, the only access to the tower was through the hall. The tower provided a

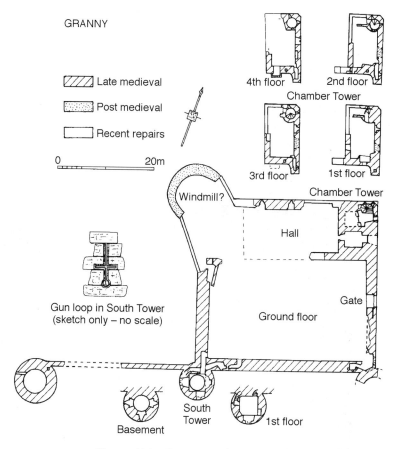

Figure 114 Granny castle: general plan

number of chambers, not linked into a suite, but probably reflecting a hierarchy of service, culminating in the lord's chamber on the fourth floor. At the same time, the central, and presumably at least the south-east, river-front tower also provided accommodation for household officers. The distinctive gunloops at Granny are also found in the east front of the Butler castle at Carrick-on-Suir. This is mainly known for the fine gallery front added in the late sixteenth century, but behind it is an earlier enclosure with two towers at the angles. Both of these now have Tudor windows, but are the remains of a strong enclosure castle, much less well preserved than Granny.

Cahir castle was the base for a cadet branch of the Butlers; like Askeaton it was set on an island, and like the others discussed, except for Granny, the site of a thirteenth-century castle. The present castle is a complex monument of several periods, again with much modern restoration (Wheeler, n.d.). In the late middle ages, the earlier hall was rebuilt as a first-floor hall over a vault. The gate tower was rebuilt as a chamber tower, with the entrance moved to the side of the

Figure 115 Granny castle: hall, chamber tower and gate from the south-west

tower. Probably in the sixteenth century, an outer screen of a curtain with projecting towers, equipped with loops for hand-guns was added.

LESSER LORDSHIPS IN THE SOUTH

Elsewhere in Munster and south Leinster are examples of lesser lords adapting or expanding earlier enclosure castles in the late middle ages. One of the Roche lords of Glanworth castle provided it with a new curtain wall on the west and south, with angle towers at the north-west and south-west, somewhat enlarging the area of the enclosure (Manning, 1987). In the area so gained, he, or another, contrived

Figure 116 Granny castle: hall window

a hall and chamber block by blocking up the entrance passage of the earlier gate tower and making a hall on the first floor, and by building on a high chamber tower to the west. The thirteenth-century hall-house was still retained, while the east curtain is probably later still, to judge by the gunloops. At Kiltinane, the thirteenth-century round great tower was retained, and the second floor saw later work, as shown by the two windows with ogee-headed lights; whether the whole second floor is a later addition is unclear. The curtain to the north was rebuilt in the late middle ages (fig. 117). The north-east tower has gunloops at the ground floor, with a late door with wicker-centred rear arch, itself typically contrived in the angle of the curtain. The first floor provided a square room internally; the wall-walks of the curtains to the south and west were of a single building phase at this level. The gate was set at the north-west angle of the enclosure, a simple

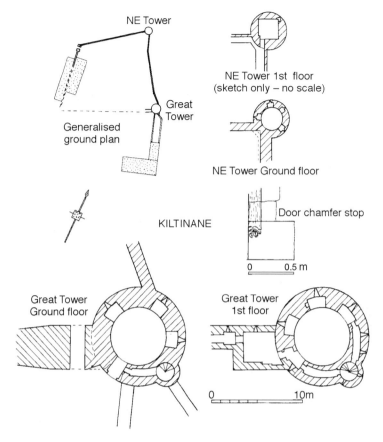

Figure 117 Kiltinane castle: general plan and floor plans of the towers

opening like that at Granny. Two angle towers survive of the de Cogan enclosure castle at Kilbolane (see fig. 88). The stair and adjacent walling (marked by an internal break in the walling) of the southern one was repaired using wicker centring for the passage, while a vault was also inserted over the room using the same centring, in contrast to the plank centring of the western embrasure which has an ogee light. A similar vault was also inserted into the western tower at the first floor, while the windows have ogee lights.

Both the halls of Castle Mora and Castle Grace have been mentioned already: both sites continued in use through the late middle ages. That the chamber tower at Castle Mora was added in this period is shown by the double loop in the south-east angle (fig. 118). It provided chambers at four levels, with the principal room at the top, as shown by its two-light window and decorated fireplace. At Castle Grace, an ogee-headed single-light window was inserted into the west wall of the hall (see fig. 91). The complexity of this wall at the northern end might indicate that it was rebuilt later than the main period; it provided a chamber at the end of the hall.

Figure 118 Castle Mora: chamber tower with arris loop

The remains of the castle of Fethard, Co. Wexford, are now walled up and inaccessible, but the main lines can be seen from the outside (fig. 119): it consists of three parts. At the eastern end is a three-storey tower whose wide, blocked arches in the north and south walls show it to have been a gate tower. At the west end lies a three-part block. In the centre is a three-storey block with a cusped ogee-headed loop on the third floor. At the south-west angle is slender three-quarter-round turret, crowned by continuous stone machicolation. There is a two-storey block to the north of the central one. A later hall with a vaulted ground floor was inserted to join the central tower and the gate tower; it was clearly added to both. Originally, therefore, the chamber tower with its attached turret and two-storey extension seems to have stood on the south side of a courtyard entered through a tower to the east.

Figure 119 Fethard castle, Co. Wexford: general view from the south

Finally, in the south of the country are Ballyloughan, Co. Carlow, and Liscarrol, Co. Cork, two cases where earlier gate houses were extensively rebuilt in the late middle ages, and so might be included here. Two notes of caution need to be sounded. The first is that the rebuilding is confined to the gate houses, and the work might be seen as being to convert them into free-standing towers beside an enclosure, effectively into tower-houses and bawns. Second, in both cases the work is at least possibly of the sixteenth century, or even later, rather than strictly in the period of this chapter.

EASTERN IRELAND

While the castles of the south of Ireland clearly show continuity of enclosure castles, this is less so in the east. Here the dominant powers were those of the English king and the lords of the Pale, in Counties Dublin, Meath and Louth. The first point to be made is to repeat the problem noted earlier, that there are crucial sites which have disappeared here. This is not just a question of individual castles, such as the Archbishop of Dublin's at Tallaght, but the systematic absence of all the major power centres of Meath (Abraham, 1991, 336), apart from Delvin: Galtrim, Gormanstown, Kells, Nobber and Rathwire. This lack of work is reinforced when the major early sites are considered: Trim, Dublin or Swords. Dublin, of course, is largely rebuilt, but there is little hint in fourteenth-century documents of significant work there. At Trim the third-floor chamber of the west side tower of the great tower received a double ogee-headed light window; and the chapel may have had a similar one, but otherwise there is little trace of later work in the castle, which was the headquarters of the Mortimer (then Yorkist and royal) lordship through the fourteenth and fifteenth centuries. The lords were often absentee, just as the Archbishops of Dublin seem to have moved their main centre from Swords to Tallaght, but it is surprising that so little trace remains. As with the later thirteenth century, there seems to be a real lack here of surviving buildings.

In the north of the area, responsibility for the small part of Ulster which was English (and the border between Louth and the Irish lordships of the North) devolved upon the royal administration with the demise of the Earldom of Ulster. The northernmost point short of Ulster is Carlingford castle, which is difficult to understand. At present the roughly oval castle, dating from *c.* 1200, with the loops and windows of the buildings set against the western half of the curtain, is divided into two parts by a massive (over 3 m (10 ft) thick) north–south cross-wall (see fig. 26). This wall is clearly later than the original castle, for it partially blocks a window embrasure at its south end. Its construction presumably required the buildings around the courtyard to be demolished as well. The area east of the wall is divided into two unequal spaces by a strong east–west wall. To the north is a room, some 10 m by 20 m (33 × 66 ft), which was floored as a unit and not as a range around a light well, because the offsets on the west and east walls align, with the one in the south wall set a little lower, implying a longitudinal support system below. Below the south-east corner of this room is a vaulted basement. South of the east–west wall are the remains of a chamber tower, in the south-east angle of the castle, now half lost because of cliff falls. The walls of this chamber tower are clearly added to the two massive cross walls. They divide the four floors of the tower into various rooms; one of the divisions is an arcade with an octagonal pier and punch-dressed, late medieval masonry.

Leask (1977, fig. 37) followed by others since (Buckley and Sweetman, 1991, 320–3) ascribes the building of the north–south cross wall to the thirteenth century, and describes the larger room to the east as the great hall of the castle. This produces difficulties. The most remarkable feature of the supposed hall is that it has no windows, except for some in the east wall. There are none in the south wall, because of the presence of the chamber tower, and none in the north wall because there is a mural passage within it, but the absence of windows in the west wall (the massive north–south cross wall dividing the castle in two) is difficult to understand. This should be the most protected side of the building, facing the castle courtyard, and therefore the safest to be pierced by windows. The thickness of the wall, its crenellations (although many internal buildings had them), and the lack of windows all make it look as though this was an external wall to the castle. This would mean that the internal range of buildings was demolished and the curtain wall to the west simply formed an outer screen to the castle proper, now confined to the hall and chamber block. There is a marked contrast between the western half of the present castle, with its many windows piercing the curtain, and the eastern one. As a thirteenth-century castle and great hall the eastern half does not convince.

While there can be no doubt that the present, late medieval internal walls of the chamber tower are additions to the fabric, the same may not be true of the basement at the south-east of the hall. This has a barrel vault, built over wickerwork centring. The vault shows no sign of being added to the east wall, where it integrates well with the embrasure of a window, built over plank centring. We have seen the presence in the same structure of the two forms of centring at Askeaton, so that this is not in itself very surprising. To the south this basement seems to link with the basement of the chamber tower as rebuilt. The vault does seem to be late medieval in date, and it may indicate that the whole eastern half of the castle is too. This would mean that the present internal walls of the chamber tower, undoubtedly late, may be simply rather later rebuildings along the lines of the original, but not necessarily very much earlier building.

The Earldom of Ulster proper brought the Crown possession of two large castles, Greencastle in Co. Down, and Carrickfergus. At Greencastle, the entrance to the thirteenth-century great hall was changed from the first floor to a new one in the ground floor, which received barrel vaults, with wickerwork centring, carried on three transverse walls. The upper parts of the hall were rebuilt with battlements, turrets and mural passages in the manner of a tower-house (Jope, 1966, 216–17). As with Liscarroll and Ballyloughan, this is, perhaps, how we should see the changes, as converting a great hall in a courtyard to a tower-house with a bawn. Carrickfergus was kept in a state of some repair from the early fourteenth to the middle of the sixteenth century, but no more. Twice (in 1381–2 and 1477) we hear of sums being assigned for work, but this seems to have been purely to maintain the fabric, not to add to or change it significantly (McNeill, 1981, 6–8).

By the 1560s it was in such poor shape that the gate house had to be rebuilt (without the back) and the great tower was repaired but, for the rest, it was simply an enclosure.

IRISH ENCLOSURE CASTLES

As with the castles of the earlier period, if we wish to discuss castles built by Irish lords, we should start with Carrigogunnell (fig. 120). North and east of the remains of what appears to be an earlier hall was built a large accommodation block. It was in two parts: to the east two storeys of great chambers with large windows and fireplaces and to the west a four-storey chamber tower, the whole like the inner block at nearby Askeaton (fig. 121). The chamber block also resembles Askeaton in its use of rounded angles to the rooms, not just to the stair (fig. 122). The whole top of the rock is surrounded by a wall, without projecting mural towers, and with the entry through a simple gate without the elaboration of a gate house. The condition of the castle is regrettable, for this is, after all, a key monument, a first-rate Irish castle in Munster.

The de Burgh Earldom of Ulster and Lordship of Connacht was the major casualty for the English in the changes of the fourteenth century, with Irish or Scottish successor lordships in the first, and cadet de Burghs (Burkes) disputing the latter with a revitalised O'Connor kingdom. In both cases lands and major castles were left without their former English owner. In the north of Ulster lies Dunluce, dramatically sited on a rock stack connected to the mainland by a narrow bridge. Most of the present remains date to after its seizure by the MacDonnells in the late sixteenth century, but the enclosure itself is older (fig. 123). It is roughly square, with round towers preserved at two of the angles. Because of the form of these towers, with their base batters, they have often been attributed to the thirteenth century and the Earls. The receipts of the 1350s from the lands of Elizabeth de Burgh, widow of John de Burgh and mother of the last resident Earl of Ulster, however, show that Dunluce was not the *caput* of John's appanage, or even the *caput* of a manor (McNeill, 1980, 68–9; 136–44). His estates in Ulster were almost certainly centred on the castle and town of Coleraine, which he had been granted along with his other lands. The origins of the castle must lie after 1360, and be attributed to the descendants of the Earl's mercenary Scottish soldiers, the MacQuillans, who emerge in the fifteenth century as the lords of north Antrim.

The outer ward of the early castle of Dundrum in Co. Down has again been attributed to the thirteenth century (Jope, 1966, 210). Like Carrigogunnell, however, the wall is thin and without projecting towers: the entrance is also a simple gate surmounted only by a box machicolation and without a gate house or even tower. At the south-west angle it is pierced by loops for hand-guns, which do not appear to be insertions. They are sited there to control the vulnerable line of approach, but may also be associated with a building later used as the core of a seventeenth-century house. The whole of the outer ward is to be attributed to the late middle ages (fig. 15). The top storey of the great round tower of the castle has a mural passage and chambers, some of which have vaults built over wickerwork centring,

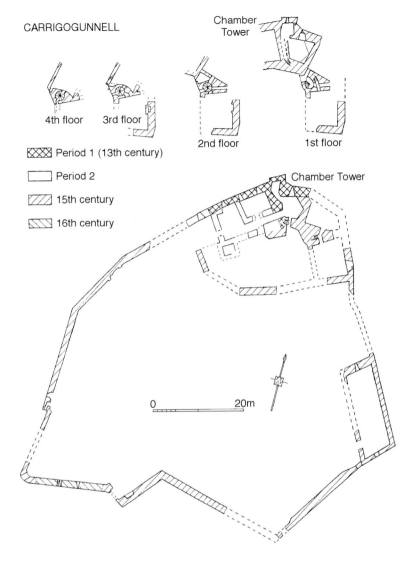

Figure 120 Carrigogunnell castle: general plan and plans of the chamber block

and others corbelled roofs. The use of both techniques has led to the assumption that the whole upper storey is late (Jope, 1966, 210). The great tower was clearly changed during this time: a door was forced through at ground-floor level to replace the first-floor entry, and it is controlled by an added box machicolation. On the other hand, the chimney flue and the internal floor system demand an upper floor, and the extent of later rebuilding may have been exaggerated. Clearly, however, the castle not only survived as an enclosure castle but was extended with the

Figure 121 Carrigogunnell castle: the chamber block from the south-east

addition of the outer ward wall. This was not undertaken, as far as we know, by the English, but by the Magennises, who certainly controlled the castle in the sixteenth century.

The impressive Greencastle in Co. Donegal was likewise not abandoned in the late middle ages. It was taken over by the Irish lords of Inishowen, the O'Dohertys, who added a square tower to the north side of the castle. This is now reduced to the ground-floor walls alone, but it appears to have been a tower house: like the castles of Ballyloughan, Liscarroll or Greencastle, Co. Down, this may have been

Figure 122 Carrigogunnell castle: the private chamber tower from the north

a case more of converting the castle into a tower house and bawn than truly continuing its use.

The evidence of the continuing use of the major castles of Connacht by the succeeding Irish is not found in their fabric but in the Annals of the late fourteenth century; in these cases all are quoted from the Annals of Connacht. During the thirteenth century the English castles appear most frequently as being captured and destroyed by the Irish (Lynn, 1986). This changes during the fourteenth century to records of their occupation and use of the castles. Some of these are of castles on islands; traditional sites, such as Lough Oughter, where Magnus O Ruairc was held prisoner in 1390, but escaped, only to be killed alighting from his skiff at the castle of Lough Scur. The Rock of Lough Key, scene of thirteenth-century sieges, was used as a prison by Mac Diarmata in 1342. It is also mentioned as being captured by a dissident section of the Mac Diarmata, who bribed the garrison in 1401 but it was then recaptured 'with great bravery' the following year, which sounds less as if it were used as a refuge or prison, and more as if the castle was a seat of power.

The first mention of the Gaelic use of earlier English castles in Connacht is in 1340 when Toirrdelbach O'Connor was forced to take refuge in Ballymote (the Annals of Clonmacnoise state that it was in the castle there). The history of Roscommon castle, the key to the English royal presence in Connacht, is more interesting in the context of its use as refuge, prison or power centre. Again, the first reference to its use by an O'Connor is as a prison, when Toirrdelbach O'Connor sent his nephew Aedh there in 1340; in the next year is a confused report that the castle was handed over to Toirrdelbach after Aedh betrayed it to him. In 1342 Toirrdelbach was again in trouble in the north of Connacht: expelled by a confederation of enemies he tried to reach Mac Diarmata's house. 'At the causeway to the house' he was ambushed, but rescued by Mac Diarmata's men, and taken to Lough Key for safety. This proved insecure, so he was escorted by Mac Diarmata back to Roscommon, which seems to have been his main base. A later O'Connor, Toirrdelbach Ruadh, gave the castle to Ruadhri O'Connor in exchange for Ballintubber castle, another of the key castles of Connacht.

The background to this is the continuing dispute between the two factions of the O'Connors through the later fourteenth century and beyond: between the O'Connor Ruadh and the O'Connor Donn lineages (Cosgrove, 1987, 577–8). In this struggle, Roscommon castle played a pivotal role. After the murder of the leader of the O'Connor Donn faction in 1406, Cathal O'Connor assumed its leadership. He was captured by O'Connor Ruadh in 1407 and a bargain was struck: he would be released in return for Roscommon castle. The bargain was not fulfilled and for the next thirteen years he was kept in captivity while the Ruadh forces besieged the castle. It was relieved in 1409 and 1413; in 1418 O'Kelly, on behalf of O'Connor Ruadh, built a siege castle opposite the main one. The situation was only resolved when O'Connor Ruadh and O'Kelly were both captured by the Clan Rickard Burkes. They were released in exchange for Cathal, who was allowed possession of Roscommon castle.

There is no trace in the physical remains of Roscommon castle to link with its days under the O'Connors, but equally there is no reason to believe that the whole castle was not being used. It was also clearly being seen as an essential part of the kingship of the O'Connor to control it, as it would in the feudal world. In this it moves further, perhaps, than the castles of Carrigogunnell or Harry Avery's, which were not as central to their respective lords' power. It is also interesting to note how here, or at Ballymote and Dundrum, a Gaelic lord was apparently wanting more than a tower for himself and his immediate household. In this, Dunluce is even more emphatic: the site may have belonged to the Gaelic tradition but the new building did not. This represents a major shift in the symbols, if not the reality, of Gaelic power.

Figure 123 Dunluce castle: general view from the mainland

The other side to this coin is in the Anglo-Irish world, where the period has been portrayed as one of gaelicisation of the great lords and their tenants. Clearly, the period did not see a shift away from the greater enclosure castles, for we can see them being maintained, added to, or constructed anew. The result, at Askeaton for example, is one of the finest castles of Ireland. It is surely significant, too, that the element which appears most prominent in this story is that of the great hall, the archetypical feature of the classic feudal castle. The continuing practice of the southern lords building castles, for large households like those of their predecessors, hardly aligns with a major shift towards the Gaelic life. For decline, we must look to the royal power in the east, where the financial resources and administrative needs had dwindled with the decline in power.

TOWER-HOUSES
DATES AND DISTRIBUTION

———— •◆• ————

It seems to have been Parker in 1860 who first used the term 'tower-house' to describe the small castles of Ireland. At the time, he made a number of shrewd observations about them; their outward similarity but actual variability, that the principal rooms were on the upper floors, and he compared some of their architectural details with those of medieval churches. To Parker, the difference between the tower-houses and the larger castles, such as Maynooth or Trim, was simply one of resources or class; the tower-houses were for the gentry, the large castles for the magnates. Westropp (1900) stated the case for the late medieval date of the tower-houses of Clare, in contrast to the earlier large castles such as Quin, which he considered to be mainly of thirteenth-century date. He based this partly on a list of founding of the castles, unacknowleged in his article, but identified by Donnelly (1994, 18) as later published in O'Grady (1926) and partly on the identification of the Irish towers with those of the Anglo-Scottish Border, an identification which he reinforced by calling them 'peel towers'. He also listed the main internal features, such as loops, vaults, etc., and, without making it explicit, showed that these related to churches which were to be ascribed to the fifteenth century in a broad sense.

The chapters devoted to tower-houses are probably the strongest part of Leask's book on Irish castles (1977, chapters 9–11). He listed the sort of features found inside many of the towers, as well as noting that there were variations among the towers; whether regional or chronological in origin he did not say. Since his work, there has been no more reason to doubt that the type exists, nor what features allow us to recognise one in the field: he set the agenda for all later discussion. When Stell (1985), therefore, arguing primarily about the castles of Scotland, makes the point that the internal categorisation within the whole population of castles should not be taken too far, his principal point is to resist attempts to use the categories for rigid date schemes, rather than to deny that there are such things as tower-houses. Tower-houses, as defined by Leask, are square or rectangular towers (occasionally equipped with side turrets), normally with a vault over at least one floor, usually the ground floor, and with the upper floors marked by better windows, fireplaces, etc.; entry was usually through a door on the ground floor. Features associated with the the tower-houses include the vault constructed on wickerwork centring, punch-dressed stone for window and door jambs, ogee-headed windows and angle loops; the wall head equipped with box machicolations and battlements with stepped merlons: these are the types of feature which define the work of the period.

CHRONOLOGY

To Westropp, the tower-houses were mostly built in the fifteenth century, with a few from the late fourteenth, and more from the sixteenth (1907, 55–75). Leask, as we have noted, thought that there was very little, if any, building in Ireland during the fourteenth century and into the first two decades of the fifteenth. To him, the stimulus for the start of tower-houses came with the passing of an Act in the Irish Parliament in 1429: 'an origin for the towers might be sought in what were called "the £10 castles". These were the fruit of a statute of the 8th year of Henry VI (1429)' (1977, 76). He went on to state that 'in 1449 a limit was put to the numbers to be built' (Leask, 1977, 77). Both these statements are oversimplifications (Abraham, 1991, 325–9). An Act of 1428 had been passed for Co. Louth; it was this which was extended to Meath, Dublin and Kildare in 1429 (Berry, 1910, 17, 33–5). The Act did not apply to a direct grant from royal funds, but permitted the commons of each separate county to levy a subsidy to provide the £10. The Act of 1449 (Berry, 1910, 176) withdrew this power for Meath. In fact, grants of the same sort continued to be permitted, specifically £10 and for towers of similar dimensions, into the later 1450s in Kildare and Wicklow (Berry, 1910, 285, 299, 457, 633). The reasons for abandoning the grant policy may lie in the way that, around this time, a number of men had fines for not constructing castles discharged, possibly because the £10 grants had not been forthcoming. The grants may, in fact, have cost the royal government money in fines. This, linked to the reluctance of the county commons to subsidise the richer landowners' new houses, is the probable reason for abandoning the grants.

It would be very unwise to use either the Act of 1428–9 or that of 1449 as arguments for the chronology of tower-houses. Although the 1429 Act did lay down dimensions (of 20 ft by 16 ft, and 40 ft high), no tower-house has been convincingly identified with them. It is, of course, unclear as to whether the Acts stimulated the first buildings of the type, or whether they required them to be in existence as models; whether they are points of origin or proofs that the tower-houses already existed. Even more, the Act of 1449 was not about limiting the building of tower-houses, as stated by Leask, and followed, among others, by Barry (1993, 212): it relates to the ending of a possible subsidy, not an end to building as such. It has never been possible to see £10 as a large enough sum either to cause a man to build who did not intend to anyway, or its withdrawal as really enough of a disincentive to stop building, if the owner wanted a castle. At best, it can only have swayed a small minority of potential builders.

In recent years, there have been several attempts to see a significant number of towers as having been built in the fourteenth century. The origin of this lies with the criticism of Leask's idea of the gap in building during that century, but it is applied not just to building in general but to tower-houses in particular. Three sorts of argument have been proposed: two based on interpretations of documents and one on the physical remains (summarised in Barry, 1993). In the first argument, unspecific references to fortified houses or to towers in castles are identified as being to the particular type of the tower-house, as for example the *inspeximus* taken in 1331 of a letter patent of 1310 (Jope and Seaby, 1959). This document allowed Geoffrey de Mortone to build two towers along the line of Dublin city wall, one at the end of the great bridge, and two houses against the city wall between them. Because the houses were to be made defensible, this has been taken to indicate that they might be urban tower-houses: similarly, references to towers in extents of castles have been identified as 'some of the ancestors of the later urban tower-houses' (Barry, 1993, 215). A similar, second line of argument identifies the word '*fortalicium*' with tower-houses in the fourteenth century (Cairns, 1987, 9; Barry, 1993, 215). The word was, of course, used mainly because it was not a precise term to contemporaries, nor did it carry the social and administrative overtones of '*castellum*'. It means simply a small fortified site, no more and no less. The third argument musters physical evidence which tends to be in the form of negative evidence: the absence of identified late medieval features being used as an indication of an earlier date, as with Kilteel (Barry, 1993, 215). All these arguments are also deployed by O'Keeffe in an article which seeks to date two building to the fourteenth century: a stone tower at Ballyloo and a gate house at Rathnageeragh. He uses a mixture of arguments, from the absence of features said to be firmly datable to either the thirteenth or fifteenth century to an appeal to the distribution of castles related to a reconstruction of the political history of the county (O'Keeffe, 1987).

In this situation there are really only two statements that we can make with confidence. One is that Leask's stress on the Acts of 1429 and 1449 was wrong; they are unlikely to have affected the building of tower-houses much, either in stimulating or depressing activity. The second is that the great majority of tower-houses, as Leask pointed out, display a common set of features, which in turn are linked to the late Gothic style of architecture found in Ireland, notably in the friaries known to have been founded in the fifteenth century. The origins of that style are to be sought in the earlier fourteenth century for churches, and it is inherently unlikely that there were no castles built in the fourteenth century (see, for example, Greencastle, Donegal, Newcastle West or Harry Avery's castles), but that does not tell us about the specific history of the building of the tower-houses as an identified type of castle. In the absence of new, better evidence, we may stick with Westropp: a few tower-houses may have been built in the later fourteenth century, with numbers rising steeply from the start to the middle of the fifteenth century, and then declining, particularly after the earlier sixteenth century, although with a small burst of activity associated with British Plantation schemes of the early seventeenth century. Jordan (1991) reviewed the evidence for the general dating, but, more importantly, attempted to discriminate between early and late tower-houses in Wexford, without much success, as he stated.

In this context it is pertinent to recall Stell's warnings about drawing too firm lines within the population of castles and exaggerating the special nature of tower-houses as opposed to hall-houses in particular. Within Ireland there are a number of castles which lie in between the two classifications. One is Ballisnihiney in Co. Galway (Knox, 1910). This has the proportions and apparently open internal space of a hall, with the joist holes of an external, first-floor entry. Over the first floor, however, is a vault built over wicker centring, like a tower-house (see fig. 97). Castle Carra, in Co. Antrim, has the features of a hall-house, but the outside dimensions of a tower-house (McNeill, 1983, 118–20). Moylough castle, and the other hall-houses, apparently isolated in the countryside without associated stone buildings around them, cannot have been very different in effect from tower-houses. This would allow the strict typologist to see these as hybrid structures and to propose the idea of the tower-house developing from them internally in Ireland, which is one of the thrusts of the argument for continuous building through the fourteenth century, with the emergence of the type then.

Against the idea of an essentially internal evolution of the tower-houses of Ireland may be opposed the idea that they were introduced from overseas. O'Danachair (1979) put this forward overtly, but based his argument rather curiously on the internal distribution of towers within Ireland. Because they are found most often in the south-west, from Galway to Limerick counties and east of there, he concluded that the idea of the tower-house entered Ireland there, probably from France, and then spread like vegetation. The argument is most remarkably mechanical and ignores the ease of communications within medieval Ireland, where people moved freely and regularly from one end of the island to the other.

The question of the outside introduction still remains, however. The idea of a blueprint of a tower-house being introduced to Ireland from somewhere and copied we may dismiss. There are few, if any, parallels close enough to argue that case, and the regional varieties of tower-houses in Ireland militate against such an idea. The nearest to such a case would be the similarity of the twin-turreted 'gate house' type found in Co. Down (Jope, 1966, 120–1) to the tower at Belsay in Northumberland. The general plan of the towers, with the entrance place between two turrets linked by an arched machicolation, is similar, but the masonry at Belsay, its vaults, corbelled rounds and crenellations are all different. At best, the overall scheme of the one inspired imitation in the other; communication could have been at the level of a description by the patron, and almost certainly did not involve a mason travelling, because the technical details of the masonry are so different. Nor is it clear in which direction the communication went.

In England, however, there is a clear line of development of chamber towers, sometimes in lesser castles: one could instance Stokesay in Shropshire or Longthorpe near Ely around 1300. In the north of the country, where tower-houses became very popular in the fifteenth century, one of the Feltons added a fine chamber tower to his hall-house at Edlingham in Northumberland during the second half of the fourteenth century; it was square and vaulted over the ground floor, while at Etal in the same county a similar tower was built during the same period. The chamber tower in all these cases was not an isolated structure but linked to a hall, but the idea was there. The tower had always been important as a symbol of lordly authority (Dixon and Lott, 1993) and it is possible to imagine how a lord might reduce his castle to the tower alone. Chamber towers were found in Ireland, too, and the same might have happened there.

Although there are no more hard-and-fast rules for the end date for the building of what we may define as tower-houses than there are for the beginnings, we can see tendencies. There are a number of features which we may associate with buildings of the later sixteenth and seventeenth centuries. The first dated occurrence of the use of brick in Ireland appears to be at Carrickfergus castle in the 1560s (McNeill, 1981, 47–8). Significantly, the brick was employed there to insert cannon ports into the medieval structure. The use of guns in war in Ireland seems to become common from around 1500 and we may consider as sixteenth century or later those loops specifically designed for the use of hand-guns, which means the loops which are reduced to a small hole at the outer face, or those with double splays. A feature of later Tudor buildings is the elaborate fireplace, often with a flue leading to an elaborate set of chimneys. Some or all of these features tend to be found in those tower-houses which have no vault, so its absence may also be linked to a later date.

DISTRIBUTION

O'Danachair put the castles listed by Leask on to a map of Ireland: whether he took out the sites which are not tower-houses is not stated (O'Danachair, 1979), and this remains the best indication of their distribution which we have. With due regard for its inaccuracy, it can be seen from it that the greatest number of tower-houses lie in the south and west of the island and the Midlands; the extreme south-west, however, has relatively fewer. Apart from the south of Wexford, where there are many, the east coast in general shows only a moderate density. The northern third has the sparsest distribution, except for a considerable number in the south-east of Co. Down and a number in north Donegal. The areas with a high density of tower-houses are those where the fourteenth century saw the greatest instability and change in land ownership. Where the three great fourteenth-century Earls carved out their lordships, Desmond, Ormonde and Kildare, are many tower-houses. Similarly, those parts where new lords succeeded the thirteenth-century order, as with the Burkes of Connacht or the English remnant of the Earldom of Ulster, occupied by the savages moving from the north, are areas of dense tower-house building.

This is parallel to the distribution of tower-houses outside Ireland. In Britain, they are most common along the Anglo-Scottish border as it emerged after the wars of Scottish independence. In France the idea of the small, strong tower is found in Normandy and the south-west, areas of fighting in the Hundred Years' War. What all areas have in common is the breakdown of central authority as it had been constituted before 1350. They are areas which were often seen by royal clerks as being lawless and violent; as with Ireland, this may not have been objectively true for it equated central government with law and order. In this light, the idea of the tower-houses being popular in Ireland is easily explained, and indeed this gives them their interest outside the country. As with the larger enclosure castles, the tower-houses of Ireland shed light on the question of the alleged breakdown of life in later medieval Ireland.

REGIONAL DISTRIBUTIONS

To examine this, we must look at detailed local studies of their distribution geographically and socially, before going on to examine the internal evidence for their construction and use. Such an exercise cannot be more than a preliminary trial of some of the approaches to be used, because the bulk of tower-houses have not been surveyed. In the first, Neill (1983) took the large South Tipperary manor of Knockgraffon for his subject. Here there were two surveys recorded for the Butler lords, in 1308 and 1508, which straddle our period (fig. 124). The first recorded a pattern which had a centre of lordship with free tenants situated in the lower parts of the land, suitable for the growing of corn. By the time of the second survey, three developments had taken place. The free tenants were now freeholders and their farms were found on new locations, mostly away from the earlier ones, and often on higher ground, rather more suitable for cattle than arable farming. There were more of the second-level centres than before, with the same family surname being found at more than one place in the manor, although, to judge by the occurrence of the same names in 1308 as in 1508, the later freeholders were descended from the earlier tenants. The distribution of the tower-houses corresponded to the later pattern of settlement. What seems to have happened in this manor at the heart of the Butler lordship was a story of change in farming accompanying (or leading to) an evolution and advancement in the status of the tenants. They celebrated their increased prosperity by building tower-houses on locations away from their older farms.

The late medieval castles of Co. Limerick are interesting in this context. On the one hand, the great Earls, of Desmond and of Kildare, built and lived in the large enclosure castles, like Askeaton, Newcastle West or Adare, which we saw in the last chapter. This leaves us with having to assume that the many tower-houses in the county (originally at least 400) were the castles of their tenants. The exception to this rule was the Earl of Desmond's own castle, Bourchier's castle, which is significantly among the largest in the county (Donnelly, 1994, 120–1). In Wexford, it was noted that the tower-houses are not located beside the moated sites in the county (Jordan, 1991, 59). There appears to have been no continuity between them.

Eastern Galway was in a different political world, an area which had been dominated by the de Burghs in the thirteenth century, with substantial baronial tenants, either English like the de Berminghams or Irish like the O'Heynes. During the later middle ages, the English parts of this area fell under the complete domination of the Burkes, although the Irish lords continued to hold the barony of Kiltartan (fig. 125). In the Burke lands, especially in the barony of Dunkellin, Mitchel (1986) noted that there was a high density of tower-houses, contrasting particularly with the density in Kiltartan. In Dunkellin, however, the tower-houses were also notably smaller and less well decorated, as might be expected as they occurred at the rate of about one for every three square miles of land, half the area per tower-house of Kiltartan. The tower-houses here represented a fragmentation of lordship among the Burke lands, which seems to have been restrained among the Irish.

In this context, it is worth recalling that in Ulster, dominated by Gaelic powers, there are only three areas of tower-house concentrations. The densest is in the area

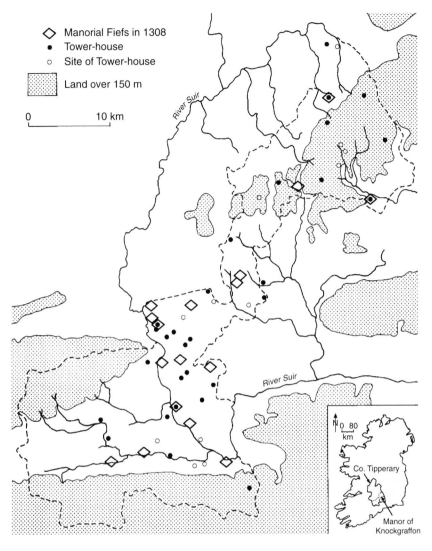

Figure 124   Map of the tenants' holdings and tower-houses in the manor of Knockgraffon

which remained in some sense English, although with an influx of new lords, the Savages, south-east Co. Down. One is an area settled by Scottish Gaelic newcomers, the MacDonnells of north Antrim. North Donegal is complex (ni Loinsigh, 1995). Here we can distinguish between two sorts of lordship, both Gaelic. The first kind are the MacSweeney lordships, established by incoming Scots mercenaries of the O'Donnells. Here there are relatively few castles, serving the centres of their lordships. By contrast, the other two lordships, the O'Donnell demesne and Inishowen, show a proliferation of castles. Inishowen, under the O'Dohertys, had had a history

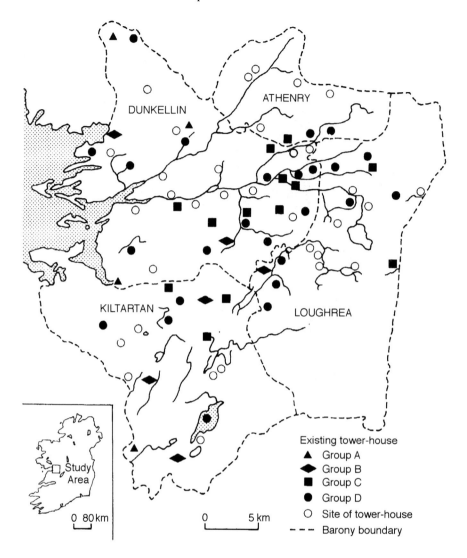

Figure 125 Map of tower-houses in south-east Co. Galway

of dispute between them and the MacLochlainns since the late twelfth century. The
O'Donnell castles are distributed around the borders of the lordship, especially
along the Foyle facing the expansive power of the O'Neills. Tower-houses prolif-
erated with the creation of new lordships, or in such places as were under military
pressure.

The most careful examination of the social position of tower-houses was that of
Abraham for the county of Meath in the English Pale (1986; 1991). He noted two
things about the tower-houses and their builders. The first was that they were not

Figure 126   Carlingford: Taafe's castle, a merchant's tower-house with an attached warehouse

built by the major lords of the county; as we have already noted, the major power centres which he identified on the basis of the status of their owners have no remains now associated with them. The tower-houses were built mainly on the estates of the lesser tenants-in-chief of the Crown, or else the larger tenants of the main lords; there were also a number of tower-houses whose owners he could not identify, another sign of their lower status. The second was that the tower-houses could be seen to vary with the rank of their owner, from the relatively simple to the more expensive. The larger ones were also the ones with subsidiary turrets, which are a feature of the tower-houses of the area. He saw no reason to attribute the building of the tower-houses either to war or to a change in land-holding in the county. If we compare his evidence with that of other areas, the amount of building in Meath appears to have been normal, given the gentry fashion for living in tower-houses. It might be taken as the expected level for the period; higher or lower densities would then require explanation.

Two other groups of people built tower-houses. The first were the richer townsmen (fig. 126) and the second were priests. Sixteenth- and seventeenth-century maps of Irish towns record a number of tower-houses in them (e.g. Robinson, 1986, for Carrickfergus) and there are towns where there is still more than one tower-house extant (e.g. Buckley and Sweetman, 1991, 323–9; Murtagh, 1988). Leask drew attention to a number of tower-houses in the Pale attached to parish churches

(1960, 18–21): Layde church in Co. Antrim also has a tower-house attached. The chantry priest's lodgings at Ardee (Buckley and Sweetman, 1991, 164–5) was also built as a tower-house. Perhaps the grandest case of this is the tower at the truncated west end of Cashel Cathedral.

The number of surviving tower-houses (Leask lists some 3,000 as marked on the Ordnance Survey maps alone, without allowing for older destruction or omissions), as well as the evidence of urban and priestly towers, shows that they were a common feature of Ireland by 1600. It is difficult to believe that Ardee or Carlingford in Co. Louth had several markedly rich men among its inhabitants, or that the parish priests of some of the churches with towers had large stipends. To build a tower-house required a reasonable investment by the standards of earlier times, but it was clearly within the resources of a surprising proportion of the later medieval population of Ireland. In spite of this, it is clear from documents of the fifteenth, sixteenth or seventeenth century that the structures which we call tower-houses were referred to consistently by contemporaries as castles. Unlike the moated sites, there seems no reason not to accept them as such. How they functioned as castles for their many owners must be the next topic.

CHAPTER FOURTEEN

TOWER-HOUSES
STRUCTURE AND USE

—— ·◆· ——

The most obvious feature of the tower-houses of Ireland is that (like every castle, of course) they are not uniform. Between the general uniformity of the type and the individuality of each lie regional groupings. Again, in discussing this, as with the discussion of the distributions and of the use, it must be stressed that the basic work of survey of the castles has not been carried out. We can only sketch out likely lines for further research, not present systematic evidence and conclusions. The regional differences may be identified, or not, in individual areas, but their boundaries cannot be defined. The differences can be expressed in terms of their overall plan or in details of construction.

An agreement survives from 1547 for building a castle for Richard Butler in return for lands which he had given to the Earl of Ormond (Curtis, 1941, 22–3). This calls for the construction of a building of three floors, with a vault over the ground floor: the walls to be 6 feet thick below the vault and 4 feet thick above it. The heights of the three floors are prescribed, the roof is to be slated and there are to be two chimneys. The door is to have an iron grate (or yett), there is to be a 'berbikan', possibly a bawn, and there are to be doors and windows and all other things necessary to a castle. The work is to be supervised by Derby Ryan and the Treasurer of Lismore, who will employ a master mason and a master carpenter. In this we have the basic organisation required to build a tower-house, for clearly that is what the castle was to be (fig. 127). Butler defines the basic limits, if only to his purse: the presence of a vault and the height of the floors; the plan dimensions were perhaps agreed when the site was chosen. The rest of the details were to be sorted out on site by the committee Butler appointed. Finally, we should note that the document mentions both a carpenter and a mason. When we look at details of the organisation of space or of the construction, the two roles of patron and craftsman need to be remembered.

STRUCTURAL TYPES

An example of the regional type defined by the plan is found in Co. Limerick (Donnelly, 1994). Combining their state of preservation and their plan, he isolated

Figure 127 Walterstown, Co. Meath: the tower-house, showing the vault and floor levels

a number of types found in the county. Of these, the commonest were his type 1A, with the plan of the rectangular tower divided into two unequal spaces: in the upper floors, the larger space housed the main chambers, with the lesser ones and the stairs in the small block. The entry was in the smaller of the two, the door leading into a lobby from which opened a subsidiary chamber on the one side and the spiral stairs on the other. This, and the closely allied tower-houses of his types 1B–C, were all to be found within an area about 18 miles by 8 (28 × 13 km), the central part of the county, south and west of Limerick city (Donnelly, 1994, 104–5). Within this area these are the predominant form of the tower-houses, while they are not to be found in the neighbouring counties, especially Tipperary. Given that many Limerick tower-houses have been destroyed, of course one cannot be dogmatic about it, but this does look very much like a definite local type of plan.

Jope (1966, 120–1) pointed out the occurrence of a particular plan type in south-east Co. Down, based on two projecting turrets on one side. They are linked by an arch at the level of the battlements, which provided a wide machicolation commanding the door which led into one of the turrets below (fig. 128). They are found neither in the rest of the county, nor in Antrim to the north, nor in Louth to the south. In the latter, interestingly, the 'Courthouse' in Ardee has two turrets projecting on one side, and the entry door leads into the stairs within one of them. However, the plan seems almost deliberately to eschew the Co. Down scheme by placing the door in the outer wall of the turret concerned (Buckley and Sweetman, 1991, 343–5). Killagh in Co. Meath does the same with the door on the side opposite from the two turrets (Abraham, 1991, fig. 36).

The tower-houses of Louth, Meath and the Pale in general are notable for their use of subsidiary turrets, though not on the one side as in Co. Down. Where there are two, they tend to be at diagonally opposed corners, like the Scottish Z-plan. Unlike it, however, the door is not placed in the angle so as to be protected from one of the flanking turrets (fig. 129). There are also tower-houses with turrets at each of the four corners. The type has not been defined more tightly, in terms either of the diagnostic traits or of its boundaries. In Wexford, the so-called Coolhull type of castle has been linked to tower-houses (Jordan, 1991, 36–7). It combines a hall with a narrow, higher chamber turret at one end; the western core of Fethard castle is one such, although it is here included with enclosure castles because it has a gate tower as well. In general, the Wexford tower-houses lack the turrets of the Pale (Jordan, 1991, 36). In the south-west, in Clare and Tipperary (but not Limerick), are found a number of tower-houses which are round in plan (fig. 130) but otherwise share the same internal and external features of the other tower-houses (Craig, 1982, figs 65 and 67). Similarly, the two rectangular blocks with angle turrets at Delvin, Westmeath and Dunmoe in Meath should be linked to tower-houses although they are formally different in plan.

The size and plan would clearly have been the patron's business for they would have dictated how the building would function and how much it cost. In the contract quoted earlier the presence of a vault was specified; this is a feature which seems to reflect some regional variation as well as a possible chronological pattern. The tower-houses of Munster as a whole are more elaborate than those of the east and north. In Limerick and Tipperary, a substantial minority of tower-houses have a vault over more than one floor. This is unknown in Ulster or in Louth and there is only one example in Meath (Newcastle – Abraham, 1991, 611). The amount of decoration would also be a matter for the patron, and does seem to vary regionally. Loops in the arris of the tower (see fig. 118) are found quite frequently in the south but not at all in eastern Ulster or in Louth, and only once in Meath, at Summerhill (Abraham, 1991, plate 76). Likewise, the elaborate corbelled-out angle turrets found in the south and west are only found (and then in rather different

Figure 128 Audley's castle, Co. Down: the door of the tower-house protected by the two turrets and a machicolation arch

form) in Ulster in seventeenth-century Scottish Plantation contexts (Jope, 1951) and are absent from the Louth and Meath.

A curious, and unexplained, procedure can be seen in the construction of some of the tower-houses of the west. Here their plans are rectangular, with the smaller rooms collected at one end, as is common elsewhere. What is odd is that it is clear, from the breaks visible in the masonry, that the section with the smaller rooms was built before the rest. It is difficult to believe that the building of a tower-

Figure 129 Roodstown, Co. Louth: the flanking turret does not protect the door of the tower-house

house was such a formidable undertaking that it was split into two parts, to allow the patron to collect his resources in two stages. Even if it was, it seems equally strange to envisage a period of time when only the lesser rooms were used, until the main ones were built.

Details which may owe more to the craftsman than the patron include those studied by Duggan, looking at the timberwork in a selection of tower-houses in the south, and McKenna, who compared the remains of timberwork (floors and

Figure 130 Ballynahow castle: a round tower-house

roofs) in Counties Tipperary and Down, to investigate these traditions (Duggan, 1982; McKenna, 1984a). Duggan distinguished between floors constructed with the joists supported by a number of beams with their ends sunk into wall sockets (his 'double floors'), and floors where the ends of the joists rested on two wall-plates (one on each opposing wall) supported by corbels and with their ends sunk into sockets in the end walls. He tried to distinguish between them in terms of date, arguing that the double floors were earlier. As an argument this has not stood up to testing. With one exception (Audley's castle, where the floor joists were supported on offsets of the walls), all the floors in the Co. Down tower-houses were built in what McKenna called her type 2, Duggan's double-floor system. This system used more timber and was more difficult to repair than the one normally used in Co. Tipperary, McKenna's type 3, Duggan's wall-plate system. While this system was used in all the Tipperary tower-houses McKenna looked at, in two of them the Co. Down system was used on one of the floors as well (McKenna, 1984a, 24–5), which seems to dispose of any chronological distinction between the two systems. In Limerick, Donnelly (1994, 140–1) also found both systems in use in different tower-houses, with no hint of a chronological difference involved. The Pale tower-houses also use both systems, sometimes in the same tower-house, like Glaspistol, Co. Louth (Buckley and Sweetman, 1991, 313–15).

The question of roofs is more complex. The first oddity, as noted by Craig (1982, 107–9), is that only one apparently original wooden roof has survived, at Dunsoghley. For the rest, we must try to reconstruct the arrangements of the wood from the sockets in the stone, left when the original timber was removed. McKenna pointed out (1984b, 42–3) that the form of the roof was intimately linked to the use of the attic space and the arrangements of the parapet and wall-walk. In Co. Down the attics were very simple with a floor carried apparently on the tie beams of the roof trusses: any windows in the gables at this level were very small and there were no other domestic features. In Co. Tipperary, the windows at attic level were larger and better made, indicating that the attics were seen as spaces for more than just storage or low-grade accommodation and their floors were carried on wall plates like those below them. In order not to block the attic space, the roof trusses must have been based on collar beams rather than tie beams: at Ballindoney, for example, the gable has sockets for collar purlins.

TOWER-HOUSE DEFENCES

The tradition of craftsmanship, as expressed in the form of the roof, was tied to the use of the building as a whole. This applies even more to the building of the gables and the wall-walks, which were related to the effectiveness of the defences of the tower-house. Tower-houses present a defensive aspect to the world outside; this is why they were and are accepted as castles. The defensive capability of the tower-house could be concentrated in three areas: the bawn wall, if it existed; the entrance, and the parapet. Bawns are rarely seriously defensive, as we would understand the word from castles of other periods or areas. They usually lack angle towers and the gates into them are rarely more than simple dorways: they may be too large for realistic defence. Perhaps the best example of realistic defensive intent is to be seen at the minute bawn of Clara, Co. Kilkenny (Leask, 1977, fig. 48). A later addition to the tower-house and set in front of the tower door, it bristles with loops for handguns, but it must be admitted that many of the loops face down into the ground and command little, while it is difficult to take an enclosure only 7 metres by 3 metres (23 × 10 ft) very seriously. Bawn walls, in fact, look usually like enclosures meant to prevent theft rather than real defences.

The entry to the tower-house was obviously controlled by a door, whose draw-bar hole is usually visible in the jamb: the doors themselves are quite small, only wide enough for two people at most to enter at once, and too low for anything other than people on foot. Apart from the single door, the only other equipment found is an iron grate, or yett, acting as an outer door in some tower-houses. Its presence is betrayed by a rebate of the outer jamb to take the yett, and a hole for a chain to secure it (fig. 131). This is by no means a standard feature on all tower-houses: in Co. Limerick, for example, there were 15 examples of tower-houses with physical evidence of one, and two more with documentary evidence (Donnelly, 1994, 127). They do not appear to be regionally distributed, but it may be significant that the three examples so far noted in Ulster (Narrow Water and Kirkistown in Co. Down – Jope, 1966, 238, 241; Termon McGrath, Co. Donegal – Lacy, 1983, 351) are late tower-houses. The normal method of defence of the door was with a box machicolation over it, elaborated in Co. Down, as we have seen, to an arch between projecting turrets. An alternative defensive feature associated with the door is that the door often led, not directly into the main body of the ground floor of the tower-house, but into a lobby. This was often divided from the rest of the tower by doors, which could be secured from the inside, and there was often a hole in its roof for dropping stones on to anyone who had penetrated thus far.

The main defence of a tower-house was conducted from above. In the main, this meant battlemented parapets, with machicolations of varying sorts. While emplacements for wooden hourds may perhaps (for they are not easily understood) survive from this period at Threave in Scotland (Stell, 1981, 32), there appear to be none from Ireland in the later middle ages. Stone, not wooden, machicolation was probably universal. In the south of the island, the embattled crowns of the tower-houses make a fine display, which culminates in the long pointed corbels which are a prominent feature of the strong houses of the later sixteenth and seventeenth centuries. The turrets corbelled out at the angles, to provide machicolations in their bases, do seem to be a feature of the south and west: in Ulster they occur only as an imported Scottish feature of the Plantation strong houses (Jope, 1951), except the grand O'Donnell castle of Donegal, while they are not found in Louth and Meath. There the box machicolation was deemed sufficient defence from the wall head. Also a feature of the south and west was the little chamber corbelled out at the angle, not at the top of the wall but at second- or third-floor level, to perform the same role.

The most interesting part of McKenna's work on the roofs of the tower-houses she studied was her recognition of the interlocking of roof design, the use of the attic floor, and the defensive effectiveness of the wall-walk. In Co. Down, the main gables were carried up from the inner side of the walls below, so that the wall-walk could continue unimpeded between them and the parapet: angle turrets were reached directly from the wall-walk. In Tipperary, by contrast, the gables were carried up from the outer face of the walls, which provided better light to the windows that could not be overlooked from the wall-walk. This meant that the wall-walk was impeded and the two long sides were only linked with difficulty. Often this was by passages in the thickness of the gable, which were difficult to contrive, awkward to combine with the windows, and which were often not

Figure 131 Ballynahow castle: the tower-house door with the emplacement for a 'yett'

continued through the full length of the gable. At Ballindoney, and elsewhere, the two sides were linked by a perilous set of steps projecting from the gable, up and over the roof (McKenna, 1984b, 56). Clearly, the elaborate wall crowns in the south (fig. 132) might be as much about display as about defensive effectiveness: the more modest tower-houses of Co. Down, especially those with the high arch between turrets, were probably more effective.

This combines with other aspects which cast serious doubt on tower-houses as defensive structures. Rarely are they sited in positions which gave the defence much

Figure 132 Two Mile Borris, Co. Tipperary: a Munster tower-house, without turrets but with machicolated corner turret

help, although a number are situated on promontories projecting out into lakes, while a few are only reached by causeways. The great majority are simply sited in a place convenient to the ordinary life of their lord. A feature which distinguishes the tower-house from hall-houses is the way the tower-house doors are situated on the ground floor: more convenient, undoubtedly, but a significant move away from defensive priorities. This is compounded by the way the defence of the door is frequently neglected in other ways. In general, the turrets are very poorly equipped with loops to provide covering fire. Too often, they are filled with stairs and latrines which would make the use of any loops very awkward in practice, even if they are provided. They may look on a plan as though they were there to give cover, as with the Z-plan, but in fact they were built to give extra room, not extra defence.

Abraham's conclusions in Meath crystallise this argument. Here he was able to see a range of tower-houses, from the small ones without turrets to larger ones which also had turrets at all four corners. The principal defensive feature was the entrance lobby with a murder hole in its roof. Perhaps, surprisingly, this was a feature found only in the lesser tower-houses, and not even in all of them. If the lord had more resources, he seems to have put it into more rooms, not more defence; indeed, he seems to have provided less defensive capacity. The men who felt in need of defence were the lesser lords. Combined with the lack of castles at all at the centres of the major estates, it is difficult to see defence as the prime motive for building the tower-houses of Meath.

LIVING IN TOWER-HOUSES

When we discuss the domestic use of tower-houses, we immediately encounter a major problem: we do not know whether the tower that we see now constitutes the whole accommodation of the castle. We cannot make proper allowance for other possible buildings beside the towers because we do not know whether they existed or, if they did, what they were. Especially if we consider a source for tower-houses to lie with chamber towers of the fourteenth century, we should recognise the possibility, if no more, that the tower was attached to a hall. The presence of a hall or of other domestic buildings would obviously totally alter our view of the life for which the tower-houses were designed. In Scotland, this is a question raised by the excavation of halls outside the tower-houses of Threave and Smailholm, formerly considered to be free-standing (Tabraham, 1988). While we may sound two cautionary notes (Threave and Hermitage, on which much of the argument depends, were the residences of earls, and at Threave, the construction of the fifteenth-century enclosure meant abandoning the hall), the point is an important one. We have taken the self-sufficiency of tower-houses for granted in the past, rather than demonstrating it.

There is support from Ireland for Tabraham's view. Richard Stanihurst, writing from Dublin in the late sixteenth century, says:

> Adjoining them [sc. castles] are reasonably big and spacious palaces made of white clay and mud. They are not roofed with quarried slabs or slates, but with thatch. In the palace they have their banquets but they prefer to sleep in the castle rather than in the palace because their enemies can easily apply torches to the roofs.
>
> (Lennon, 1981, 146)

It should be pointed out, however, that Stanihurst is here describing the life of the Gaelic Irish princes, not his own Anglo-Irish. The tower-house of Athclare in Co. Louth has the roof-line of a substantial building attached to the west side: the dressed quoins of the tower on the south-west angle only start from the eaves level of the attached building. This was therefore built with the tower and may have been a hall. In Meath, in the grass of the former bawn of Walterstown tower-house, are the remains of a rectangular building, which again might on excavation prove to be a hall.

It must be admitted, however, that the limited excavation that has been done outside tower-houses (summarised in Donnelly, 1994, 168–9) has given little support to the idea of substantial buildings set beside tower-houses, but the halls need not have left substantial traces. More to the point is that we would expect halls to be located in bawns. This is not an absolute rule: Threave hall pre-dated the enclosure, but it is sited on an island, and was guarded by the formidable presence of Archibald Douglas, the Grim. Bawns in Ireland are by no means universally associated with tower-houses. A fairly consistent figure of around one tower in five having evidence of a bawn comes from the surveys of Counties Down, Louth, Meath and Limerick. In the latter county, the Civil Survey of the 1650s mentions bawns at just 20 per cent of the towers it lists (Donnelly, 1994, 168). Clearly, the argument is undecided: we cannot assume either the presence or absence of other buildings associated with any individual tower-house in Ireland.

With all this said, we have to proceed with the evidence available to us: perhaps in the future a programme of excavation around tower-houses will shed light on the problem, but there is no sign of it coming yet. This means that we have to judge the tower-houses as free-standing structures. The rooms within them may be graded and assigned uses with the same confidence, or lack of it, that we can bring to the earlier castles in Ireland or to castles elsewhere in Europe. This is not easy, and there are clearly areas of doubt: the use of the ground floor of the tower-houses shows the problem. In many tower-houses the ground floor is covered by a vault and has only poor windows: to Leask (1977, 79) this was used for storage, while the vault was defensive in purpose, stopping fire which an attacker might start through the ground-floor windows from spreading to the upper floors. The latter was clearly not universal, because (particularly in the south) vaults were not confined to the ground floor. Nor were the ground-floor rooms always just for storage. In Meath, several tower-houses have doors which lead straight into the main ground-floor room, which a visitor must cross to reach the stairs. Mainly in the smaller towers in the same county, the vaults have lofts providing a first-floor level: at Summerhill, the loft is fully equipped for domestic life with two windows, fireplace and latrine (Abraham, 1991, 285–7). In Limerick, there are fireplaces in the ground-floor rooms of some tower-houses, which seems to preclude their being designed for storage (Donnelly, 1994, 161–2).

The most detailed analysis of the domestic arrangements of tower-houses is that of Abraham in Meath. The towers provided different levels of accommodation: the small towers had effectively only one room on each floor, with stairs and latrine taking up the rest of the available space. Against these are the tower-houses with lesser rooms usually provided in the turrets, either one or more, as well as the stair and latrine, but the builder at Summerhill contrived a lesser chamber without a turret. The main room was the one occupying the main block on the floor above the vault; it is distinguished by having the largest fireplace and windows and if any window seats are in the tower-house they will be found at this level. In the small tower-houses, where there was no provision of lesser chambers, there are hints of a division of space on this floor. The doors from the stair and the fire-place are at one end, while the best window and latrine are at the other; if the fireplace was used for cooking, it would have allowed a more private space away from servants at the other end of the room. Above this level, the second floor has the next largest windows and fireplace, and also has a latrine. The top floor, on the other hand, has neither fireplace nor latrine. Conventionally this looks like an arrangement of the hall above the vault with a great chamber over it, and then accommodation for servants above that (Abraham, 1991, 283–300).

The arrangement within the turrets is interesting. The smaller tower-houses seem to provide simple small chambers for sleeping, one per floor. The larger tower-houses permitted a more elaborate arrangement. At Liscarton, the turrets provided what Abraham called mini-tower-houses in themselves (Abraham, 1991, 307–8). The south-west turret had three floors of chambers with fireplaces and good windows. They were linked, not to the main block on each floor, but to each other via a private stair in the turret. The north-west turret provided two identical floors; in effect two suites of lodgings were provided in the turrets there, leaving, presum-ably, the lord to occupy the main block with a hall, great chamber and service above. This has moved rather far from the idea of the simple stack of rooms that tower-houses can be visualised as providing.

As such Liscarton invites comparison with the elaborate provision of side rooms in the very large tower-house of Bunratty castle in Co. Clare, the base of the O'Briens of Thomond (Leask, 1977, 116–17). In Limerick, the large tower-house of Bourchier's castle, owned by the Earl of Desmond, had four main floors, of which the first and fourth are covered in vaults. In other Limerick tower-houses there is more than one vaulted floor: Cappagh has three vaults, over the first, third and fourth floors. This multiplication of vaulted rooms, which weakened the struc-ture of the tower, makes it less easy in Limerick to identify a main room than in Meath or in Ulster.

Finally, we may note cases of the special adaptation of tower-houses to serve a particular need. The first of these is for the life of the urban merchant. The Bridge castle in Thomastown, Co. Kilkenny (Murtagh, 1988), and the two tower-houses in Carlingford town, Co. Louth, Taffe's castle (see fig. 126) and The Mint (Buckley and Sweetman, 1991, 323–9), all have ground floors with entrances separated from the rest of the tower floors. Both the Bridge castle and Taffe's castle have doors in their ground floors which open out on to what were the sites of the medieval quays. These were the equivalent in Ireland of the later medieval merchants' houses, for example in Southampton (Platt and Coleman-Smith, 1975), where the ground floor or cellar had a separate entrance from the rest of the house. It acted as a warehouse, or might be let out as a shop by the owner if he did not want to use it himself. In Co. Down, Nendrum and Sketrick castles were both sited on islands: both have vaulted rooms on the ground floor, apparently to house boats (Jope, 1966, 244–5; 1250–2).

CHAPTER FIFTEEN

THE LATER MIDDLE AGES AND THE END OF CASTLES IN IRELAND

——— ·◆· ———

The later middle ages in Ireland saw a great proliferation in the building of stone castles. It covered the full range of society able to afford such buildings, and it covered most of the island. The continuing use of the larger enclosure castles and, more importantly, their improvement and new construction, shows that for the magnates the period may well not have seen a great change in the style of life. This was still organised around the great hall, with their own immediate house-holds accommodated in separate chamber blocks, and other chambers for more independent members of their wider retinues. This is the same organisation as in the preceding centuries. It is worth dwelling a little on the fact of the existence of some of the late enclosure castles, simply because examples such as Askeaton are as fine as any earlier castle. There is no hint here of the so-called 'decline of the castle' before the sixteenth century, any more than there is in other countries. The main difference, other than stylistic detail, is in the further winding down of defences, exemplified by the end of the imposing gate house to the complex. At best a single tower guarded the entry, while the perimeter was defended only from the wall-walk, with no provision in most of the castles of mural towers, or any means of flanking fire. Askeaton, Dunluce or Cahir were the most formidable of the late castles, but because of their siting, not because of artifice.

We may take the building of the enclosure castles as a guide to the balance of power in Ireland. It is clearly biased to the lands south of a line from Dublin to Limerick. This is the area of the great earldoms which dominated the later middle ages in Ireland. They replaced the English king as the ultimate source of power in Ireland during the fourteenth century, and the state of the royal castles shows it. In the case of the major lords of the northern Pale, the magnates of Meath who seem to have been able to do without significant castles, this may represent the calmness of their lives, ordered around unfortified timber houses. This cannot be the case for the royal power elsewhere, however: allowing the castles he inherited, from Carrickfergus to Trim, to drop down to a care and maintenance basis at best, or to large hall and chamber blocks alone, as at Greencastle, Co. Down, or Carlingford, reflects severely on the capacity for royal action.

It is important to recognise the change in lordship that the period saw, when compared to that of the thirteenth century. Earlier lordships in Ireland were on the whole relatively compact blocks of land, with a degree of internal territorial integrity. It was a land where there were many boundaries between competing lordships. The existence of these boundaries brought forth the type of small border castle to respond to the situation. The later medieval lordships were not so well defined. Not only were they geographically less coherent, but the relations between the magnates and their tenants had changed. The tenants had moved, in the areas of English lordship at least, much more into a position of freeholders, tied to the greater lords more by political than tenurial obligations. Their power was much less than that of the great lords, but their freedom of manoeuvre was greater than that of their predecessors.

The dominant feature of the period, in terms of sheer numbers and investment in stone building, is the proliferation of the tower-houses. This is not, of course a phenomenon confined to Ireland, but is as much a feature of Scotland and northern England and parts of France. In spite of the attempts, in Ireland as in Scotland or England, to push this surge of building back to the earlier fourteenth century, we must resist these and continue to regard it as something which started only at the end of the century (Dixon, 1993, 33–6). The dates matter for two reasons. The attempts to extend the date range of tower-houses dilute their concentration in time and blur the impact of their existence. As a result, they cease to be a separate phenomenon requiring explanation or shedding a peculiar light on the history of the fifteenth century in those areas where they occur so prolifically.

In the past, the tower-houses have usually been seen as sending a message of the warlike nature of the men and society who built them. Undoubtedly, the Anglo-Scottish border was the scene of much conflict, although it may be that this is a picture derived more from the sixteenth than the fifteenth century. The parts of France where towers seem most common, Normandy and the south-west, were the areas of conflict during the Hundred Years' War. The Annals report an endless number of wars in Ireland during the period and the writers of political history find themselves recounting numerous stories of violence and upheaval. In these circumstances, it is only natural to link the two things together. Tower-houses look defensive, with their narrow windows and the prominent wall-head array of defensive features; they were meant to present a military face to the outside world.

Just because it seems so self-evident should not stop us from examining critically the assumption of the warlike purpose of tower-houses. Historically, it is a moot point whether Ireland was truly more caught up in war than the England of the Hundred Years' War or the Wars of the Roses. The lords of Meath do not seem to have given the needs of defence a high priority when they built the more elaborate tower-houses in the county. The fine display of wall-head turrets and machicolations of Tipperary was just that, display, when compared with the more modest but more effective defences of the tower-houses of Co. Down. A wall-walk which requires defenders to double back or climb over the roof in order to follow an attacker round the corner leaves a lot to be desired. No tower-house contains a well; Ireland is an island with a plentiful supply of rainwater, of course, which might ensure a steady supply in case of need. The siting of tower-houses is not designed to give them great strength. The violence that tower-houses were designed to respond to was that of a quick raid by a small number of men. If they could be prevented from rushing the door or immediately getting in through a window, they would go away. The tower-houses are meant to cope with a siege lasting hours rather than days. The moated manor house in the English country-side now presents a very peaceful aspect but, if the walls were crenellated and manned and windows barricaded with furniture, it would have been as effective as a tower-house in this context.

It is much more profitable to examine the social implications of tower-houses rather than their possible military purpose. In La Perche district of Normandy, the rebuilding of the manors with towers was associated with the replacement of the earlier gentry with a new group in the aftermath of the Hundred Years' War (Gautier-Desvaux, 1993, 142–3). On both the Scottish and English side of the Border, the building of towers can be related to shifts in the pattern of lordship and the prosperity of the lords (Dixon, 1979; 1993). The initiative was first taken by the English lords of the lowlands; in the late fifteenth and sixteenth centuries, it was the turn of the Scottish lords. In both cases the ability to build the towers was linked to the tenurial position of the lords concerned and to the profits of their lordship. In England, the lesser lords continued to be dominated by the greater, while in Scotland they achieved a position of much greater independence; at the same time, the profits of raiding the weakly defended English lands gave them the money to build.

There are at the very least hints from the distribution of the tower-houses in Ireland that they too were linked to the emergence of a new class of freeholding lesser lords, the descendants of the tenants of the thirteenth century. The social stability in Meath shows that this was not the whole story; it is an explanation for the greater density elsewhere, in Galway, Limerick or Tipperary. The lesser lords here took advantage of the looser lordship of the late middle ages, with its shifting boundaries, to express their confidence in the building of tower-houses. The building of so many is a powerful argument for the prosperity of their builders, as Dixon has shown (1979, 245–6; 1993, 38–41). Here it is interesting to compare the pattern of tower-house building to that of the enclosure castles. The tower-houses of the south, as exemplified by those of Tipperary or Limerick, are notable for the number of their floors, and particularly the vaulting of more than one of them, and for the elaboration of their wall-heads. As one proceeds north and east from there through the Pale to Co. Down the tower-houses become steadily smaller and simpler. This reflects the same pattern of wealth and power seen in the larger enclosure castles concentrated in the south. Not only the three great Earls, but their supporters, controlled the greatest wealth in Ireland.

The wealth was presumably derived from agriculture and trade. After the economic upheavals of the fourteenth century, like so many other regions of Europe, Ireland concentrated on specialised production. This meant cattle, whose hides could command a ready market. More of the land was suitable for cattle than for arable and so the potentially profitable area increased: there are more tower-houses in some areas than there had been thirteenth-century manorial centres. In this, there is a parallel from the churches: the fifteenth century saw the building of many parish churches, especially in the Pale, the rebuilding of some monasteries in the south, such as Holy Cross and Kilcooly, and the building of friaries in the

West. They could not deploy the elaborate architectural detail or wealth of the late Gothic styles of Europe, but in their window tracery and incidental carving they represent a significant level of expenditure compared to earlier periods in Ireland.

This building, of tower-houses and churches, spread across most of Ireland, whether English or Irish in its political allegiance. We find examples of the Irish continuing to use large enclosure castles, as well as large tower-houses that were almost full castles like Bunratty, as well as the more normal tower-houses. The efforts made by the disputing O'Connors to control Roscommon at the beginning of the period, and the way in which possession of Dunluce seems to have clinched the seizure of the northern route for the MacDonnells of Antrim in the later sixteenth century, both speak of a new attitude to castles among the Irish. The pattern of O'Donnell castles in north Donegal reflects their concern to hold on to territory. It can be no coincidence that this came at a time during which the Irish lords were adopting a new attitude to their lordships (Simms, 1987). On the one hand they were scaling down their claims of kingship, while on the other they were increasing their demands on the lands and men under their control. In this, the possession of castles must have been an important asset.

Even among the lordships normally considered Irish, there were variations in the extent of the proliferation of castles. In the south-west and Connacht, they were considerably more in evidence than among the Irish of the hegemony of O'Neill in Ulster, although the O'Donnells of north Donegal built a fair number. It is unclear why this should be: at least three explanations can be put forward. The Irish who built most castles, especially the O'Donnells, may have been under more military pressure from the relatively dominant O'Neills. The number of castles may have been a measure of the dispersal of power within the lordship, with the O'Neill ruling family conceding least, as might be indicated in a comparison between the intruding and fissiparous Burkes and the long-established O'Heynes in Galway. Finally, inland Ulster might be the area least touched by the market economy of the fifteenth century and so least able to command the resources for castle building, in contrast to the men of Connacht exporting through Galway, while the fish of Donegal may have brought prosperity to the north-west. If this were so, however, the O'Neills of Clandeboy in the east of Ulster, with access to (if not control of) the port of Carrickfergus, should have had more than the three castles they had; and one of them, Castlereagh, is of the sixteenth century.

Whatever the answer to this, the very fact of widespread (as opposed to the sporadic activity we have been able to record before) Irish castle building is significant. The lifestyle, the economy and the structure of power implied by castles was new to the Irish world. This fits ill with the idea of a 'Gaelic Revival' as propounded by Eoin MacNeill or Curtis. Instead, this must surely be a case of the Irish borrowing a significant feature of cultural and political life from the English. Clearly in this respect, the two sets of lords had grown together, as much through the anglicisation of the Gaels as through the gaelicisation of the English. A considerable part of the image of the gaelicised Ireland of the later middle ages comes from the very sources that stressed the warlike state of the island, the royal officials in Dublin. The evidence of the building of castles during the fifteenth century would seem to contradict both propositions. This is not to say that Ireland was a peace-fully idyllic place in the late middle ages, for there was patently a persistent presence of low-level violence there, but it was low-level.

It was in the century and a half from the 1530s to the 1690s that Ireland became significantly more violent, the period which saw the end of castle building. The determination of the Tudor kings and queens to control Ireland was matched by the militarisation of Gaelic society, most notably in the war state created by Shane O'Neill in Ulster. The Reformation and the rivalries of England and Spain added fuel to the fire. The wars were punctuated by famous sieges of castles in which artillery played a notable role: Maynooth in 1535, Askeaton in 1580 or Cahir in 1599 (Johnson, 1975), and culminating in the campaign of the New Model Army through Ireland in 1649–50. As a result it is easy to link the two together and give guns and war as the two causes of the end of castle building: 'The advent of gunpowder and artillery rang the death knell of castles' (Leask, 1977, 143); 'The Cromwellian invasion and pacification killed off the tower-house: partly this was because of . . . artillery . . . but, more fundamentally because he brought to an end the ancient tradition of petty war in Ireland' (Cairns, 1991, 13).

There are two ways in which guns may affect castles. The first is the use of hand-guns for defence, and the second is the use of heavy artillery, either for attack or defence. We first hear of guns in Ireland in the fourteenth century, when English expeditions brought them over, but it is not for another century that mentions of them become at all frequent (De hOir, 1983, 80–1). As we have seen, castles of the sixteenth century do have loops with the small apertures or double splay associated with the use of hand-guns in defence: guns replacing bows. The gunports for heavier weapons, with wider mouths and mounted low in the wall, which we find in Scottish tower-houses of the sixteenth century, are either not found in Ireland, or are extremely rare. The first gunports for artillery seem to be those of the 1560s at Carrickfergus castle, and some of them are mounted too high, probably to reuse existing arrow loops to save money. The lack of evidence in the structures for the mounting of heavy guns during the sixteenth century matches the lack of references to the making of guns in Ireland noted by De hOir (1983, 84).

In fact, as McComish pointed out: 'castles continued to play a dominant role in Irish warfare until the end of the seventeenth century', for which he gave a number of reasons: the lack of guns and skilled gunners, and the great difficulty moving artillery around the country (1969, 15–19). The Civil War in England showed that medieval castles still retained a reserve of real military strength, even against artillery, although this was usually because the garrison constructed outer works in earth to keep the attackers' guns at a distance (Thompson, 1987, 138–57). The wars of the 1640s in Ireland saw the same prominence for castles, often tower-houses. It could be argued that this was simply due to the inefficiency of the artillery in use, until the arrival of the well-organised siege train of the New Model Army with Cromwell in 1649.

By then, however, men had been building replacements for castles for half a century. During the seventeenth century, but particularly in the first half, there were a number of houses built which grafted on to what were essentially Jacobean houses more or less provision for defence. In the tradition of the tower-houses, the defence was a matter of deploying hand weapons in a more or less systematic and widespread way. This is a development which need not detain us here, when it has been well charted by others, especially with the buildings associated with the most thorough of the Plantation schemes, that of Ulster (Jope, 1960; Waterman, 1963; Craig, 1982, ch. 8; Johnson, 1988; Johnston, 1980). These show that the move away from anything which we can really call a castle, and towards country houses, had started well before the wars of the middle of the century. Artillery which did not become effective before the 1650s cannot have caused a change visible before 1600.

In another way, it is right to identify the invasion by Cromwell, and the wars of the seventeenth century, as crucial to the end of castles. The result, especially by the 1690s, was that there was a massive change in the land ownership of Ireland, as the victors stripped the losers of their estates. During the seventeenth century itself, a whole series of compromises over where to live took place, from reoccupying the old castles or tower-houses to building new strong houses. After the definitive victory of the Boyne, the new lords were now confident of their position. The old castles were inconvenient and outmoded for the life they intended to live, and they were abandoned wholesale. In England, the Civil War provided a military motive for the slighting of castles. In Ireland the land revolution was accompanied by a massive assault on the forests of Ireland, turning the land into the most treeless of Europe in a century. This surely explains the remarkable lack of surviving timber in Irish castles, especially from the roofs. The wood was looted (or recycled), even if the stonework was not, for the new houses of the new aristocracy, if not for the fires of their tenants. The Georgian houses of Ireland rang the death knell of the castles.

EPILOGUE

—— .◆. ——

The castles built in Ireland in the two generations after 1169 set the agenda for their later history in four ways. They show the confidence and resources of their builders; they divide fairly clearly into the major castles of the few most powerful men and the castles of the lesser lords; they illustrate the balance of power between the king and his barons; and, interestingly perhaps, the Irish lords figure little in the story. Between them, these themes bring the great bulk of the story that castles have to tell in Ireland within their purview.

The confidence expressed in the original castles of the greater lords was remarkable. In their new lands, they invested heavily in large stone castles as well as timber and earth ones, bringing over skilled men to design them, if not the gangs of craftsmen needed to carry out the work. The most obvious of the local resources which they deployed was that of the materials, stone, lime and timber, needed to build them, but there must have been a major importation of resources from outside. There is no reason to suppose that either the expertise or the numbers of craftsmen required could have been found from the resources available in Ireland before 1169. It also seems unlikely that the castles were built out of the rents and profits of the initial years of the lordships: these would take time to show such profits, but in the meantime the lords must have somewhere to live. If they were prepared to make an investment in their new lands, derived presumably from their estates in England, they seem to have done so in the spirit of confidence that their future was secure. In contrast to their contemporaries in Wales, they seem not to have made defence the main priority for their castles. Instead, the aim was to provide a comfortable and, above all, magnificent setting for the exercise of their new power.

By the standards of late twelfth-century England or France, a number of these early magnate castles in Ireland were fine castles. Trim is the most obvious example, but the round great tower of Nenagh and the stonework of the great hall at Adare were excellent designs, well carried out; Carlingford castle had an impressive line of a curtain wall and buildings behind it, while the great tower of Carrickfergus was also impressive, if a little old-fashioned and set within a cramped courtyard. The slightly later royal castles at Dublin and Limerick took their place, too, in the assemblage of fine castles.

In the century and a half after 1220, the pace seems to slacken somewhat, although Castle Roche and Ferns maintain the tradition of first-rate castles, but there are few other candidates. This is not because of any isolation from the ideas or from the craftsmen who worked on contemporary castles: Roscommon castle was clearly a product of the ideas which led to the construction of Edward I's Welsh castles, while the details of Greencastle, Donegal, have such close links with those of Harlech that we must imagine that a mason from the Welsh royal works was responsible. If the date of Ballymoon lies within this period, it too may take its place as a first-rate castle for its accommodation and organisation, but not for its defensive aspect. The great towers of Lea or Carlow show that there were masons in Ireland with their own ideas of how to design castles, and that there could be more to building castles in Ireland than importing men and ideas from overseas. The relative lack of first-rate castles in these years is made up of two strands. The most obvious is the lack of resources. If the earlier castles depended in part on the profits of English lands being invested in Ireland, with the development of the lordships of Ireland this would die away. Ireland was not as rich a land as it appeared to the likes of Gerald of Wales, a place where great fortunes were to be made, if only the land were to be run in properly organised estates. Money was therefore short compared to overseas, and so was the basic resource of good building stone; inevitably the castles in Ireland suffered from the lack.

The smaller scale of the castles was reflected mainly in their defensive aspects, seen as clearly as anywhere at Roscommon. The ideas were there but they were not followed through into a full concentric castle, presumably because the Justiciar thought that the threat did not justify the expenditure of the proportion of the resources available. The lord's personal accommodation in baronial castles does not show the same scaling down of size and expense, although the smaller size of the castles, and the relative lack of provision of suites and chambers for others, may show that households in Ireland were rather smaller than in England. Again, this would reflect the fact that the estates of the baronage of Ireland were not as profitable as those of their contemporaries in England.

If we knew more about the buildings of Askeaton, Newcastle West or Adare castles we would be in a better position to see whether they followed the same trend that we have seen in an earlier period: that of building castles to accommodate smaller households in Ireland than their social equivalents in England. For the Butlers, the problem is summed up in the question as to how we regard Granny and Kilkenny as representatives of their achievements: Granny is small and provides mainly for the lord, while Kilkenny must have been at the most adapted from the earlier castle. As such, they are not the castles we might expect of a fifteenth-century English earl. The western castles, especially Newcastle West, may well have been able to accommodate a significantly larger household, but nowhere do we really see the sort of symmetrical architectural composition which, along with sheer size, marks out the finest late medieval castles in England and France. They continue the story of the early fourteenth century in their aims and their vocabulary of design, just as the church buildings of the period did, for the building industry of the late middle ages had its origins then. They are fine castles by the standards of Ireland rather than elsewhere; Trim would be a fine castle anywhere.

The distinction between the great early stone castles and their timber and earth-work contemporaries is an easy one to understand now, and probably was at the time they were built. While the basic division was between the grades of men who held the land and built the castles, this was not the whole story. The mottes do not occur everywhere where English lords settled, while they proliferate particularly towards the borders of some lordships. Behind the pattern of their construction lies a balance of choices: prestige, pressure from an overlord perhaps, and the perceived military threat. This balance was clearly felt differently in different parts of the island, and, in particular, there are suggestions of the use of mottes with baileys in a more military role along the frontiers after they had stabilised. This was succeeded apparently by the development of the small polygonal enclosures for the same pur-pose during the thirteenth century. Border castles during the thirteenth and four-teenth centuries are strikingly informal structures, whether of earth and timber or of stone, relating effectively to the nature of the war they were designed to fight.

Behind the borders, however, lay the bulk of the lordships. Here the earlier pres-ence of the mottes shows up the absence of the later equivalent sites the more clearly. There are various explanations which we may suggest to account for this. Traces of them above ground may have been destroyed. The remains of the halls excavated on the mottes in Ulster were hardly robust and can only have survived because they were isolated from the destructive forces of later agriculture by being perched on the tops of the mottes: as such they contrast with the stone-built hall-houses of Connacht. There may not have been many manorial centres in the thirteenth century, because the main thrust of settlement may not have been so much based on the manors as on the dispersed farmsteads of the free tenants. In the south and east, free tenants are probably represented by the moated sites, but they too are not found everywhere where we would expect them; they are conspic-uously absent from the area which later was known as the Pale. The crucial absence from the manorial sites of Ireland (and the farmsteads of the free tenants of Meath) is a surrounding enclosure, which would survive above ground to be found by archaeologists now. The paucity of the sites known to archaeologists is another case of the dependence of Irish archaeology on the above-ground remains of sites for their discovery.

This is a gap remedied with a vengeance after 1400, with the tower-houses. The idea of a tower providing accommodation and security for the minimal household of a lesser landholder in the late middle ages was taken up as enthusiastically in Ireland as anywhere else in Europe. It is tempting to see them as evidence of the continuity of settlement, with mottes, moated sites and tower-houses somehow all serving similar functions in a line of continuity, but this would be too simplistic. We must remember that the mottes were not built either for a single class in society or for a single purpose; nor were the moated sites. Although some sites show two or more examples of the types together in apparent succession, the great majority of sites of each type are found isolated in the landscape. There is as much evidence that the tower-houses represent the fruits of a new order of land-holding and settle-ment as that they are the products of an old order in a new dress. Comparing them to the mottes does, however, remind us of one thing. They were designed so that their defensive functions were precisely defined and limited: elaboration rarely expressed itself in greater military effectiveness or expenditure. Prestige, not war, lay at the root of the tower-houses, and this may be a message we should look at for the mottes as well.

Again, like mottes, their distribution, although it is hardly yet known for much of the island in detail, is not even, nor can it be representative of the distribution of all settlement of the period. In parts, particularly in the south and west, they seem to represent a fragmentation of lordship and its replacement by a new pattern of settlement. The contrast between the Irish lords' control of tower building and its absence from the lands of English lordship is impressive. Similarly, the regional nature of their designs, with local 'schools' of tower-house construction, fits with the picture of the towers as a phenomenon of the fragmentation of the large, strong lordships of the preceding century. In this world clear boundaries dissolved and with them went the idea of the specifically border stronghold; in the fifteenth century there were too many borders to bother about.

The later middle ages saw the collapse of the power of the English king in Ireland, the end of the story of the medieval balance between the two forces of king and baron, which began with the expedition of Henry II in 1170. He may have asserted his power then, but the pattern of castle building shows how the balance shifted. In the next thirty years, royal castles were decisively outstripped by those of the lords. John, having failed in 1185, tried to recover his position after 1205, with the building of Dublin and Limerick castles. Even then he could only muster at most six stone castles in Ireland in 1210, and of those Ardfinnan may not have been of stone at the time, while neither Wicklow nor Athlone was very impressive. On the other hand, there were at least a dozen baronial castles of stone by then in Ireland and the imbalance simply reflected the position in terms of acreages. It is little wonder that John tried to seize the lordships of Limerick, Meath and Ulster in an attempt to recover the royal position.

His attempt had failed by 1227 when Henry III granted back the Earldom of Ulster to Hugh de Lacy, and the king never really dominated Ireland again. In the later thirteenth century we can see his weakness in the castles again with Roscommon, a castle which we may judge in two ways. Within Ireland at least, it was a first-rate castle, but Richard de Burgh, Earl of Ulster and lord of Connacht, built three such castles, at Ballintubber, Ballymote and Greencastle, Donegal, as well as rebuilding the outer gate of Carrickfergus. He could show a far greater strength in castles than could the Justiciar, just as he controlled directly far more land. Likewise, while Roscommon was a fine castle, Edward I spent less on it than he did on each of half a dozen castles in Wales, and built bigger and stronger castles for his money. On either count the royal resources in Ireland come out poorly from the comparison.

After 1300, the royal works stopped building new castles altogether. The royal castles might be repaired at times but were often run on a care and maintenance regime at best; some, like Dungarvan, passed from royal to baronial control, especially outside the area close to Dublin. Many of the great castles of the fifteenth century were held by the three great Earls, of Kildare, Ormond and Desmond, but there were also O'Brien at Carrigogunnell and MacQuillan at Dunluce, controlling major castles which they had either built or rebuilt. When the Tudors wished to reassert their power over Ireland in the sixteenth century, their lack of castles reflected the slenderness of the resources they had inherited from their predecessors.

One of the most problematic topics raised by this study is to understand the attitude of Irish lords to castles. They do not seem to have been concerned to build castles, except in rare and exceptional circumstances, before the middle of the fourteenth century, which is puzzling for several reasons. The more we stress the lords' knowledge of the forms and power of feudal lordship before 1169, the more likely it is that they would have been receptive to the building of castles. This might not have happened before 1169, but it should have opened the way for it afterwards. In the Highlands of Scotland, Gaelic lords were prepared to equip themselves with castles from the early thirteenth century at least, while the Welsh lords did the same. The latter did so under pressure to retain their lands from the rapacity of the English lords pressing in on them. After the arrival of the English lords in 1169, the same pressure should have applied to the Irish.

The clearest illustration of the problem is to consider the case of the O'Connor kingdom of Connacht. In the earlier twelfth century it may have been at the fore-front of the move towards the new powers; the evidence of the Annals suggests that the kings were ready to install their men in fortifications as part of a scheme of military control. They had close, if not friendly, relations with Kings Henry II and John until 1215, so that they must have thought of the idea. Under Henry III they faced a continuous attack from Richard de Burgh and royal officials which ended with a massive loss of territory as they were confined to the Five Cantreds. During this attack in particular, we would expect that the obvious device for the O'Connors to hold on to their lands and power would be to build castles from which to defend their estates. It might not prevent the piecemeal confiscations of slices of land by the king's officials but it would surely have made the dismem-bering of the kingdom by de Burgh much harder. We can only speculate that it would have required a systematic organisation of their lands into estates, each centralised on a castle, and the whole centralised on the person of the king. This was a political restructuring which no single O'Connor was able to do himself, or willing to allow another to do.

If this is the explanation, then the beginnings of the systematic building of castles by the Irish lords after the middle of the fourteenth century becomes more inter-esting. The widespread presence of castles would imply that the Irish had accepted or initiated an alteration in their power structure. This is something that has already been suggested by historians, but the systematic building of castles is a powerful piece of additional evidence to the debate. An extension of this would be the way that, once initiated, the Irish lords seem to have been successful at preventing a fragmentation of their power such as may have occurred in the greater English lordships in the south. At the same time, we are far from understanding how the Irish lords who took over castles from the English used them, especially in peace. A castle such as Roscommon was designed to provide accommodation for a consid-erable household, which is not something we might expect from an Irish lord. Were many of the rooms simply abandoned, as the possible shrinkage of Greencastle, Donegal, down to a tower-house, with the rest of the castle acting as a bawn, might indicate?

This brings us to the nub of the question of how we should view the castles in Ireland: what picture of their times do they represent? The traditional view has always been to stress them as structures associated primarily with war. In Ireland, where so much of the past may be seen in terms of the present, this has on occasions been extended to seeing them as the products of a particular war, that of the partial English conquest of the island. In truth, castles are much more complex than that: their military role was only one of their functions. In Ireland especially, as we have seen continuously through this study, in many castles it was clearly not the main feature. Castles were pre-eminently structures which articulated and concentrated political power. This might be military but it had peaceful dimensions which occupied much more of the life of the castle. The basis of power was control over land, either to command the men who lived on it, or to gather the rents and produce from it. The castle served to administer this control, and then to allow the lord a base from which he could translate the control of the land attached to the castle to the wider political scene. The display of power and wealth, and the provision of accommodation for the household who maintained his power, were clearly integral to the process.

From this it follows that when we study castles, in Ireland as elsewhere, what we are studying are the structures of power, literally and metaphorically, in the society of the middle ages. Actions speak louder than words, and the investment required for a castle tells us much about the lord's aims and power when he caused a castle to be built. The nature of that power will be reflected in the structure of the castle, and so we should be able to deduce it from the study of the structure. Until then, the castle is dumb, so we must not carry to the castle preconceived ideas of its role. Even if one castle was built for a certain purpose, another castle, even if it was built by the same man (lord or craftsman) at the same time, might have been for a different purpose. Each castle stands alone at the beginning of any study. Apart from any other reason, this is why this work will need to be revised as we recover more information from individual castles.

Future scholars will only be able to do this if the castles survive, and they have not been well treated in the last three hundred years in Ireland. They seem to have been abandoned relatively quickly after the middle of the seventeenth century, as places not fit for gentlemen to live in. Thereafter they proved to be useful sources of stone and timber for building being carried on nearby, a process exacerbated on occasions by their association with the English lordship at a time when the rising tide of nationalism made this unpopular. It would be good to be able to think that these times have changed and that castles are now more valued by modern people, because of the insight they give into the conditions of their time, interpreted in a less military or militant way. Certainly they are now forming an integral part of the heritage industry, which is such a prominent part of the Irish landscape at the end of the twentieth century. This may preserve them in part, but the cost may be high, as the value of their study may be lost in the demands of facile presentation and over-enthusiastic restoration. The most alarming development in this direction is the treatment of Carrickfergus castle, with new walls and staircase destroying the understanding of the great tower, and the construction of a ticket office and shop as recently as 1991, which involved the digging of foundations in a large part of the outer ward down to the bedrock without any archaeological excavation. This was the work of the state organisation dedicated to the preservation of historic monuments: if the guardians act like this, maybe we should abandon hope.

If we abandon hope, we allow two important stories, which are contained within the stones of these monuments, to be lost for the future. Their castles tell us of the life experiences and expectations of the new aristocracy of medieval Ireland. Their adaptation to the land informs us of their life outside Ireland, from which many of them and their ideas came: the castles of Ireland are part of the story of Europe. They also shed a clear light on the experiences of Ireland during these crucial centuries, between the relative isolation of the early middle ages and the violence of the early modern period.

GAZETTEER OF SELECTED CASTLES

——— .◆. ———

The aim of this list is to give to the potential visitor a flavour of the variety of castles to be found in Ireland; in no way is it a complete listing of the many sites which might be included. Other lists exist, of State Care monuments and that of Salter (1993). No one knows how many castles either survive or once existed in Ireland, although Leask guessed at about 3,000. About 350 mottes survive, or are known to have been destroyed, while the great majority of the rest are (or were) tower-houses. Both because of the numbers, and because of their similarity to each other, I have been ruthlessly selective with these types. For mottes, I have chosen sites which are accessible, mostly those in State Care. For tower-houses, I have tried to select a large and a small example from several parts of the island, to try and embrace the variety of the whole. Those castles not in State Care are marked with an asterisk; the numbers in bold after the site names refer to illustrations.

ADARE Co. Limerick R472466 **(22–4)**
Perhaps originally the town was beside the castle and the parish church. Consists of two enclosures: the outer with two halls (c. 1200 and 13th cent.) and a small gate tower. The inner one may be late medieval, like the upper parts of the tower (Leask's 'keep').
Dunraven, 1865; Rynne, 1961; Sweetman, 1980; Barry, 1983, 307

ASKEATON Co. Limerick R340502 **(104–5, 108–12)**
Inner enclosure for the Earl of Desmond's household dominated by the 15th-cent. chamber tower. The outer enclosure contains the fine, first-floor great hall rebuilt in the 15th cent. over the 13th-cent. one.
Nuttall, 1988

ATHCLARE Co. Louth O054860
Tower-house with the roof-line visible of a contemporary attached hall.

ATHENRY Co. Galway M506209 **(48, 85)**
Dominated by the decorated 13th-cent. hall block. The enclosure along the east, river side shelters a chamber block of the same date.
Papazian, 1990

ATHLONE Co. Westmeath M035415 **(82)**
Much of the present castle dates from its conversion to an army barrack 200 years ago. The central tower may enclose a motte: two round, 13th-cent. angle towers.
Orpen, 1907b

AUGHNANURE Co. Galway M152416
Elaborate (cf. Rockfleet) six-storey tower-house with a high vault, low-set bartizans and large bawns.
Craig, 1982, 104

*BAGINBUN Co. Wexford S801030
Cliff-top enclosure inserted into an earlier, larger promontory fort.

BALLINTUBBER Co. Roscommon M729745 **(56, 58)**
A large enclosure with the western half better preserved than the east: north-west tower much rebuilt in the 17th cent.
O'Conor Don, 1889; Claffey, 1975

*BALLYDEROWN Co. Cork R847007
Claimed to be an early 13th-cent. tower but with a first-floor window in the west wall which appears much later, as does the thin walling.
O'Keeffe, 1984

BALLYLAHAN Co. Mayo G273988 **(73)**
A polygonal enclosure *c.* 30 m across with a twin-towered gate house. Foundations of one square and one rectangular building are visible within the enclosure.

BALLYLOUGHAN Co. Carlow S747584 **(68)**
A rectangular enclosure with the surviving remains of two square angle towers and a gate house; earthworks to the north-east may represent a deserted settlement or the garden of a post-medieval house to the north.
De Paor, 1962

BALLYMOON Co. Carlow S744614 **(65–7)**
The most enigmatic castle in Ireland: a rectangular enclosure with few defences, yet first-rate accommodation for the lord and his household. Beside it are the remains of a village or town settlement.

BALLYMOTE Co. Sligo G662155 **(56)**
An irregularly rectangular courtyard with strong corner towers, twin-towered gate house and towers along the east and west walls; a postern tower planned for the south was never built, nor was the castle given a moat.
FitzPatrick, 1927; Sweetman, 1986

BALLYNAHOW Co. Tipperary S082602 **(130–1)**
Round tower-house.
Craig, 1982, 105

*BALLYWALTER Co. Antrim J266885
A very typical Ulster motte, in both its siting and dimensions.

CAHIR Co. Tipperary S060246
Occupies an island in a river. 13th-cent. inner enclosure with a gate tower and north tower. The gate tower was blocked and a great hall built against the tower in the late middle ages; the outer works are 16th cent.
Wheeler, n.d.; Johnson, 1975

CARLINGFORD Co. Louth J118119 (25–7)
An oval enclosure set on a rock outcrop above the port, divided into two by a massive north–south wall. In the town are the remains of at least three merchants' tower-houses.
Buckley and Sweetman, 1991, 320–3

CARLOW S717763 (70)
The surviving east wall of the donjon shows that there were originally three stories.

CARRICKFERGUS Co. Antrim J415873 (13–14, 33, 35)
The most complex castle of Ireland; it still dominates the town and harbour. The inner ward and great tower are late 12th cent., middle ward and east tower 1215–23 and outer ward second quarter of the 13th cent. The earliest surviving cannon ports in Ireland inserted in the 1560s and the gate rebuilt; converted to an infantry barrack and then an artillery fort in the 19th cent.
McNeill, 1981

CARRIGOGUNNELL Co. Limerick R499550 (120–2)
Set on a steep hill. Windows with sandstone dressings probably survive from a 13th-cent. building against the west curtain of the inner ward. The rest of it is dominated by a 15th-cent. block with great chambers and five stories of private chambers. The outer ward has a simple late medieval gate.

*CASTLE KEVIN Co. Wicklow T184985 (92)
A rectangular platform defined by deep ditches, with traces of stone revetment; a gate tower and a possible outer enclosure to the east.
Orpen, 1908

CASTLE KIRKE Co. Galway L995502 (102)
Irish hall-house on an island in Lough Corrib.
Lynn, 1986, 102–3

*CASTLE MORA Co. Cork R560927 (89, 118)
Hall-house with later chamber tower set in a ditched enclosure; also known as Castle Barret.

CASTLE ROCHE Co. Louth H991118 (45–7)
An inland promontory site with an outer ward or town to the east. 13th-cent. oval enclosure with hall and gate house.
Buckley and Sweetman, 1991, 333–7

CLARA Co. Kilkenny S575578
Elaborate, well-preserved five-storey tower-house in a tiny bawn.
Leask, 1977, 79–86

CLONMACNOIS Co. Offaly N007305 **(43, 83)**
Originally a large motte and bailey set beside the Shannon south of the early monastery. Hall and enclosure of stone then built on the motte and inner bailey.

CLONMINES Co. Wexford S845929
Two towers exist within the remains of a deserted town. One was a merchant's; one the tower of a fortified church.

CLONMORE Co. Carlow S961763 **(64)**
Rectangular enclosure with hall and chamber to the east; late 13th-cent. lodgings added. Earlier motte and bailey half a mile east.

CLOUGH Co. Down J409403
Motte and bailey, where the entire top of the motte was excavated, revealing the hall and attached stone tower.
Waterman, 1954a

DELVIN Co. Westmeath N600626
Motte, with a 15th-cent. (?) rectangular tower and angle turrets east of it, partially destroyed by a shop.
Flanagan, 1993

DROMORE Co. Down J206532 **(42)**
Large motte and bailey.
Jope, 1966, 203–4

DUBLIN O155339 **(29)**
The medieval fabric now reduced to rebuilt towers surrounded by later buildings, still the centre of government.
Maguire, 1974; Lynch and Manning, 1990

DUNAMASE Co. Laois S530980 **(19, 20)**
Hill-top castle with earlier fort. Late 12th-cent. hall tower and gate tower; early 13th-cent. gate house, looped curtain and outer gate.
Hodkinson, 1995

DUNDRUM Co. Down J404369 **(15, 34)**
Late 12th-cent. inner enclosure with early 13th-cent. round tower and later gate house. Late medieval outer ward wall enclosing a 17th-cent. house.
Jope, 1966, 207–11

DUNGARVAN Co. Waterford X263930 **(28)**
Late 12th-cent. inner enclosure with a 13th-cent. outer enclosure with twin-towered gate house and round great tower; the whole later occupied by a barrack.

DUNLUCE Co. Antrim C904414 **(123)**
Late 14th-cent. towered inner ward on a rock stack, mainly occupied by a 16–17th-cent. manor house, extended to the landward side, with gardens and a town.

DUNMORE Co. Galway M500640 **(86)**
13th-cent. walled enclosure on a rock with a possible twin-towered gate house and a hall, later raised to a tower.

DUNSOGHLEY Co. Dublin O118433
Elaborate tower-house of the Pale (cf. Roodstown), with four attached turrets for lesser chambers and a stair; it also has the only original roof left on a castle in Ireland.

FERNS Co. Wexford T098498 **(69, 74–5)**
South and east walls of the later 13th-cent. donjon tower, probably originally four separate ranges around a light well; fine chapel in the south-east corner tower.
Sweetman, 1979

GLANWORTH Co. Cork R756040
13th-cent. inner enclosure at the edge of a cliff with a hall and gate tower; in the 15th cent. the gate was blocked and a chamber turret added.
Waterman, 1968; Manning, 1987

GLENQUIN Co. Limerick R247126
Large (six-storeyed, with a vault over two of them) tower-house typical of the county, with the door leading to an entrance lobby from which doors lead to the main chamber, the stair and a guard room (cf. Lissamotta).

GRANARD Co. Longford N330808
The large motte and bailey still dominate the town, disfigured by a statue of St Patrick.

GRANNY Co. Kilkenny S575144 **(113–16)**
15th-cent. quadrilateral enclosure, extended along the river frontage; dominated by the hall and chamber tower attached to it.
McFadden, 1990

GREENCASTLE Co. Donegal C653403 **(59–61)**
Early 14th-cent. oval enclosure with a twin polygonal-towered gate house at one end and a more ruined large polygonal tower at the other; a tower-house added later.
Waterman, 1958; McNeill, 1980, 73–6; Lacy, 1983, 365–7

GREENCASTLE Co. Down J247119 **(48–9)**
13th-cent. quadrilateral enclosure; the ditch and dam being exposed by excavation on the east. A hall in the centre and chamber block against the east curtain.
Waterman and Collins, 1952; Jope, 1966, 211–19; McNeill, 1980, 23–7; Gaskell-Brown, 1979; Hamlin and Lynn, 1988, 66–9

GREENMOUNT Co. Louth O062930
Motte and bailey with foundations of a ?hall visible in the bailey.

HARRY AVERY'S CASTLE Co. Tyrone H392852 **(101, 103)**
Gaelic Irish castle. A polygonal enclosure surrounds a natural hill, fronted by a double-towered gate house
Jope et al., 1950; Rees-Jones and Waterman, 1967

*INCHIQUIN Co. Cork X039747 **(34)**
Round great tower, now standing isolated beside a marsh; later vault inserted over the ground floor.
Hartnett, 1945, 42–4

KILBOLANE Co. Cork R422210 **(88)**
The north-western half of a rectangular enclosure with two surviving angle towers. The rear of the southern one was rebuilt in the 15th cent., with modern repairs too.

KILCLIEF Co. Down J597457
Tower-house of the Bishop of Down (cf. Strangford) with the door set between two frontal turrets.
Jope, 1966, 233–5

KILKENNY S508556
Early 13th-cent. masonry quadrilateral with angle towers replaced an earth and timber enclosure.
Friel, n.d.; Murtagh, 1991; 1992

KILMACDUAGH Co. Galway M403201 **(95)**
Hall-house within the monastic enclosure.

KINBANE Co. Antrim D087438
Dramatically sited castle of the Gaelic Scots with a small tower and enclosure.
McNeill, 1983, 109–12

KNOCKGRAFFON Co. Tipperary S044287 **(36)**
A large motte and bailey; the latter has a stone curtain wall and a building within it. Nearby is a medieval church and tower-house.

LEA Co. Laois N571120 **(71–3)**
Overgrown outer enclosure with a 13th-cent. gate house, later blocked and converted to a tower-house. Inner enclosure on a possible motte, dominated by a donjon.
Leask, 1937, 173–5

LIMERICK R573572 **(3, 29–32, 35)**
An early earthwork enclosure succeeded by the stone castle of *c.* 1210, an incomplete quadrilateral with three corner towers and a gate house. The south-east angle completed with a 16th-cent. angle bastion; converted to barracks *c.* 1800.
Wiggins, 1991

LISCARROLL Co. Cork R452124
A large 13th-cent. enclosure with a gate tower to the south; at the north end, a latrine tower and doors at first-floor level are evidence of buildings. The gate house was much rebuilt in the 15th cent.
Leask, 1936, 189 and fig. 23

*LISSAMOTTA Co. Limerick R419386
A small (four stories and attic, one vault) tower-house of the county plan, with entrance lobby leading to the main chamber, stairs and guard room (cf. Glenquin).

*MAINHAM Co. Kildare N870300
Typical motte, sited on a ridge top and beside a medieval church.

MAYNOOTH Co. Kildare N934376 **(21)**
A 12th-cent. hall tower (with inserted ground-floor vault) dominates the enclosure, perhaps with the site of a hall to the east; much rebuilt in the early 17th cent. and damaged by later road through it.
FitzGerald, 1914

MOUNT SANDAL Co. Londonderry C870300
Small enclosure castle set high over the River Bann.
McNeill, 1980, 8, 14–15

NENAGH Co. Tipperary R867794 **(16–17, 51–3)**
A quite small enclosure, with only the gate house and the round great tower now surviving; the tower of *c.* 1200 built higher in the mid-13th cent.
Gleeson and Leask, 1936

*NEWCASTLE MCKYNEGAN Co. Wicklow O293042 **(80–1)**
A wide, round earth platform with a 13th-cent. gate house much rebuilt in the 1560s and 1570s.
Orpen, 1908

NEWCASTLE WEST Co. Limerick R278335 **(106–7)**
The original enclosure is now split between the OPW monument and the house next door. There are three principal buildings surviving: the 15th-cent. first-floor hall built over a 13th-cent. chapel (?); an early 14th-cent. hall or chapel partially rebuilt in the 15th cent. and much damaged recently; and a 15th-cent. chamber block.
Westropp, 1909

RATHMACKNEE Co. Wexford T034138
Five-storey tower-house with a well-preserved bawn containing modern buildings.

RINNDOWN Co. Roscommon M006540 **(76–8)**
Overgrown enclosure within the walls of a deserted town with a hall, a simple gate, and an added hall (?) to the west.

ROCKFLEET Co. Mayo L930952
A small, four-storey tower-house set beside the sea (cf. Aughnanure).

ROODSTOWN Co. Louth N996925 **(129)**
Small tower-house of the Pale (cf. Dunsoghley) with two turrets, but the door only defended by an internal murder-hole.
Buckley and Sweetman, 1991, 337

ROSCOMMON M874652 **(54–7)**
Formal rectangular courtyard with angle towers and gate house, all of 1275–85; 16th-cent. house built in the northern half and the gate house.
Leask, 1936, 185–7

ROSCREA Co. Tipperary S135890 **(79)**
13th-cent. enclosure with two angle towers (not projecting fully) and a gate tower, with turning bridge, later blocked.
Stout, 1984; Manning, 1989; 1990; Wren, 1992

SHANID Co. Limerick R243450
Motte and bailey with part of a polygonal shell-keep wall on the motte.

STRANGFORD Co. Down J589501
A plain merchant's tower-house without turrets (cf. Kilclief).
Jope, 1966, 253; Waterman, 1967

SWORDS Co. Dublin O183460 **(62–3)**
Large enclosure with a simple gate to the south. Tower with two chambers at the north; hall (?) and lord's chamber to the east; chapel and Constable's lodgings on either side of the gate.
Leask, 1914; Fanning, 1975

TERRYGLASS Co. Tipperary M860010
Ground floor of an unfinished towered donjon.
Leask, 1943

TRIM Co. Meath N802568 **(6–12)**
Ireland's largest and finest castle. The towered curtain wall has two gate towers and encloses the massive great tower and a hall complex against the north wall.
Sweetman, 1978; McNeill, 1990a; Stalley 1992

GLOSSARY

———— •◆• ————

Assart A clearing made in the forest, or other unploughed land, bringing it into production. Often separated from village settlement and occupied by farmers who were personally free (not serfs), paying rent and living in isolated farmsteads.

Bartizan An overhanging corner turret providing machicolations for defence of the ground beneath.

Bawn A word derived from the Irish for a cattle enclosure, which came to mean the walled enclosure attached to a tower-house.

Bretasch (Latin *bretagium*) A wooden tower.

Caput The chief place of an estate, whether a barony or an individual manor, where the lord lived or which was the centre of its administration in his name.

Chamber A room meant primarily for living in by the lord or upper members of his household, normally equipped with good windows, a fireplace and access to a single latrine. Chambers may be linked into suites with an outer great chamber, for daily life, connected to an inner private chamber for sleeping.

Crannog An artificial island, usually *c.* 30 m (100 ft) across, constructed of wood and stones in a lake in order to provide a platform for a defended house. Frequently found throughout Ireland in the medieval period and also in Scotland.

Great tower The pre-eminent building of a castle. In its military aspect (expressed by the use of the sixteenth-century term **keep**) it is the strong tower, containing all the essential rooms of the castle, grouped in a tower used as the place of last resort in a siege. It may have a more formal and longer lasting domestic role (expressed in the French **donjon**) accommodating the lord's inner household in a dominating tower.

Gate house A structure uniting the gate passage and two projecting towers, protecting and flanking it on either side, into a single building; its unity is often visible in the joining of the space over the passage with the interior of one or both towers, at first-floor level. It contrasts with both the **gate tower**, where the passage is contained within a single tower, occupying virtually all the ground-floor space, and with an arrangement whereby the gate is placed between two towers but the elements are not united into one building.

Hall The formal centre of the wider life of the castle; the large room where public feasts, courts, etc. were held by the lord. It is identified by its size, rectangularity and the display of large windows, fireplace, decorative stonework and, often, access to multiple latrines.

Hourds Wooden structures oversailing the wall-top to allow rocks to be dropped on the base of the wall below. When carried out in stone, they are known as **machicolations**.

Justiciar The chief governor in place of the king.

Liberty A lordship where the lord, not a royal official like the sheriff, was responsible for most normal administration of justice.

Machicolation A line of small arches or corbels projecting from the front of a wall top. A wall, built on the arches, protects men dropping rocks, etc., on to the base of the main wall from holes between the arches or corbels.

Motte A high mound of earth surrounded by a ditch, in the British Isles almost always round and artificially constructed (not a natural hill) as the strong point of a timber and earthwork castle. As height is its principal quality for defence, it may be defined as needing to be at least 2 m (6 ft 6 in) high above the surrounding land around the entire perimeter.

Rath or **Ringfort** A circular enclosure of the early medieval ('early Christian') period in Ireland, providing space for the house of a single family. Usually the enclosure is defined by a bank and external ditch, but it may also be made by levelling a hilltop to produce a scarp around most of the perimeter (**platform rath**). With time its interior may be raised to give a **raised rath**, although the entrance remains marked by a causeway over the ditch and a ramped access to the interior. If the enclosure is defined by a dry-stone wall, it is termed a **cashel**.

Ringwork A term coined in the 1960s to describe castles of earth and timber which were small enclosures without mottes.

Shell-keep A wall enclosing the top of a motte, often to provide a ring of buildings or a tower.

Tower-house A small castle of the late middle ages, where the lord's household accommodation is contained within a stone tower and any other buildings are quite separate, even if contained within a walled enclosure, and are, in Ireland at least, very rarely of stone. The tower is more or less defensible as a unit.

Western Transitional style The style of church architecture transitional between Romanesque and Gothic, found in Connacht; defined in Leask, 1960.

BIBLIOGRAPHY

———— •❖• ————

Abraham, A. S. K., 1986: 'The social context of tower-houses in late medieval Meath and southern Louth', BA dissertation, Archaeology Department, Queen's University of Belfast
—— 1991: 'Patterns of landholding and architectural patronage in late medieval Meath', Ph.D. thesis, Queen's University of Belfast
Addyman, P. V., 1965: 'Coney Island, Lough Neagh, prehistoric settlement, Anglo-Norman castle and Elizabethan fortress', *Ulster Journal of Archaeology*, 28, 78–101
Annals of Clonmacnoise, edited by D. Murphy, Royal Society of Antiquaries of Ireland, Dublin, 1896
Annals of Connacht, edited by A. M. Freeman, Institute for Advanced Studies, Dublin, 1944
Annals of Lough Key (Loch Ce), edited by W. M. Hennessy, Rolls Series, London, 1871
Annals of Ulster, edited by W. M. Hennessy and B. MacCarthy, Dublin 1887–1901; vol. I, ed. S. Mac Airt and G. MacNiocaill, Institute for Advanced Studies, Dublin, 1983
Austin, D., 1988: *Barnard castle*, English Heritage, London
Barry, T. B., 1977: *Medieval moated sites of south-east Ireland*, British Archaeological Report no. 35, Oxford
—— 1983: 'Anglo-Norman ringwork castles: some evidence', in T. Reeves-Smyth and F. Hamond (eds): *Landscape archaeology in Ireland*, British Archaeological Report no. 116, Oxford, 295–314
—— 1987: *The archaeology of medieval Ireland*, Methuen, London
—— 1993: 'The archaeology of the tower-house in late medieval Ireland', in H. Andersson and J. Wienberg (eds): *The study of medieval archaeology*, Almquist & Wiksell, Stockholm, 211–17
Barry, T. B., Culleton, E. and Empey, C. A., 1984: 'Kells motte, Co. Kilkenny', *Proceedings of the Royal Irish Academy*, 84(C), 157–70
Beresford, G., 1987: *Goltho: the development of an early medieval manor*, English Heritage, London
Berry, H. F., 1910: *Statute Rolls of the Parliament of Ireland, reign of King Henry VI*, HMSO, Dublin
Brooks, E. St J., 1950: *Knights' fees in Counties Wexford, Carlow and Kilkenny*, Irish Manuscripts Commission, Dublin
Brown, R. A., 1955: 'Royal castle building in England, 1154–1216', *English Historical Review*, 70, 353–98
Buckley, V. M. and Sweetman, P. D., 1991: *Archaeological survey of Co. Louth*, Stationery Office, Dublin
CDI: *Calendar of documents relating to Ireland* (ed. H. S. Sweetman), 5 volumes, Public Record Office, London
Cairns, C. T., 1987: *Irish tower-houses*, Group for the Study of Irish Historic Settlement, Athlone

—— 1991: 'The Irish tower-house, a military view', *Fortress*, 11, 3–13

Châtellain, A., 1981: 'La nouvelle architecture militaire du XIIIe siècle en Ile de France', in T. J. Hoekstra, H. L. Janssen and I. W. L. Moermann (eds): *Liber castellorum*, Zutphen, 66–75

Childe, V. G., 1938: 'Doonmore, a castle mound near Fair Head, Co. Antrim', *Ulster Journal of Archaeology*, 1, 122–35

Claffey, J. A., 1975: 'Ballintubber castle, Co. Roscommon', *Journal of the Old Athlone Society*, 1, 143–6, 218–21

Collins, J. T., 1945: 'Ui Mac Caille: A.D. 1177 to 1700', *Journal of the Cork Historical and Archaeological Society*, 50, 31–9

Cosgrove, A. (ed.), 1987: *A new history of Ireland*, vol. 2, Oxford University Press, Oxford

Cotter, C., 1986: 'Ferrycarrig, Newtown, Co. Wexford', *Excavations 1986*

—— 1987: 'Ferrycarrig, Newtown, Co. Wexford', *Excavations 1987*

Craig, M., 1982: *The architecture of Ireland*, Batsford, London

Cruden, S., 1960: *Scottish castles*, Nelson, Edinburgh

Culleton, E. and Colfer, W., 1975: 'The Norman motte at Old Ross', *Journal of the Old Wexford Society*, 5, 22–5

Cunningham, G., 1987: *The Anglo-Norman advance into the south-west Midlands of Ireland*, Parkmore, Roscrea

Curnow, P. E., 1980: 'Some developments in military architecture', *Proceedings of the Battle Conference on Anglo-Norman Studies*, 2, 42–62

Curtis, E., 1932–43: *Calendar of Ormond deeds*, 6 vols, Irish Manuscripts Commission, Dublin

Davies, O. and Quinn, D. B., 1941: 'The Irish Pipe Roll of 14 John', *Ulster Journal of Archaeology*, 4, supplement; see also Quinn, 1943

Davison, B. K., 1962: 'Excavations at Ballynarry, Co. Down', *Ulster Journal of Archaeology*, 24–5, 39–87

—— 1977: 'Excavations at Sulgrave, Northamptonshire, 1960–76: an interim report', *Archaeological Journal*, 134, 105–14

De hOir, S., 1983: 'Guns in medieval and Tudor Ireland', *Irish Sword*, 15, 76–88

De Paor, L., 1962: 'Excavations at Ballyloughan, Co. Carlow', *Journal of the Royal Society of Antiquaries of Ireland*, 92, 1–10

Dickinson, C. W. and Waterman, D. M., 1960: 'Excavations at Castle Skreen, Co. Down', *Ulster Journal of Archaeology*, 23, 63–77

Dimock, J., 1867: *Giraldi Cambrensis opera*, vol. 5, Rolls Series, London

Dixon, P., 1979: 'Towerhouses, pelehouses and border society', *Archaeological Journal*, 136, 240–52

—— 1993: 'Mota, aula et turris: the manor houses of the Anglo-Scottish border', in G. Meirion-Jones and M. Jones (eds): *Manorial and domestic buildings in England and northern France*, Society of Antiquaries, occasional papers, 15, London, 22–48

Dixon, P. and Lott, B., 1993: 'The courtyard and the tower: contexts and symbols in the development of late medieval great houses', *Journal of the British Archaeological Association*, 146, 93–101

Donnelly, C. J., 1994: 'The tower-houses of Co. Limerick', Ph.D. thesis, Queen's University of Belfast

Drage, C., 1981: 'Nottingham castle: the gatehouse of the outer bailey', *Transactions of the Thoroton Society of Nottinghamshire*, 85, 48–55

Duggan, S., 1982: 'Structural woodwork in 15th and 16th century Irish tower-houses', MA thesis, University College, Cork

Dunbar, J., 1981: 'The medieval architecture of the Scottish Highlands', in L. MacLean (ed.): *The middle ages in the Highlands*, Inverness Field Club, Inverness

Dunraven, Lord, 1865: *Memorials of Adare manor*, Parker, Oxford

Ellis, P., 1994: *Beeston castle, Cheshire*, English Heritage, London

Empey, C. A., 1981: 'The settlement of the kingdom of Limerick', in J. Lydon (ed.): *England and Ireland in the later middle ages*, Irish Academic Press, Dublin, 1–25

Fanning, T., 1975: 'An Irish medieval tile pavement: recent excavations at Swords Castle, Co. Dublin', *Journal of the Royal Society of Antiquaries of Ireland*, 105, 47–82

Faulkner, P., 1963: 'Castle planning in the fourteenth century', *Archaeological Journal*, 120, 215–35

FitzGerald, W., 1914: 'Historical notes on Maynooth castle', *Journal of the Royal Society of Antiquaries of Ireland*, 44, 281–94

FitzPatrick, J. E., 1927: 'Ballymote castle', *Journal of the Royal Society of Antiquaries of Ireland*, 57, 81–99

Flanagan, D. E., 1973: 'The names of Downpatrick', *Dinnseanchas*, 4, 89–112

Flanagan, M. T., 1989: *Irish society, Anglo-Norman settlers, Angevin kingship*, Oxford University Press, Oxford

——— 1993: 'Anglo-Norman change and continuity: the castle of Telach Cail in Delbna', *Irish Historical Studies*, 28, 385–9

Frame, R., 1982: *English lordship in Ireland, 1318–1361*, Oxford University Press, Oxford

——— 1984: 'War and peace in the medieval lordship of Ireland', in J. Lydon (ed.): *The English in medieval Ireland*, Royal Irish Academy, Dublin

Friel, P., n.d.: *Kilkenny castle*, Stationery Office, Dublin

Gaskell-Brown, C., 1979: 'Excavations at Greencastle, Co. Down', *Ulster Journal of Archaeology*, 42, 34–50

Gautier-Desvaux, E., 1993: 'Les manoirs du Perche', in G. Meirion-Jones and M. Jones (eds): *Manorial and domestic buildings in England and northern France*, Society of Antiquaries, occasional papers, 15, London, 141–57

Gleeson, D. F. and Leask, H. G., 1936: 'The castle and manor of Nenagh', *Journal of the Royal Society of Antiquaries of Ireland*, 66, 247–69

Graham, B. J., 1980: 'The mottes of the Norman Liberty of Meath', in H. Murtagh (ed.): *Irish Midland Studies*, Old Athlone Society, Athlone

——— 1988: 'Medieval timber and earthwork fortifications in the west of Ireland', *Medieval Archaeology*, 32, 110–29

Gwynn, A. and Hadcock, G. N., 1988: *Medieval religious houses: Ireland*, Longman, London

Hamlin, A. and Lynn, C. J., 1988: *Pieces of the past*, HMSO, Belfast

Hartnett, P. J., 1945: 'Some Imokilly castles', *Journal of the Cork Historical and Archaeological Society*, 50, 42–53

Heliot, P., 1965: 'La genèse des châteaux de plan quadrangulaire en France et en Angleterre', *Bulletin de la Société national des antiquaires de France*, 57, 238–57

Herrenbrodt, A., 1958: *Der Husterknupp, eine niederrheinische Burganlage des frühen Mittelalters*, Bohlau, Cologne

Higham, R. and Barker, P., 1992: *Timber castles*, Batsford, London

Hodkinson, B., 1995: 'The Rock of Dunamase', *Archaeology Ireland*, 9 (no. 2), 18–21

Holland, P., 1987: 'The Anglo-Normans in Co. Galway', MA thesis, University College, Galway

——— 1988: 'The Anglo-Normans in Co. Galway: the process of colonisation', *Journal of the Galway Archaeological and Historical Society*, 41, 73–89

Johnson, D. N., 1975: 'A contemporary plan of the siege of Caher castle, 1599, and some additional remarks', *Irish Sword*, 12, 109–15

——— 1988: 'Portumna castle – a little known early survey and some observations', in J. Bradley (ed.): *Settlement and society in medieval Ireland*, Boethius, Dublin, 477–503

Johnston, J. D., 1980: 'Settlement and architecture in Co. Fermanagh', *Ulster Journal of Archaeology*, 43, 79–89

Jope, E. M., 1951: 'Scottish influences in the north of Ireland: castles with Scottish features, 1580–1640', *Ulster Journal of Archaeology*, 14, 31–47

——— 1960: 'Moyry, Charlemont, Castleraw and Richhill: fortification to architecture in the north of Ireland', *Ulster Journal of Archaeology*, 23, 97–123

——— 1966: *An archaeological survey of Co. Down*, HMSO, Belfast

Jope, E. M., Jope, H. M. and Johnson, E. A., 1950: 'Harry Avery's castle, Newtonstewart, Co. Tyrone', *Ulster Journal of Archaeology*, 13, 81–92

Jope, E. M. and Seaby, W. A., 1959: 'A new document in the Public Record Office: defensive houses in medieval towns', *Ulster Journal of Archaeology*, 22, 115–18

Jordan, A. J., 1991: 'Date, chronology and evolution of the County Wexford tower-houses', *Journal of the Wexford Historical Society*, 13, 30–81

Kenyon, J. R., 1992: *Medieval fortifications*, Leicester University Press, Leicester

King, D. J. C., 1978: 'Pembroke castle', *Archaeologia Cambrensis*, 127, 75–121

Kirker, J. R., 1890: 'Cloughoughter castle, Co. Cavan', *Journal of the Royal Society of Antiquaries of Ireland*, 21, 294–7

Knight, J. K., 1987: 'The road to Harlech: aspects of some early thirteenth century Welsh castles', in J. R. Kenyon and R. Avent (eds): *Castles in Wales and the Marches*, Cardiff, University of Wales, 75–88

—— 1991: *Chepstow castle*, Cadw, Cardiff

—— 1992: 'Excavations at Montgomery castle', *Archaeologia Cambrensis*, 142, 97–180

Knox, H. T., 1910: 'Ballisnihiney castle', *Journal of the Galway Archaeological and Historical Society*, 6, 178–9

Lacy, B., 1983: *Archaeological Survey of Co. Donegal*, Donegal County Council

Lawlor, H. C., 1938: 'The castle of Magh Cobha', *Ulster Journal of Archaeology*, 1, 84–9

Leask, H. G., 1914: 'Swords castle', *Journal of the Royal Society of Antiquaries of Ireland*, 64, 259–63

—— 1937: 'Irish castles, 1180 to 1310', *Archaeological Journal*, 93, 143–99

—— 1943: 'Terryglass castle', *Journal of the Royal Society of Antiqaries of Ireland*, 73, 141–4

—— 1960: *Irish Churches and monastic buildings*, Dundealgan Press, Dundalk

—— 1977: *Irish castles and castellated houses*, 3rd edition, reprinted, Dundealgan Press, Dundalk

Lennon, C., 1981: *Richard Stanihurst the Dubliner*, Irish Academic Press

Lynch, A. and Manning, C., 1990: 'Dublin castle – the archaeological project', *Archaeology Ireland*, 4, 65–8

Lynn, C. J., 1982: 'The excavation of Rathmullan, a raised rath and motte in Co. Down', *Ulster Journal of Archaeology*, 44–5, 65–171

—— 1985, 'Excavations on a mound at Gransha, Co. Down', *Ulster Journal of Archaeology*, 48, 81–90

—— 1986: 'Some 13th century castle sites in the West of Ireland', *Journal of the Galway Archaeological and Historical Society*, 40, 90–113

McComish, W. A., 1969: 'The survival of the Irish castle in an age of cannon', *Irish Sword*, 9, 15–21

McFadden, E., 1990: 'Grannagh castle and the Earls of Ormond in the 14th and 15th centuries', BA dissertation, Archaeology Department, Queen's University of Belfast

McKenna, M., 1984a: 'Evidence for the use of timber in medieval Irish tower-houses – a regional study in Lecale and Eastern Tipperary', BA dissertation, Archaeology Department, Queen's University of Belfast

—— 1984b: 'Evidence for the use of timber in medieval Irish tower-houses – a regional study in Lecale and Eastern Tipperary', *Ulster Journal of Archaeology*, 47, 171–4

McNeill, T. E., 1977: 'Excavations at Doonbought fort, Co. Antrim', *Ulster Journal of Archaeology*, 40, 63–84

—— 1980: *Anglo-Norman Ulster*, John Donald, Edinburgh

—— 1981: *Carrickfergus castle*, HMSO, Belfast

—— 1983: 'The stone castles of northern Co. Antrim', *Ulster Journal of Archaeology*, 46, 101–28

—— 1986: 'Church building in the 14th century and the "Gaelic Revival"', *Journal of Irish Archaeology*, 3, 61–4

—— 1990a: 'Trim castle, Co. Meath, the first three generations', *Archaeological Journal*, 147, 308–36

—— 1990b: 'Early castles in Leinster', *Journal of Irish Archaeology*, 5, 57–64

—— 1991: 'Excavations at Dunsilly, Co. Antrim', *Ulster Journal of Archaeology*, 54, 78–112

—— 1992: *Castles*, Batsford, London

—— forthcoming: 'Castles and the changing pattern of border conflict in Ireland', *Château Gaillard*, 17

Maguire, J. B., 1974: 'Seventeenth century plans of Dublin castle', *Journal of the Royal Society of Antiquaries of Ireland*, 104, 5–14

Mallory, J. P. and McNeill, T. E., 1990: *The archaeology of Ulster*, Institute of Irish Studies, Belfast

Manning, C., 1987: 'A sheila-na-gig from Glanworth castle, Co. Cork', in E. Rynne (ed.): *Figures from the past*, Glendale Press, Dublin

—— 1989: 'Roscrea castle', *Excavations 1989*, 46

—— 1990: 'Clogh Oughter castle, Cavan', *Breifne*, 8, 1–44

Mitchel, P., 1986: 'The distribution and location of tower-houses in eastern Galway', BA dissertation, Archaeology Department, Queen's University of Belfast

Müller-Wille, M., 1966, *Mittelalterliche Burghugel (Motten) im nordlichen Rheinland*, Graz, Cologne

Murtagh, B., 1988: 'The bridge castle, Thomastown, Co. Kilkenny', in G. MacNiocaill and P. Wallace (eds): *Keimelia*, Galway University Press, Galway, 536–56

—— 1991: 'Kilkenny castle', *Excavations 1991*, 29–30

—— 1992: 'Kilkenny castle', *Excavations 1992*, 39–40

Neill, K. A., 1983: 'The manor of Knockgraffon', MA thesis, Queen's University of Belfast

ni Loinsigh, M. S., 1995: *The castles of north Donegal and their relationship to the land-holding structure of late mediaeval Gaelic lordships*, M.Phil. thesis, Queen's University of Belfast

Nuttall, R. A., 1988: 'The history and archaeology of Askeaton castle', MA thesis, Queen's University of Belfast

O'Brien, E., 1989: 'Excavations at Dundrum castle, Dundrum, Co. Dublin', *Archaeology Ireland*, 3 (no.4), 136–7

O'Conor Don, 1889: 'Ballintubber castle, County Roscommon', *Journal of the Royal Society of Antiquaries of Ireland*, 19, 24–30

O'Conor, K., 1992: 'Irish earthwork castles', *Fortress*, 12, 3–12

—— 1993: 'The earthwork castles of medieval Leinster', Ph.D. thesis, University College, Cardiff

O'Corrain, D., 1974: 'Aspects of early Irish history', in B. G. Scott (ed.): *Perspectives in Irish archaeology*, AYIA, Belfast, 64–71

O'Danachair, C., 1979: 'Irish tower-houses', *Bealoideas*, 45–7, 158–63

O'Grady, S., 1926: *Catalogue of the Irish manuscripts in the British Museum*, London

O'Keeffe, T., 1984: 'An early Anglo-Norman castle at Ballyderowne, Co. Cork', *Journal of the Royal Society of Antiquaries of Ireland*, 114, 48–56

—— 1987: 'Rathnageeragh and Ballyloo: a study of stone castles of probable 14th century date in County Carlow', *Journal of the Royal Society of Antiquaries of Ireland*, 117, 28–49

Orpen, G. H., 1906: 'Mote and bretasche building in Ireland', *English Historical Review*, 21, 417–44

—— 1907a: 'Motes and Norman castles in Ireland', *Journal of the Royal Society of Antiquaries of Ireland*, 37, 123–52

—— 1907b: 'Athlone castle: its early history, with notes on some neighbouring castles', *Journal of the Royal Society of Antiquaries of Ireland*, 37, 257–76

—— 1908: 'Novum castrum McKynegan, Newcastle Co. Wicklow', *Journal of the Royal Society of Antiquaries of Ireland*, 38, 126–40

—— 1911–20: *Ireland under the Normans*, I-IV, Oxford University Press, Oxford

—— 1915: 'The mote of Oldcastle and the castle of Rathgorgin', *Journal of the Galway Archaeological and Historical Society*, 9, 33–44

Otway-Ruthven, J., 1949: 'Dower charter of John de Courcy's wife', *Ulster Journal of Archaeology*, 12, 77–81

Papazian, C., 1990: 'Athenry castle', *Excavations 1990*, 32–3

Parker, J. H., 1860: 'Observations on the ancient domestic architecture of Ireland', *Archaeologia*, 38, 149–76

Phillips, J. R. S., 1984: 'The Anglo-Norman nobility', in J. Lydon (ed.): *The English in medieval Ireland*, Royal Irish Academy, Dublin, 87–104

Platt, C. and Coleman-Smith, R., 1975: *Excavations in medieval Southampton*, Leicester University Press, Leicester

Quinn, D. B., 1943: 'Index and corrigenda to Irish Pipe Roll of 14 John', *Ulster Journal of Archaeology*, 6, supplement

RCHM, 1970: Royal Commission on Historical Monuments of England: *Dorset*, vol. II, part 2, HMSO, London

RDKPRI: *Reports of the Deputy Keeper of the Public Records of Ireland*, HMSO, Dublin

Rees-Jones, S. and Waterman, D. M., 1967: 'Recent work at Harry Avery's castle, Co. Tyrone', *Ulster Journal of Archaeology*, 30, 76–82

Reeves, W., 1850: *Acts of Archbishop Colton in his metropolitan visitation of the diocese of Derry*, Irish Archaeological Society, Dublin

Renn, D. F., 1968: 'The donjon at Pembroke castle', *Transactions of the Ancient Monuments Society*, 15, 35–47

—— 1969: 'The Avranches traverse at Dover castle', *Archaeologia Cantiana*, 84, 79–92

—— 1987: 'Chastel de Dynan: the first phases of Ludlow', in J. R. Kenyon and R. Avent (eds): *Castles in Wales and the Marches*, Cardiff University Press, Cardiff, 55–73

Robinson, P., 1986: *Carrickfergus*, Irish Historic Towns Atlas, no. 2, Royal Irish Academy, Dublin

Rynne, E., 1961: 'Was Desmond castle, Adare, erected on a ringfort?', *North Munster Antiquarian Journal*, 193–202

Salter, M., 1993: *Castles and stronghouses of Ireland*, Folly Publications, Malvern

Saunders, A. D., 1977: 'Five castle excavations: reports of the Institute's project into the origin of the castles in England', *Archaeological Journal*, 134, 1–156

Scott, A. B. and Martin, F. X., 1978: *Expugnatio Hibernica, the conquest of Ireland, by Giraldus Cambrensis*, Royal Irish Academy, Dublin

Simms, K., 1987: *From kings to warlords*, Boydell, Woodbridge

Stalley, R. A., 1971: *Architecture and sculpture in Ireland*, Gill & Macmillan, Dublin

—— 1984: 'Irish Gothic and English fashion', in J. Lydon (ed.): *The English in medieval Ireland*, Royal Irish Academy, Dublin, 65–86

—— 1987: 'A misunderstood Gothic masterpiece: the Cantwell effigy at Kilfane, Co. Kilkenny', in E. Rynne (ed.): *Figures from the past*, Glendale Press, Dublin, 209–22

—— 1992: 'The Anglo-Norman keep at Trim: its architectural implications', *Archaeology Ireland*, 6, 16–19

Stell, G., 1981: 'Late medieval defences in Scotland', in D. H. Caldwell (ed.): *Scottish weapons and fortifications*, John Donald, Edinburgh, 21–54

—— 1985: 'The Scottish medieval castle: form, function and "evolution"', in K. J. Stringer (ed.): *Essays on the nobility of medieval Scotland*, John Donald, Edinburgh, 195–209

Stout, G., 1984: *Archaeological survey of the Barony of Ikerrin*, Roscrea Heritage Society, Roscrea

Sweetman, P. D., 1978: 'Archaeological excavations at Trim castle, Co. Meath', *Proceedings of the Royal Irish Academy*, 78 (C), 127–98

—— 1979: 'Archaeological excavations at Ferns castle, Co. Wexford', *Proceedings of the Royal Irish Academy*, 79 (C), 217–45

—— 1980: 'Archaeological excavations at King John's castle, Limerick', *Proceedings of the Royal Irish Academy*, 80 (C), 207–29

—— 1986: 'Archaeological excavations at Ballymote castle, Co. Sligo', *Journal of the Galway Archaeological and Historical Society*, 40, 114–24

Tabraham, C., 1988: 'The Scottish medieval tower-house as lordly residence in the light of recent excavation', *Proceedings of the Society of Antiquaries of Scotland*, 118, 267–76

Tatton-Brown, T., 1982: 'The great hall of the Archbishop's palace', in *Medieval art and architecture in Canterbury before 1220*, British Archaeological Association Conference Transactions, 112–19

Taylor, A. J., 1977: 'Castle building in Wales and Savoy', *Proceedings of the British Academy*, 63, 265–92

—— 1986: *The Welsh castles of Edward I*, Hambleton Press, London

Thompson, M. W., 1987: *The decline of the castle*, Cambridge University Press, Cambridge

—— 1991: *The rise of the castle*, Cambridge University Press, Cambridge

Warren, W. L., 1981: 'King John in Ireland', in J. Lydon (ed.): *England and Ireland in the later middle ages*, Irish Academic Press, Dublin, 26–42

Waterman, D. M., 1951: 'Excavations at Dundrum castle, 1950', *Ulster Journal of Archaeology*, 14, 15–29

—— 1954a: 'Excavations at Clough castle, Co. Down', *Ulster Journal of Archaeology*, 17, 103–63

—— 1954b: 'Excavations at Dromore motte, Co. Down', *Ulster Journal of Archaeology*, 17, 164–8

—— 1955: 'Excavations at Seafin castle and Ballyroney motte and bailey', *Ulster Journal of Archaeology*, 18, 83–104

—— 1958: 'Greencastle Co. Donegal', *Ulster Journal of Archaeology*, 21, 74–88

—— 1959a: 'Excavations at Lismahon', *Medieval Archaeology*, 3, 139–76

—— 1959b: 'Piper's Fort, Farranfad, Co. Down', *Ulster Journal of Archaeology*, 22, 83–7

—— 1961: 'Some Irish seventeenth century houses and their architectural ancestry', in E. M. Jope (ed.): *Studies in building history*, Odhams, London, 251–74

—— 1963: 'Excavations at Duneight, Co. Down', *Ulster Journal of Archaeology*, 26, 55–78

—— 1967: 'A note on Strangford Castle, Co. Down', *Ulster Journal of Archaeology* 30, 83–7.

—— 1968: 'Rectangular keeps of the thirteenth century at Grenan (Kilkenny) and Glanworth (Cork)', *Journal of the Royal Society of Antiquaries of Ireland*, 98, 67–73

—— 1970: 'Somersetshire and other foreign building stone in Ireland', *Ulster Journal of Archaeology*, 33, 63–76

Waterman, D. M. and Collins, A. E. P., 1952: 'Excavations at Greencastle, Co. Down, 1951', *Ulster Journal of Archaeology*, 15, 87–102

Westropp, T. J., 1900: 'Notes on the lesser castles or "peel towers" of the County Clare', *Proceedings of the Royal Irish Academy*, 21(C), 348–65

—— 1907: 'The ancient castles of the County of Limerick', *Proceedings of the Royal Irish Academy*, 26(C), 55–108; 143–264

—— 1909: 'The Desmond castle, Newcastle West, Co. Limerick', *Journal of the Royal Society of Antiquaries of Ireland*, 39, 42–58; 350–68

Wheeler, H., n.d.: *Cahir castle*, Office of Public Works, Dublin

White, N. B. (ed.), 1932: *The Red Book of Ormonde*, Irish Manuscripts Commission, Dublin

Wiggins, K., 1991: 'Strange changes at King John's castle', *Archaeology Ireland*, 5 (no. 3), 13–15

Wren, J., 1992: 'Roscrea Castle', *Excavations 1992*, 52

INDEX

———— •◆• ————